Without
Justice
for All

Recent Titles in
Contributions in Political Science
Series Editor: Bernard K. Johnpoll

Without
Justice
for All

The Constitutional Rights
of Aliens

ELIZABETH HULL

Foreword by Senator Dick Clark

Contributions in Political Science, Number 129

Greenwood Press
Westport, Connecticut · London, England

Library of Congress Cataloging in Publication Data

Hull, Elizabeth.
  Without justice for all.

  (Contributions in political science, ISSN 0147-1066 ;
no. 129)
  Bibliography: p.
  Includes index.
  1. Aliens—United States. 2. Emigration and immigra-
tion law—United States. I. Title. II. Series.
  KF4800.H84 1985   342.73'083   84-19798
  ISBN 0-313-23670-4 (lib. bdg.)   347.30283

Library of Congress Catalog Card Number: 84-19798
ISBN: 0147-1066
ISSN: 0-313-23670-4

First published in 1985

Greenwood Press
A division of Congressional Information Service, Inc.
88 Post Road West
Westport, Connecticut 06881

Printed in the United States of America

10 9 8 7 6 5 4 3 2 1

Contents

Foreword

American refugee policy in the four decades since World War II has been remarkably consistent in one respect: we have been very liberal about allowing persons fleeing communist regimes to come to the United States and become citizens, while following a very restrictive policy toward those fleeing "right-wing" repressive regimes. Forty thousand Hungarians were given asylum in the United States when the Hungarian Revolution failed in 1956. We have now resettled more than 750,000 Indochinese in the last decade. We have accepted 700,000 Cubans since Castro took over in 1959. President Lyndon Johnson even made a speech at the foot of the Statue of Liberty inviting all Cubans to come to the U.S., and we accept virtually all immigrants who can get exit permits from the Soviet Union if they desire to come here.

By comparison we refused to take more than a token number of Chileans when the elected government of Salvador Allende was overthrown by General Pinochet's military regime in September of 1973. Those fleeing "Baby Doc's" right-wing regime in Haiti have found asylum in the United States very difficult to obtain. The same is, of course, true of those who have fled El Salvador and Guatemala in recent years.

No doubt close to 99 percent of all the refugees who resettled in the United States since World War II were persons fleeing communist governments. Such a policy is disconcerting to those Americans who believe that we should live up to agreements wherein we become signatories to an international convention and protocol which requires us to apply equal standards to all those seeking asylum—regardless of the ideological nature of the persecuting regime.

Nevertheless, it is not surprising that presidents have treated refugee policy within the broader context of American foreign policy. Like other human rights issues in our foreign policy, refugee policy is treated as only another aspect of the East-West struggle. Containment of communist expansion has been the paramount goal of American foreign policy ever since the Truman Administration and the humanitarian aspects of American foreign policy have been made more successful in escaping the confines of the Cold War than any other.

This does not mean that there was no humanitarian motivation in our refugee policy—there certainly was and continues to be—but that motivation remained secondary to the broader political goal in the minds of most high ranking policy makers.

Dr. Hull explains alll this very well in her study.

Although our refugee policy has followed the prevailing outlines of our foreign policy with consistency, little else has been consistent about refugee policy.

It was not until the Refugee Act of 1980 was passed that the government began to operate under a comprehensive law. Prior to this decade our policy and practice in dealing with refugees was almost ad hoc. When the Eisenhower Administration suddenly decided to bring 40,000 Hungarians to this country in 1956 they cited as legal justification a rarely used provision of law which allowed the Attorney General to issue pardons to individual foreigners seeking asylum. That provision of the law became the legal basis bringing in virtually all of the refugees from Indo-China, Cuba, and the Soviet Union in the 1960s and 1970s. They were pardoned in by the attorney general. The meager law which did exist made provision for a very small number of refugees who were fleeing communism or the areas of the Middle East.

The process was very informal. An Administration—represented by someone from the Bureau of Human Rights and Humanitarian Affairs in the State Department after its creation in the mid-1970s—would explain its recommendations to the House and Senate Committees of the Judiciary on the types and numbers of refugees they planned to bring into the country for re-settlement each year. After the reactions of these committees was received the Attorney General would announce his parole and the process would proceed for another year.

In 1979 there was an urgent need to assist the thousands of "boat people" who were escaping from Vietnam and landing in nearby countries. This required greater effort and leadership by the United States. It meant significantly increasing our admission numbers and working with other western democracies to have them do likewise. These factors, combined with the largest migration ever to leave the Soviet Union (55,000), convinced President Carter of the necessity to appoint a U.S. Coordinator of Refugee Affairs who was given jurisdiction over both the foreign and domestic aspects of refugee policy. The coordinator was also charged by the president to prepare a comprehensive law—which would govern the admission and resettlement of refugees in the United States. Congress passed such a law, the Refugee Act, in 1980.

This study by Dr. Elizabeth Hull does an excellent job of analyzing and criticizing how this new law works—or often fails to work. Dr. Hull presents the most comprehensive, and certainly the most interesting, discussion of United States immigration policy that I have read to date. The book is marvelous: Dr. Hull forces us to think as she confronts us with hard questions and provocative policy options. As members of Congress—for the third consecutive term—begin debate on a broad new immigration bill, it would behoove them to read *Without Justice for All*. For that matter, this book should be priority reading for anyone who is interested in the way we treat the stranger at our gates.

Senator Dick Clark

Acknowledgments

In writing this book I received abundant assistance from friends and associates. Dr. Susan Buchanon and Janice Sottilaro provided me with their expertise and editorial assistance, the staff at the Center for Migration Studies gave generously of their time and resources, and G. Marvin Bogart offered both sound advice and inspiration.

I am grateful to my colleagues in the Political Science Department at Rutgers-Newark for their ongoing support, both moral and material; Dr. Kenneth Miller, the chairman of my department, provided me with particular encouragement.

Above all I am grateful to the person whose wise counsel, indulgence, and good humor sustained me during the many months in which I researched and wrote this book—my husband, Jeff Ambers.

Introduction

Each year hundreds of thousands of aliens[1] fly, drive, walk, swim, or sail into the United States. They come despite the uncertainty of their reception, for Americans have always been ambivalent hosts, greeting newcomers with alternate warmth and aversion. Such contradictory responses should perhaps be expected in a country that is itself a land of contradictions—created by people who were both slaveholders and children of the Enlightenment; nurtured by others who possessed both the missionary's spirit and the xenophobe's bile.

Americans have demonstrated their ambivalence time and again: They have received more than forty-eight million aliens since 1820,[2] yet at the same time they have sustained one nativist alliance after another—the Know Nothings in the 1850s, the American Protective Association in the 1890s, and the Ku Klux Klan from the 1920s thereafter. They have provided sanctuary to millions fleeing potato famines, political insurrections, or religious repression. Yet in 1938 and 1939, when news of Hitler's extermination camps was fairly widespread, a Gallup Poll revealed that well over half the American people favored a total ban on refugee admissions.[3]

Similar inconsistency has characterized the country's immigration policies. In 1892 Congress passed the Chinese Exclusion Act, and twenty-nine years later it passed the National Origin Quota Act. Together these provisions discriminated for decades against more than half the world's population. Yet for almost two centuries Congress has retained the world's most liberal naturalization laws, and in 1980 it passed an act institutionalizing one of the most generous refugee admissions policies in history.

Recently the United States has absorbed twice as many immigrants as the rest of the world combined,[4] and at least as many as it did during the mass European migration early this century. Between 1978 and 1980 alone, well over one and one-half million aliens entered legally, and between 1978 and 1982 another 500,000 or so have slipped in surreptitiously each year.[5] The sheer size of this influx will assuredly compound the public's traditional ambivalence toward aliens, and it may even trigger a nativist resurgence.

There are already signs of this resurgence: According to a recent public opinion poll, 80 percent of the American public want a substantial reduction in legal immigration;[6] states and localities are passing a number of laws and regulations designed to discomfit their alien residents;[7] and a plethora of new groups, dedicated to an "America first" philosophy, are burgeoning.[8] Senator Alan K. Simpson, co-sponsor of a major immigration reform bill, concluded that Americans are suffering from "Compassion fatigue."[9] *The New York Times* goes further, discerning in public attitudes what it calls "a rising, ugly nativist sentiment."[10]

The Times may overstate the case, but Americans *are* beset with anxieties, for which aliens now, as in the past, provide convenient scapegoats. Unemployment is high, and national resources are dwindling. Exacerbating their anxiety, moreover, is fear lest the country's assimilative capacities be overtaxed, or indeed, that its very character be imperiled by the preponderance of nonwhite, Spanish-speaking newcomers.[11]

Projected immigration trends are unlikely to assuage the public's anxieties. According to one recent study, sponsored by Senator Mark Hatfield, "the pressures to immigrate to the United States will increase over the next decade, making immigration and refugee policy the most pressing social issue in the world."[12] These pressures are substantial. Most demographers agree that at least two billion people—an astonishing one-half of the world's population—are poor.[13] The International Labor Organization

(ILO) estimates that the labor force will grow 600 to 700 million over the next two decades, creating more young people looking for work than are employed today by all the industrialized nations;[14] famine in Africa and conflict in Afghanistan, Southeast Asia, the Middle East, and Latin America have fostered a refugee population ranging somewhere between eleven and sixteen million.[15]

Many of these people will seek refuge in the United States, whose glories have been trumpeted throughout the Third World nations, particularly by the Voice of America. Even among developed countries the United States is particularly enticing because of its traditional receptiveness, its accessibility, and its strong and supportive immigrant communities. Hoping to forestall this potential "deluge," government leaders are debating several proposed amendments to the Immigration and Naturalization Act (INA).[16]

Whether the proposals ultimately adopted are humane or vindictive, the INA will continue to reflect—more than any other statute—the predominant values of the American people. The act reveals their biases, their illogical and intolerant characteristics, as well as their decent and even noble aspirations. By examining the INA one learns whether, among the lovely, Americans are willing to admit some who are not so lovely; whether they are secure enough to receive an occasional ideological provocateur, or even-handed enough to treat asylum seekers from Haiti or El Salvador as equitably as Soviet defectors.

This book examines the way American law and legal practice affect the country's noncitizens. Noncitizens consist of "immigrants," who have made the United States their home, and "nonimmigrants," who may be just passing through; "undocumented," or "illegal" aliens, whose entrance or continued presence in the United States is unauthorized, and "refugees," who are fleeing persecution. Source material is anything that lends insight into the noncitizens' legal rights and obligations—the INA, judicial opinions, state department edicts, personal testimonies.

This book is not written by a lawyer, nor from a lawyer's perspective. Rather, it is written from the perspective of a citi-

1

American Immigration Law and Policy: An Historical Overview

Chief Ben American Horse of the Sioux Indian tribe once gave the following advice to Alben Barkley, who was then Vice president of the United States: "Young fellow . . . [b]e careful with your immigration laws. We were careless with ours."[1] America's immigration laws have, in fact, demonstrated less "carelessness" than simple confusion, reflecting the public's own uncertainty regarding their country's mission: Should the United States be a refuge for the "tired and poor," or an outpost, properly off-limits to the "wretched refuse" of the world?

The United States has always been more a refuge than an outpost, notwithstanding sustained and often temporarily successful efforts by nativists to maintain restrictive admission policies. These nativists have historically longed for a legendary America, peopled by proud and proper Anglo-Saxons.[2] In actuality, however, the country has always been home to immigrants of many nationalities and social castes. Even after Great Britain laid claim to North America, it permitted foreigners to settle in its overseas territory. As a result, the British established homesteads alongside delegations from Spain, France, Portugal, and Germany. Moreover, for every "proper" Englishman who was lured to America by the promise of a royal land grant, there was the ragged jailbird who connived his freedom by agreeing to emigrate, or a group of down-and-out commoners who sought better fortunes abroad.

The United States was never the pristine land for which nativĩsts yearn, but it has always been a bold republic, whose innovative policies have distinguished it from other nations. Foremost among these policies has been its willingness to welcome the stranger. Although initially America's leaders did nothing to encourage immigration—preferring, as Thomas Jefferson exhorted, to let people enter, but without "the expediency of inviting them by extraordinary encouragement"[3]—they nevertheless abided by an unrestricted open-door policy for almost a century.

An "open door" was essential because the United States depended on newcomers to settle its frontiers, lay its railroad ties, and harvest its sugar cane crops. Notwithstanding its neutralist rhetoric, the government consequently encouraged immigration in a number of ways. Until 1875 it passed no restrictive immigration laws, with the exception of the short-lived Alien Act of 1798, which authorized the President to deport any foreigner whom he considered dangerous to the country's security.[4] The government offered homesteaders cheap and abundant land. Finally, Congress enacted the most liberal naturalization laws in existence, thereby encouraging newcomers to participate in the governmental process.

The ease and manner with which immigrants may acquire citizenship, in fact, represent still another distinctive feature of the American republic. Since the country passed its first naturalization laws in 1798, aliens have had to satisfy only minimal requirements in order to become citizens. Most notably, they must reside in the United States five years before seeking naturalization; they must renounce foreign allegiances and titles of nobility; and finally, they must profess loyalty to republican ideals as embodied in the United States Constitution.[5] As historian Arthur Mann pointed out, in 1795 an ideological test for naturalization was unprecedented.[6] In other nations, a subject acquired citizenship by swearing allegiance to the person of the monarch, not to a set of beliefs. In other nations, moreover, naturalization was not a right potentially available to every inhabitant, but an act of sovereign grace typically bestowed, as in England, on only a privileged elite.

American leaders, influenced by their Enlightenment tutors, believed that expatriation is a fundamental human right, and accordingly that individuals should be free to pledge allegiance to the polity of their choice. By reflecting this belief, in still another way American immigration policy distinguished itself from that of other countries, where the theory persisted—well into the nineteenth century—that subjects owed irrevocable allegiance to their sovereign.[7]

From the infant days of their republic, Americans have shared a fundamental conviction that, in a final way, has differentiated them from other political bodies: America is at once the Promised Land and the Great Experiment, her people both "chosen" and "duty bound" to offer the rest of the world not only an example of Enlightenment ideals made manifest, but also a sanctuary and a new beginning.[8]

Americans considered their land, then, as a haven, and for many decades this benign self-image coincided neatly with the country's economic needs. Yet from colonial times this idealism has coexisted with intolerant and even xenophobic attitudes that have also represented a resilient strain in the American psyche. Thus George Washington spoke for his fellow citizens when he declared that "the bosom of America is to receive not only the Opulent and respectable stranger, but also the oppressed and persecuted of all Nations and Religions."[9] About the same time, however, Benjamin Franklin expressed views no less popular when he inveighed against the Germans because of their "clannishness," their fecundity, and "their little knowledge of English," and dismissed the Irish as "a low and squalid class of people."[10]

Franklin was offended by those "habits and peculiarities" he associated with new immigrants—their poverty and radicalism, their Catholicism and their "foreign" predilections. Successive generations of Americans have shared similar views—a phenomenon analyzed by historian John Higham in his classic *Strangers in the Land*. Higham noted that the anti-poor, anti-radical, and anti-Catholic tradition defined what America was not and must not become.[11]

Anti-Catholic sentiment continues to linger in some enclaves, but it has proved generally less durable than Americans' fear of foreign radicals, whom they associated at one time with the licentiousness of the French Revolution, and whom they continue to associate with anarchy and communism. Americans traditionally have borne a related animus toward the foreign poor, who were considered susceptible to, if not purveyors of, European-style radicalism. The poor, moreover, have represented an affront to American sensibilities, signifying the absence of character, of grace, or of assimilative capacity.[12]

Although the United States has always housed substantial numbers of poor people, Catholics, and even radicals, xenophobic tendencies nevertheless remained tempered until the 1830s and 1840s, when hundreds of thousands of Irish and German Catholics immigrated to the United States, the former fleeing a potato famine, and the latter a depression. These newcomers excited biases that had lain relatively dormant for decades, and contributed to the rise of the Know-Nothing party. This nativist alliance consisted primarily of chronic bigots and the disaffected, of workers who resented the competition posed by alien labor, and Southerners who feared the growth in Northern population and political power.[13] The party, which emerged coterminously with a virulent anti-Chinese movement on the West Coast, was relatively successful at the polls in the 1850s. Although it never regained its political strength after the Civil War, it has served as a prototype for kindred organizations that have erupted thereafter. Many of these organizations have exercised significant, if indirect, political power, particularly by influencing the content of immigration-related legislation.[14]

During the second half of the nineteenth century, while membership quadrupled in these "America first" associations, Congress made fundamental changes in the country's immigration laws. In 1875 it passed the first in a series of restrictive acts, thereby heralding the official end of America's "open-door" policy.[15] Between 1875 and 1920 Congress prohibited the entry of any person who possessed a criminal record, was afflicted with a "loathsome or dangerous disease," or who might become a public charge; it banned epileptics and idiots, lunatics, the insane, paupers, polygamists, and those whose past actions suggested moral turpitude.[16] Legislators also passed a head tax of fifty cents per immigrant,[17] and responded to the importunings of organized labor by prohibiting the admission of contract workers.[18]

In 1882, Congress made a radical breach with tradition when it passed the Chinese Exclusion Act, which effectively prohibited members of an entire nationality from entering the United States.[19] This act was passed in response to the fervent anti-Chinese sentiment that had mounted during the late nineteenth century, particularly on the West Coast where almost 100,000 Chinese had settled by 1880.[20] Most of these Cantonese laborers had been recruited to lay railroad ties or pick ore in the mines of the Southwest, but with the completion of the transatlantic railroad and the Depression of the 1870s, their labor was no longer necessary. Many nevertheless elected to remain, and their industry and thrift, coupled with their linguistic and cultural dissimilarities, provoked the intense animosity of their Anglicized neighbors.[21]

Demagogic politicians, capitalizing on this sinophobia, claimed the Chinese as a class were incapable of assimilation and prone to criminality and prostitution.[22] Legislators passed a rash of laws in several states prohibiting the Chinese from owning property or engaging in a number of occupations.[23] After enacting a package of particularly severe penalties in 1876, the California Senate crowned its action with the resolution that "[t]he Chinese are inferior to any race God ever made."[24]

Americans' antipathy toward the Chinese ultimately extended to almost everyone indigenous to the Asian continent. In 1907, the United States and Japan negotiated a "Gentlemen's Agreement" that limited the right of Japanese nationals to settle in this country.[25] By 1917, Congress had excluded virtually every resident of the so-called "Asiatic barred zone," a vast territory that extended from the Kirghiz (Russian) Steppes and the Arabian Peninsula to what is now Indonesia.[26]

During the late nineteenth century Congress also concluded that citizenship, like the right of entry, was a privilege properly granted on a race-conscious basis. Although the Constitution's Fourteenth Amendment provides that "all persons born" in the United States are citizens,[27] Congress determines who among the foreign-born can qualify for naturalization.[28] It accordingly declared in the Act of 1870 that "[t]he naturalization laws are hereby extended to aliens of African nativity, and to persons of African descent."[29]

Congress inserted the racially-qualifying phrase in the 1870 Act at the behest of Western legislators, who feared that without restrictive language the Chinese might eventually qualify for citizenship.[30] As Arthur Mann pointed out, however, because of this language American nationality "could accommodate only two kinds of people: white and black."[31] In subsequent years, Congress and the courts were thus compelled to wrestle with a succession of awkward racial questions: Who was "white?" "Black?" Into which categories did groups such as Indians, Puerto Ricans, and Hawaiians fit?

The Indians presented a particularly vexatious case: Until 1887 Native American tribes qualified for collective citizenship if they agreed, essentially, to adopt the mores of the prevailing culture. What, then, was to be done with those Indians who sought citizenship in their individual capacity? In 1884 the Supreme Court held that John Elk could not become a United States citizen, despite the fact that he paid taxes and had served in the militia.[32] The Court reasoned that since he was born on tribal lands, which were not subject to American jurisdiction, he did not fall within the Fourteenth Amendment's definition of a native-born citizen.[33]

A Canadian-born Indian was similarly ineligible for citizenship. In the 1880 case of *In Re Camille*,[34] an Oregon state court reasoned that the petitioner, who was born in British Columbia of a white father and an Indian mother, was "as much an Indian as a white person, and might be classed with one race as properly as the other. Strictly speaking, he belongs to neither."[35] It then resurrected a judicial maxim relied upon by the antebellum courts to determine the legal status of American mulattos—i.e., to qualify for American citizenship the petitioner must be "nearer white than nonwhite."[36]

Canadian Indians did not qualify for citizenship, but according to an 1887 court ruling this ineligibility did not extend to their Mexican brethren. Despite the statutory requirement that an applicant for naturalization be either white or black, a Texas district court reasoned that by granting citizenship to everyone who was living in the territory acquired from Mexico in 1848 and 1853, Congress intended to include even those inhabitants who were of Indian descent.[37] In 1889, the United States acquired Puerto Rico, and in 1917 Congress again obfuscated the black-white distinction by granting citizenship to all residents of this island, including those of Indian descent.[38] Finally, in 1924, Congress declared that regardless of residence all Indians born in the United States were citizens.[39]

In 1889 the Supreme Court concluded that while the American-born children of Chinese aliens were constitutionally entitled to citizenship, their parents "have never been allowed, by our laws, to acquire nationality."[40] Twenty-four years later it held that Japanese immigrants were also ineligible for citizenship.[41] A federal court similarly concluded that the son of a German father and a Japanese mother cannot acquire citizenship, since "it cannot be said that one who is half white and half brown or yellow is a white person as commonly understood."[42] Nor is a Hindu born in India, even of high caste, a "white person" eligible for citizenship, although another court decreed that Armenians from Asia Minor qualify, since they are of Alpine stock and European persuasion.[43]

While policy-makers were maintaining selective citizenship rosters, the United States was undergoing a demographic transformation. By the end of the nineteenth century, for the first time in the country's history, new arrivals from Italy and Greece and Poland surpassed in volume those from northern and western Europe.[44] At first the new immigrants were received with relative enthusiasm. Their arrival reconfirmed the "success" of the American experiment, and they also supplied the labor necessary for a society that was being rapidly transformed. In time, however, the new immigrants also provided a ready scapegoat for a citizenry growing anxious and disoriented by this transformation. Slums were sprouting up, crime rates were soaring, and the working class was flexing its muscles. As the new arrivals became associated with these various ills their presence provoked resentment and even hostility, not only from the established gentry, but also from the Irish and Germans, who had themselves been regarded as a motley and threatening lot only a few decades earlier.

The new immigrants were particularly "visible": They coalesced in cities, where they lived in unsightly ghettos and in-
dulged their peculiar customs and curious speech. To established residents they represented a stark symbol of the "new,"
as opposed to the "old" and already mythologized America.
Visiting his homeland after many years abroad, the novelist
Henry James subsequently recorded the nostalgia and disloca-
tion experienced by many of his erstwhile compatriots. What,
he asked, was to become of America "ethnically . . . physiog-
nomically, linguistically, personally?"[45]

In increasing numbers Americans began to support a drive
for restrictive immigration laws. A series of theories, based on
so-called "scientific racism," served to accelerate and further
justify this drive. These doctrines, which historians and social
scientists popularized in the late nineteenth and early twentieth centuries, comprised much of the conventional wisdom of
the day. Influenced by the theory of evolution and the social
Darwinism of Herbert Spencer, they consisted of "highly questionable assumptions" and "an alchemist's smorgasbord of
'measurement' techniques from Cephalic indexes to Somatic
types."[46] On their authority, pundits first consigned blacks to
inferior status, then Asians, and finally immigrants from southern and eastern Europe.

Edward Ross, a respected academician at the time, described
the Jews as being "the polar opposite of the pioneer breed: Un-
dersized and weak-muscled, they shun bodily activity and are
exceedingly sensitive to pain."[47] Worse yet, one "can't make
boy scouts out of them."[48] Ross noted that Italians "lack the
power to take rational care of themselves,"[49] because of low
craniums. He decried all new immigrants, in general, because
they are "beaten men from beaten races, representing the worst
failures in the struggle for existence."[50] These pseudoscientific
theories would be laughable today were it not for the great harm
that was done in their name—most tragically, of course, the
abominations resulting from Hitler's notions of genetic purity.
They also provided theoretical justification for the racism and
restrictionism that characterized United States immigration laws
until 1965.

In 1911 the Dillingham Commission, consisting of members

of Congress, released a forty-two volume study of the impact of immigration on United States society.[51] According to its Chairman, William P. Dillingham, the report provided irrefutable proof that the new immigrants were of inferior stock. The Commission therefore concluded that American society would be inexorably debased unless migration from southern and eastern Europe was substantially curtailed. To effect this objective the members recommended a literacy test.

The Dillingham Report both reflected and reinforced the era's prevalent nativism. Nativism had erupted at predictable intervals in the past, but it had been tamed by countervailing forces—by Americans' vigorous optimism, in general, and their confidence that the country was spacious enough to absorb large numbers of immigrants; by their assurance that these immigrants, like their forerunners, were adaptable and thus capable of acquiring the New World's ethos; by a pride in, and reluctance to foresake, a tradition that welcomed the poor and downtrodden; and, finally, by a conviction that a recurring infusion of new blood would continue to enrich and revitalize the polity. This sanguine attitude was difficult to sustain in the twentieth century: The era of Manifest Destiny had ended, and the United States frontier was officially closed; according to the public's perception, moreover, the new immigrants seemed to resist assimilative pressures, and to represent in disproportionate numbers those who were in jail or on the dole.

Although Congress waited six years to respond to the Dillingham Commission, it continued to expand the list of excludable aliens. After President William McKinley was shot by Leon Czolgosz, an anarchist and an immigrant, for the first time in American history Congress excluded aliens on the grounds of their political beliefs. In 1903 it enacted legislation excluding anarchists and any other persons who believed in or advocated "the overthrow of the United States government, all government, or all forms of law by force or violence."[52]

A decade later, the United States fell victim to a rash of anti-German sentiment. As a result, many flourishing newspapers, social clubs, and other enterprises serving the German-American community were forced to close. The Governor of Iowa prohibited the use of any language other than English in public places and over the telephone,[53] sauerkraut was renamed "liberty cabbage," and the demand for dachshund pups fell in one year by 60 percent.

During this period many public officials urged that aliens be required to demonstrate proficiency in English before being issued a visa.[54] Elaborating on a theme that has resurfaced in the 1980s, they denounced the migrants' attachment to their native language, and interpreted their apparent reluctance to learn English as a divisive and disloyal act. Although a language requirement was never instituted, in the Immigration Act of 1917 Congress enacted a law prohibiting the admission of aliens unable to satisfy a literacy test.[55]

When Congress first discussed the merits of a literacy test in 1896, Senator Henry Cabot Lodge had analyzed the probable impact of such a requirement:

The illiteracy test will bear most heavily upon the Italians, Russians, Hungarians, Greeks and Asiatics, and very lightly, or not at all, upon English-speaking immigrants or Germans, Scandinavians, and French . . . In other words . . . the races most affected by the illiteracy test are those whose emigration to this country has begun within the last twenty years and swelled rapidly to enormous proportions, races with which the English-speaking people have never hitherto assimilated, and who are most alien to the great body of the people of the United States.[56]

The 1917 Act represented a comprehensive revision of United States immigration laws, and as amended it remained in effect until 1952. The act was passed amid the furor of World War I, and reflected the xenophobia that clouded the era: It banned not only illiterates and virtually every inhabitant of Asia, but also several other categories of aliens as well.[57] A year later Congress passed the Anarchist Act of 1918, which with its subsequent revisions denied visas to anyone who had been a member of, or identified with, certain proscribed organizations, or who, essentially, believed in, advocated, or in any way disseminated politically objectionable doctrine.[58]

A direct response to the Russian Revolution, the Anarchist Act registered the government's fear that without preemptive measures dangerous and alien doctrines might undermine the United States. Under its aegis, Attorney General A. Mitchell Palmer commanded his agents to launch midnight raids, invade private dwellings, stop suspected trouble-makers, interrogate, search, and incarcerate them. During these so-called "Palmer Raids," more than 5,000 aliens, reputed to be political activists, were arrested and deported. On a single night in January 1919, agents in thirty-three cities throughout the United States made between 2,500 and 5,000 arrests.[59]

During this time many public figures decried the illiberality that pervaded the body politic. Writers such as Horace Kallen and William James extolled the benefits of cultural pluralism,[60] and denounced the "sniveling cant" of Anglo-Saxon conformity.[61] Their message had little impact, however, during the bleak years following World War One. These were the years during which the United States rejected the Treaty of Versailles and refused to join the League of Nations, when the Ku Klux Klan was resurrected, and Henry Ford launched his crazed anti-semitic tirades.

Undaunted by the restrictive immigration laws enacted during this era, the aliens kept coming. Between 1880 and 1930, more than 27 million were processed at ports of entry.[62] Americans were alarmed by the number and composition of these new arrivals—whose ranks were dominated by southern European Catholics and Jews—and troubled as well by their potential impact: Could the United States absorb an indefinite number of newcomers, markedly dissimilar to their Anglicized forebears, without losing its animating spirit? Professor Henry Pratt Fairchild expressed their apprehension in his popular book *The Melting Pot Mistake*, when he wrote that "a preponderating influence of foreigners . . . takes away from a people its most precious possession—its soul."[63]

The country was ready for an effective counter-attack against the swarm of immigrants. It had imposed head taxes and multiplied the grounds for exclusion; it had denied visas to illiterates and political radicals and barred Asians completely. None of these expedients had curtailed immigration or reduced appreciably the number of "undesirable" entrants. Thus, in 1921

Congress passed, and President Harding signed into law, a measure designed to accomplish what its precursors had failed to do—"reclaim America for Americans."

This measure, the First National Origins Act,[64] established a ceiling on European immigration and limited the number of annual visas allocated to any one country to 3 percent of its foreign-born population in the United States at the time of the 1910 census. This formula still allowed more southern and eastern Europeans to enter than its framers had intended, however. To rectify the situation Congress subsequently passed an amended version known as the Johnson-Reed, or second "National Origins," Act, which went into effect in 1929 and remained the gravamen of United States immigration law until 1965.[65]

The National Origins Act provided that no more than 150,000 Europeans could immigrate to the United States in any one year. Its quota system was engineered to yield more satisfying results than its antecedent: By distributing visas on the basis of each nationality's contribution to the overall population of the United States, rather than on its proportion of foreign-born, the act reduced the number available for southern and eastern Europeans. In addition, it established quotas at 2 percent of the foreign-born enumerated in the 1890 census, rather than 3 percent in the 1910 census, thus reducing the number of eligible southern and eastern Europeans.

The second National Origins Act, then, was a finely-tuned contrivance designed to restore an "optimal" ethnic mix: Under its terms, Great Britain, with 2 percent of the world's population, received 43 percent of the quota; most Asians continued to be barred altogether, and the allotment for southern and eastern Europeans was significantly slashed.[66]

The act established no quota for the western hemisphere, and as a consequence sizable numbers of Mexican immigrants continued to arrive. Although many Congressmen considered them as unassimilable as the Asians, they believed that any attempt to protect the vast United States land borders from illegal penetration was futile. They were also loath to take any step that could jeopardize the country's plentiful supply of temporary Mexican labor.[67]

The National Origins Act never operated with fool-proof efficiency, but it was sufficiently effective to beget disastrous consequences. The act excluded hundreds of thousands of people attempting to escape Hitler's exterminators.[68] In what a congressional staff report referred to as perhaps "the cruelest action in United States history,"[69] in 1939 Congress also defeated a proposal to rescue some 20,000 children from Nazi persecution, despite the eagerness of American families to sponsor them.[70] The reason: The children would have exceeded the annual quota allotted to Germany.

After the Second World War, thoughtful people, appalled by the consequences of their country's immigration policies, began agitating for their revision. The quota system nevertheless remained basically intact for another twenty years,[71] although Congress frequently circumvented it by passing special legislation that resulted in the admission of hundreds of thousands of mainly "new" immigrants—war brides, displaced persons who had escaped Hitler's death camps, and later, refugees fleeing communism.[72] To secure the integrity of the national origin system, however, Congress charged these special interests against their countries' future quotas.

Refugees were also subjected to careful screening, lest saboteurs infiltrate their ranks. The government's authority to exclude confirmed or potential trouble-makers had been expanded in 1940 when Congress passed the Alien Registration, or Smith Act.[73] This act provided for the exclusion of any alien who was at present, or had been in the past, a member of any organization advocating the violent overthrow of the government.[74]

Security agents worried that despite the Smith Act's broad language, loopholes still remained through which subversives might enter. Consequently, in 1941 Congress authorized consular officers to refuse visas to any individual whose entrance into the United States would, in their opinion, jeopardize public safety.[75] The Passport Act, reenacted the same year, also empowered government officials to exclude any alien whose presence would be prejudicial to the "best interests of the United States."[76]

These security measures were a prelude to the Internal Security, or Subversive Activities Control Act,[77] passed in 1950 during the McCarthy Era when fear ran rampant—not only of communism, but of anything that smacked of unorthodoxy. In this act Congress imposed a broad-based ban on the admission of aliens who were even peripherally affiliated with the Communist party, its predecessors, successors, or with any organization registered or required to be registered with the attorney general. It also excluded those aliens who, officials believed, upon entry might engage in subversive activity or become active in any proscribed organization. The Subversive Activities Control Act authorized the exclusion or deportation not only of confirmed agitators, but also of other aliens who even years before may have joined an organization—legal at the time—which the attorney general subsequently adjudged subversive.[78]

In 1948 Congress began a serious review of its immigration policy, which many of its members still considered unduly permissive. Despite the volley of exclusionary provisions passed since 1940, a number of lawmakers agreed with Senator Patrick McCarran, co-sponsor of the subsequent reform legislation, when he warned that "[p]resent laws are shot through with weaknesses and loopholes. Criminals, Communists and Subversives are even now gaining admission into this country like water through a sieve."[79]

As a consequence of the various refugee relief measures enacted after World War II, an "excessive" number of southern and eastern Europeans were entering alongside the "fifth columnists." In response Congress passed the Immigration and Nationality Act of 1952. This legislation, better known as the McCarran-Walter Act,[80] effected a general revision and codification of the country's immigration laws, and still constitutes their basic framework. It ranks among the country's most controversial policies, and with the exception of the Internal Revenue Code represents the longest, most complicated, and certainly the most arcane piece of legislation in modern United States history.[81]

Despite increasing difficulty in justifying the national origin quota system in the aftermath of World War II, Congress steadfastly refused to abolish it. Although arguments premised on the inherent inferiority of certain races were no longer acceptable, those favoring quotas relied upon another stratagem: Certain ethnic groups were supposedly less capable of assimilation than others—they represented what Senator McCarran referred to as great "undigestible blocs"[82]—and consequently their admission should be limited.

The 1952 act abandoned the Asiatic Barred Zone, although its constituent countries generally received only minimal visa allotments, and their residents were still treated differently from other immigrants. For quota purposes non-Asians were credited to their country of birth, while Asians were counted against the country of their forebears. A second generation Argentinian of Japanese ancestry, for instance, would be counted against the small quota provided Japan, while a second generation Argentinian of German ancestry would be considered an Argentine.[83]

Through its disbursement of visas the United States registered its estimation of the relative desirability of different ethnic groups: Asians received a total of 2,990 visas a year; Africans, 1,400; Europeans, 149,667.[84] More than half a million West Indian blacks had immigrated to the United States before passage of the 1952 act. Under the provisions in the act, West Indian blacks were entitled to a nominal 100 visas a year. Colonial possessions in the western hemisphere, accustomed to drawing upon their mother countries' ample quotas, were similarly restricted to this minimal allocation.

With the exception of colonies and dependencies, countries in the western hemisphere continued to enjoy unrestricted immigration. Natives of the eastern hemisphere, however, were subject to an annual ceiling of 150,000 visas, which were distributed according to a preference system that favored skilled workers and the relatives of United States citizens and resident aliens. As journalist David Margolick observed, the act also expanded and codified the list of excludable aliens by "lump(ing) Communists and anarchists with prostitutes, polygamists, paupers, stowaways and other categories of aliens previously barred from entering the United States."[85] The act also excluded any persons who, "in the opinion" of immigration officials, were likely "at any time" to become a public charge.[86]

For thirteen years following its enactment Congress made no systematic changes in the McCarran Act, notwithstanding the mounting censure it engendered. Among its critics were the members of a presidential commission impaneled to study the country's immigration laws. The commission concluded that "[our present laws] flout fundamental American traditions and ideals, display a lack of faith in America's future, damage American prestige and position among other nations, ignore the lessons of the American way of life."[87]

Since 1952, opposition to the quota system has also been expressed in the presidential platforms of both major parties. When John Kennedy won the presidency in 1960, he vowed to use the full powers of his office to abolish it.[88] Pressure to eliminate quotas also emanated from nongovernmental and even international sources: On the domestic level, members of the emergent civil rights movement became particularly active in this endeavor, as did affiliates of church, ethnic, and civic organizations, whose postwar efforts on behalf of refugees had sensitized them to the inequities inherent in the country's immigration scheme. On the international level, the quota system became increasingly difficult to rationalize. After colonial ties were severed following the Second World War, the new nations that emerged invariably received only token quotas. Such an affront operated at cross-purposes with America's postwar campaign for the "hearts and minds" of the Third World.

Congress delivered Kennedy a fitting eulogy when, twenty-three months after his assassination, it finally repudiated an immigration policy based on race and ethnicity. When President Johnson signed the Immigration and Nationality Act Amendments of 1965[89] at the foot of the Statue of Liberty, he bode riddance to a system that, he said, "has been un-American in the highest sense."[90] The new act introduced a number of fundamental policy changes, including a new system for visa allocations. By 1968, every country in the eastern hemisphere would receive 20,000 visas a year, with the total number limited to 170,000. For the first time in its history, the United States also imposed an annual ceiling on the western hemisphere—a quota of 120,000 visas. No per country limitations were imposed, however.

In the allocation of visas, the 1965 Act continued to favor close relatives of United States citizens and resident aliens and, to a lesser extent, those with needed skills. This preference system was applicable only to the eastern hemisphere, however. Finally, the act introduced a new labor clearance procedure: Prior to the receipt of a visa, all prospective immigrants who are neither immediate relatives nor refugees must obtain certification from the Secretary of Labor that American workers are not available for the job they wish to fill, and that their presence will not adversely affect prevailing wages and working conditions.

Until 1965 those immigrating to the United States had been predominantly from northern and western Europe. The 1965 amendments effected marked changes in the composition of new entrants, as residents of Asia and southern and eastern Europe began coming in great numbers while those from traditional source countries declined (see Table 1). This transformation was not immediately apparent because by virtue of the new requirement for labor certification, immigration from the eastern hemisphere initially fell by 30 percent; a decade later, however, rates again soared because by then at least 80 percent of those immigrating to the United States were close relatives of citizens or resident aliens, and thus statutorily exempt from the certification process.[91]

The new legislation significantly reduced the flagrant racial and ethnic discrimination that had characterized earlier acts, but some aspiring immigrants were still treated inequitably: Colonies and dependencies were allocated only 200 visas a year—to be counted against both the mother country and its hemispheric ceiling.[92] The result has been to restrict dramatically immigration from certain colonial areas, where demand for entrance is high and where the population is mainly black and Asian.[93] Under the 1965 act many western hemisphere countries also fared badly because their residents, accustomed to unlimited migration, were now restricted to an annual ceiling of 120,000. Within this ceiling applicants were granted visas on a "first come-first serve" basis—a system that soon provoked criticism from many members of Congress, either because entrants from certain countries, particularly Mexico, could immigrate to the United States in what they considered inordinate

TABLE ONE
Immigration From Major Sending Areas*
1960-1979

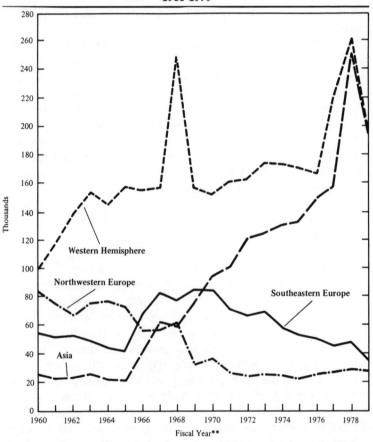

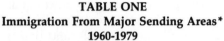

SOURCE: Based on Table 14, *Annual Reports*, Immigration and Naturalization Service, and unpublished data.

*By area of birth.

**Fiscal years 1960-1976 were from July 1-June 30; fiscal years 1977-1979 were from October 1-September 30.

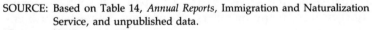

numbers, or because the new policy extended no favoritism to those with needed skills or family ties to United States residents.[94]

To rectify these perceived shortcomings, in 1976 Congress subjected the western hemisphere to the same per-country limitations and preference system that governed the eastern hemisphere.[95] Two years later legislators again amended the INA when they provided for the admission of 290,000 immigrants under a single worldwide ceiling.[96] Finally, in 1980 Congress passed the Refugee Act, which established a special procedure for admitting aliens with a "well-founded fear of persecution,"[97] and at the same time it reduced the annual quota for nonrefugee immigrants to 270,000.

These revisions eliminated some problems, but they also created new ones: According to the official explanation, each country was limited to 20,000 visas a year in order to prevent an undue allocation to any one state.[98] However, because Congress elected to impose the quotas on a per country basis, rather than allow unrestricted migration within a worldwide ceiling, applicants from high-demand nations such as Mexico and the Philippines are penalized. Moreover, they are not allowed to use any of the unclaimed quotas for undersubscribed countries—a policy that compounds the resentment of those whose plans are stymied by the long wait while those from low-demand countries immigrate virtually at will.[99] Finally, and ironically, applicants from those countries that were disfavored under the national origin quota system are also disadvantaged under the new system, since its per country limitations perpetuate the discriminatory ratios that existed prior to the abolishment of this system in 1965.[100]

In addition to the unlimited visas available for the spouses, children, and parents of adult United States citizens—so-called "non quota immigrants"—the quota system reserves two-thirds of the preference categories for the close relatives of United States citizens and resident aliens (see Table 2). Congress has placed so much emphasis on the value of family reunification that the country's immigration scheme reflects what demographers David North and Marion Houston call "a national policy of nepotism."[101] By 1978, in fact, family members comprised more than

TABLE TWO
Current Visa Allocation System

NUMERICALLY EXEMPT IMMIGRANTS

Immediate relatives of U.S. citizens

    Spouses
    Children
    Parents (of U.S. citizens at least 21 years of age)

Special immigrants

    Certain ministers of religion
    Certain former employees of the U.S. government abroad
    Certain persons who lost U.S. citizenship

NUMERICALLY LIMITED IMMIGRANTS (270,000)

Preference	Groups Include	Percentage & Number of Visas
First	Unmarried sons and daughters of U.S. citizens and their children	20% or 54,000
Second	Spouses and unmarried sons and daughters of permanent resident aliens	26% or 70,000*
Third	Members of the professions of exceptional ability and their spouses and children	10% or 27,000
Fourth	Married sons and daughters of U.S. citizens, their spouses and children	10% or 27,000*
Fifth	Brothers and sisters of U.S. citizens (at least 21 years of age) and their spouses and children	24% or 64,800*
Sixth	Workers in skilled or unskilled occupations in which laborers are in short supply in the United States, their spouses and children	10% or 27,000
Non-preference	Other qualifed applicants	Any numbers not used above*

SOURCE: "United States Immigration Policy and the National Interest," Staff Report of the Select Commission on Immigration and Refugee Policy, April 30, 1981, p. 327.
*Numbers not used in higher preferences may be used in these categories.

90 percent of all nonrefugee immigrants.[102] Such a policy further penalizes residents of those countries historically subject to restrictive quotas because they have comparatively few family members in the United States to sponsor them.[103]

Under the 1965 act the system for securing visas has become so complicated, as well as so weighted in favor of family members and the highly skilled, that aspiring immigrants who fall into neither category frequently face one of three options: They can hire expensive lawyers to help them maneuver through the bureaucratic morass; wait, like quota immigrants from Mexico, up to nine years for a visa; or enter the country clandestinely, as many people from oversubscribed countries in Latin America and Asia have chosen to do.

To a real, if indeterminate extent, developing nations are also handicapped by another feature of the 1965 Immigration Act. By also according preference to people with needed skills, Congress has contributed to the so-called "brain drain"—a phenomenon in which tens of thousands of foreign professionals have been lured to the United States from their homelands, where there is an urgent need for their skills.[104]

Certain classes of people are also disadvantaged by the country's immigration policy, since the 1965 act provides for exclusion on 33 grounds—many of which are arbitrary and archaic, some of which are unjust.[105] Congress uses a wide brush to ban people: It excludes not only the hardened drug trafficker, but also the individual found guilty of possessing one marijuana cigarette; the person convicted of a notorious crime, but also the would-be immigrant who years ago purloined a phonograph record; the individual with suspected homosexual tendencies as readily as the convicted rapist. The United States also shuts out those who are "likely to become a public charge"[106]— an expansive category, since consular offices may exclude every one who, in their estimation, may at any time in the future require public assistance. Finally, current law excludes people whose political beliefs are considered objectionable, quite apart from whether they have ever acted, or proposed to act, in a manner inimical to the security interests of the United States.[107]

In formulating their immigration policy, Americans have made their hard choices. They have decided that families should be

2

Resident Aliens

Every year the United States admits hundreds of thousands of foreigners for permanent residence.[1] These so-called "immigrants," or "resident aliens,"[2] evoke far less controversy than either undocumented migrants or refugees because policy-makers are able to exert at least rough control over their quality and numbers. Their presence in the United States still engenders debate, however, particularly over the role citizenship should play in the American polity: Should all persons who have made the United States their permanent home be accorded relative equality of legal rights, or should important privileges and benefits be reserved for those who are neither native-born nor naturalized citizens?

While resident aliens are at present subject to all the obligations of citizenship—they must pay taxes,[3] obey the law, register with the selective service, and serve in the armed forces if called[4]—they are not entitled to all the correlative rights of citizens.[5] They are ordinarily eligible for citizenship after living in the United States for five years,[6] but in the interim they occupy a somewhat ambiguous legal status, which persists for those who forgo naturalization. As a result, as far back as 1893, Justice David Brewer suggested that there be a separate class, "denizen," for a permanent resident who dwells "in a kind of middle state, between an alien and a natural born subject, and partakes of both of them."[7]

Over the years the rights accorded resident aliens have been determined largely by the legislatures and the courts. Both of these bodies, in turn, have been influenced more by the mercurial winds of public opinion than by the language of the Constitution, which draws only few and insignificant distinctions between citizens and noncitizens.[8] In a document where little is accidental, this suggests that the framers intended that all permanent residents enjoy generally equal status.[9]

The Constitution prohibits noncitizens from serving in high federal office—with the notable exception of the judiciary—but it mandates no other limits on their political participation. Every one of the original thirteen states granted aliens the franchise, and during the nineteenth century so did at least twenty-two states and territories.[10] Gradually, however, and mainly in response to fears that the "new" immigrants would debase republican institutions, states began to restrict to citizens not only the franchise, but also other civic activities such as jury service and elective office. As resident aliens' political influence waned, their ability to protect their interests declined proportionately. As a consequence even today they enjoy decent, but scarcely equal, treatment.

THE EMIGRATION PROCESS

Aliens wishing to immigrate to the United States must first secure a visa, a lengthy process that is at best cumbersome and at worst both cumbersome and discriminatory. Visas are issued by American consuls who operate in foreign countries under the supervision of the Department of State. After undergoing a thorough screening, and a mental and physical examination, an applicant will be granted an entrance permit providing he or she has established eligibility "to the satisfaction" of the consular officer. An applicant who fails to satisfy the officer is entitled to a limited intra-departmental review of his or her application. Unless a supervisory agent overturns the consul's decision, the applicant will be denied permission to enter the United States.[11]

No one has an abstract "right" to enter the country. Once the government agrees to admit aliens who satisfy stipulated preconditions, however, it is obliged to treat them fairly. Indeed, the Constitution established a system of government largely defined by its dedication to procedural due process. The means by which visas are granted or withheld, however, is arbitrary in the extreme. The consular officer who makes the crucial initial decision on visa issuance is often an inadequately trained and poorly supervised subordinate agent.[12] Neither Congress nor the Secretary of State has provided these officers with workable standards by which to assess an applicant's eligibility, and as a consequence the decisions rendered by various consulates are largely discretionary and baldly inconsistent.

In order to evaluate the equity of United States immigration laws, both substantively and in application, the Civil Rights Commission conducted lengthy hearings in the late 1970s.[13] A number of witnesses recounted experiences with what they described as "high-handed" consular officers who operate in foreign countries. According to one witness, they "became like kings in their own domain."[14] Since the Department of State has promulgated no regulations concerning whether, or under what circumstances, an alien has the right to the assistance of counsel during visa interviews, consular officers make this determination on an *ad hoc* basis according to criteria of their own devising. Visas can be denied because the consul determines that the applicant is likely to become a public charge after he or she has entered the United States, despite the fact there is frequently no basis for this determination, and occasionally even evidence suggesting the contrary.[15] Consuls' determinations, moreover, frequently receive only perfunctory review from a supervisory agency or, ultimately, from the Department of State, and the INA prohibits the federal courts from intervening, thus removing an additional institutional check.[16]

Aliens may submit evidence to rebut a finding that they are ineligible for a visa, and they are entitled to a statement citing the reasons why their request was denied. They have no right to examine adverse evidence, however, and no right to a formal review of the consul's decision. The absence of these procedural safeguards prompted immigration lawyer Laurier McDonald to conclude that "[t]he American process stops at the threshold of the American consulates abroad."[17]

If aliens are granted a visa, their chances of being admitted to the country are enhanced but not assured: At a United States port of entry they must still undergo another screening and inspection by immigration officers, who can exclude them on many grounds.[18] If they seek permanent residence in the United States, they must obtain clearance from the Public Health Service.[19] If they secured a visa based upon their potential employment in this country, they must obtain employment certification from the Department of Labor.[20]

Aliens surviving this bureaucratic gauntlet are admitted to the United States for permanent residence. At this point, they are entitled to many rights and privileges, but their "denizen" status is nevertheless apparent. They must inform the Immigration Service of their whereabouts, and travel abroad without American diplomatic protection. If their native country is either warring with the United States or threatening it with invasion, they may be arrested, expelled, or interned.[21] Should they travel abroad, there is a likelihood, but no guarantee, that they will be readmitted to the country. Finally, they live with the knowledge that they can be deported on any of 700 grounds.[22]

THE DEPORTATION PROCESS

The deportation process must rank among the country's least cost-effective ventures, as judged by the time and money expended by the government and the hardship visited upon the alien. The inefficiency of the process is illustrated by the deportation statutes themselves. Congress typically responds to international crises by adding new categories to the list of deportable aliens. As tensions subside, rather than refine or eliminate these categories, legislators provide new avenues for discretionary relief.[23] The result is an arcane, Byzantine network of laws beyond the comprehension of anyone other than a highly-trained attorney.

That Congress has the right to enact deportation statutes, complicated or otherwise, has been acknowledged at least since 1892, when the Supreme Court proclaimed that

[among] the accepted maxims of international law [is] that every sovereign nation has the power, as inherent in sovereignty, and essential

to self-preservation, to forbid the entrance of foreigners within its dominion, or to admit them only in such cases and upon such conditions
as it may see fit to prescribe.[24]

Not surprisingly, few judges contest the government's right to
expel those it deems undesirable; what *is* surprising is that so
few contest the way this expulsion is effected.

If the government were to seize individuals suspected of a
crime, detain them indefinitely without bail, deny them appointed counsel and the right to compel witnesses in their own
behalf, subject them to self-incrimination, prosecute them for
an offense perfectly legal when committed, and finally banish
them forever from the country, the American public would be
outraged: The government would have flaunted half a dozen
rights that comprise the bedrock of this country's constitutional
system.

The government's action would be perfectly legal, however,
if the suspects were aliens, facing deportation. Many members
of the Supreme Court apparently agree that expulsion from the
country may "deprive an alien of all that makes life worth living,"[25] as Justice Louis Brandeis once noted. The Court has
nevertheless continued to insist—as it has for nearly 100 years—
that deportation constitutes neither a criminal procedure nor a
punishment. According to judicial logic, deportation is a civil
undertaking by which the government merely rids itself of un-
wanted guests.[26] The consequences of labeling deportation a
"civil" proceeding are enormous. Although the government is
still theoretically obliged to observe fundamental fairness, it may
disregard many of the specific constitutional guarantees that are
applicable only in criminal cases where the defendant is threatened with imprisonment.[27]

That deportation comprises no punishment is a particularly
disingenuous myth, as the plights of Carlos Marcello and Juan
Galvan bear witness. In 1908, Marcello was brought as an infant from Tunisia to the United States. He eventually married
an American citizen, raised a family, and lived a generally un-
eventful life until 1938, when he was jailed for one year for violating the Marijuana Tax Act. When Congress amended the
INA in 1952, it made a marijuana conviction grounds for ex-

pulsion.[28] Shortly thereafter, the Immigration Service initiated deportation proceedings against Marcello and ordered him to leave the country in sixty days.[29]

Galvan's circumstances were similar. He had lived in the United States since 1918. In 1944 he joined the Communist party, which was legal at the time and had even sponsored candidates whose names appeared on state ballots. During the two years in which Galvan was a member, the 1940 Alien Registration Act[30] was in effect. One provision of this act stipulated that no alien could be deported for subversion without proof that he or she actually advocated the overthrow of the government. This provision was nullified by the passage of the Internal Security Act of 1950,[31] which made it a deportable offense to be or have been at any time a member of the Communist party. When Galvan's case eventually reached the Supreme Court, a majority concluded that the 1950 act dispensed with any need to prove advocacy. The defendant's two-year membership in the Communist party was in itself grounds for deportation.[32]

The Court has frequently intimated that it regrets its self-imposed, but longstanding doctrine that since deportation proceedings are civil in nature the government can accordingly penalize aliens for activity that was not unlawful when committed. It has nevertheless refused to abandon the doctrine, for reasons explained by Justice Felix Frankfurter in *Galvan v. Press*:

[M]uch could be said for the view, were we writing on a clean slate, that the Due Process Clause qualifies the scope of political discretion heretofore recognized as belonging to Congress in regulating the entry and deportations of aliens. . . . But the slate is not clean. As to the extent of the power of Congress to review, there is not merely "a page of history," . . . but a whole volume. . . .[33]

In deference to this "whole volume" of precedent, the majority thus refused to overturn Galvan's deportation order.[34]

Marcello and *Galvan* would be less distressing if they simply illustrated practices peculiar to an unenlightened era. In fact, however, the deportation laws are still severe; §241(a) of the INA, for instance, authorizes the deportation of any alien who joins or even affiliates with an organization associated with subversive doctrines, or who promulgates those doctrines by any means whatsoever.[35] Moreover, the Supreme Court is as unwilling as ever to challenge §241 or any other provisions of the deportation laws on substantive grounds.

One significant change has occurred, however, since the Cold War years when *Marcello* and *Galvan* were decided: Now when they interpret or apply the deportation laws, federal judges often labor creatively to mute their harsh impact. Most of them insist that standards of procedural fairness be fastidiously observed, or that any ambiguity in statutory language be resolved on behalf of the alien. On occasion they will even stretch facts, contort phraseology, or impute intentions to Congress that belie common sense. In 1957, for instance, the Court asserted in *Rowoldt v. Perfetto*[36] that Congress intended only to deport those aliens whose membership in the Communist party had been "meaningful," and six years later it concluded in *Gastelum-Quinones v. Kennedy* that the government bears the burden of proving its "meaningfulness."[37]

Adroit judges continue to benefit many individual aliens.[38] Notwithstanding their good offices, however, the deportation laws remain Draconian. Since the 1952 INA abolished all statutes of limitation involving deportation,[39] an alien labors forever under a cloud of insecurity if even long ago, and however innocently, he or she engaged in any of several hundred proscribed activities. Moreover, since the 1952 act explicitly made all the grounds for deportation retroactive,[40] the alien remains subject to expulsion even for activities that were lawful at the time of their performance. Such provisions are apparently constitutional, at least as long as the judiciary maintains the illusion that deportation results in no penalty. They are not fair, however, and as Justice William Douglas noted in a 1952 case, they are not consistent with America's tradition: "[t]he principle of forgiveness and the doctrine of redemption are too deep in our philosophy to admit that there is no return for those who have once erred."[41]

NATURALIZATION AND DENATURALIZATION

Congress could pass a law ordering the deportation of all permanent resident aliens without contravening either international or American constitutional law. It could also double or triple the number of federal laws that restrict their employment opportunities or public service benefits. Congress would probably not exercise either option, but the fact that it could underscores both the vulnerability of an alien's status, and the comparative security he or she would enjoy as a naturalized citizen.

As an adjunct of its constitutional power to "prescribe a uniform rule of naturalization,"[42] Congress determines the conditions under which an alien may become a citizen. Congress has always stipulated that applicants for naturalization satisfy certain age and residency requirements, and over the years it has attached other conditions as well. At one time, the naturalization laws discriminated on the basis of race, color, national origin, and even sex, since even women born in the United States forfeited their citizenship upon marrying an alien.[43] Qualifications based upon invidious criteria have been removed, but Congress has retained restrictions that penalize aliens who have unconventional life styles or political beliefs. The judiciary has invariably upheld these restrictions, reasoning that the granting of naturalization is an adjunct of sovereignty—and as such "a privilege, to be given, qualified, or withheld, as Congress may determine."[44]

Only those possessing "good moral character" are eligible for citizenship, although the meaning of this term is almost as ambiguous today as when it first became a requirement nearly 200 years ago. Most courts at least agree, however, that the requirement does not demand that applicants demonstrate saintlike virtue, but only that they comply with the standards held by the average citizen in the community in which they reside.[45] According to the INA, applicants shall be considered deficient in moral character if they are at present, or were in the past, a drunkard, adulterer, polygamist, prostitute, procurer, or if they engaged in any of a number of proscribed activities. Occasionally courts have also gone beyond the technical language of the act—for instance, by prohibiting homosexuals from becoming citizens.[46]

An applicant for naturalization must also be "[a]ttached to the Principles of the Constitution" and be "well disposed to the Good Order and Happiness of the United States." Although this provision is rife with imprecision, courts agree that at a minimum it requires applicants to support the basic form of government in the United States.[47] The Supreme Court *did* declare in *Schneiderman v. United States*[48] that aliens could not be barred from citizenship because they advocated peaceful and constitutional change. Anarchists, however, or aliens who have been a member of a communist organization during the preceding ten years, may be disqualified from obtaining citizenship, even if there is no proof that they personally advocated Marxist ideas or were more than nominal members.[49]

In order to qualify for citizenship, applicants must also possess a knowledge of the English language, which ordinarily is interpreted to mean that while they need not rival Henry James, they should understand "simple words and phrases."[50] Spanish-speaking applicants have challenged this requirement on the ground that it denies them equal protection of the laws, but to date no courts have supported their stance. Prospective citizens must also demonstrate an understanding of the American form of government—but again, they are ordinarily not expected, for instance, to analyze the complexities of the Tenth Amendment, but only to grasp fundamental principles, such as that the United States government is divided into three branches.[51]

Before they are naturalized, aliens must take an oath that they will "bear arms on behalf of the United States when required by law."[52] Some applicants object to this requirement, which exacts from them an affirmative pledge from which native-born citizens are exempt. As an alternative to this pledge, however, they may take an oath to perform noncombatant service in the armed forces or important civic work under civilian direction.[53]

In addition to prescribing the terms for acquiring citizenship, Congress also determines—within limits—the conditions under which foreign-born individuals may be stripped of their citizenship, or "denaturalized."[54] The judiciary rarely questioned those conditions until the late 1950s, when the Supreme Court began to acknowledge the seriousness of denaturalization.[55] Indeed, in a 1958 case, Chief Justice Earl Warren asserted that being deprived of one's citizenship was "a fate forbidden by the principles of civilized treatment."[56] Today a naturalized citizen may be involuntarily deprived of his or her citizenship only when the government is able to prove by "clear, unequivocal, and convincing evidence"[57] that it was illegally or fraudulently procured.[58]

Despite these salutary developments, by perverting the "fraudulent procurement" provision government leaders can still abuse the denaturalization process. Used as intended, the provision enables the government to prevent charlatans from reaping the benefits of their misrepresentation, or rid the country of malefactors, such as former Nazis who acquired their citizenship by concealing their past activities. When misused, however, this same provision enables the government to penalize those whose political views it finds objectionable.[59] A number of people lost their citizenship during World War I because they expressed sympathy for Germany, and again during and after World War II because they voiced support for fascist or Communist doctrines.[60]

The government justifies denaturalization in these cases with the rationale that individuals advocating fascism, for instance, or communism, or anarchism, must inevitably have obtained their citizenship through fraud, since they could not simultaneously champion such ideologies and still be attached to republican principles. Consequently, the INA stipulates that everyone who joins a proscribed organization within five years after their naturalization establishes prima facie evidence of lack of attachment to the Constitution.[61] The Supreme Court will sanction their subsequent denaturalization if prosecutors can prove they were "active" members who knowingly supported the organization's objectives.[62]

Naturalized citizens, consequently, may not exercise their political rights as fully as their neighbors who were born in the United States. Unlike their native-born counterparts, moreover, they alone can be stripped of their citizenship and banished for activities that terminated well in the past if the government can prove that timely disclosure of these activities would have rendered them ineligible for citizenship in the first place.[63] Thus, while they enjoy most of the privileges accompanying their status, in some important respects naturalized citizens nevertheless remain second class citizens.

STATE DISCRIMINATION AGAINST ALIENS

The Supreme Court has consistently held that by virtue of its "sovereign prerogatives" Congress can prescribe the terms and conditions upon which aliens may enter and remain in the United States.[64] Less clear is the extent to which individual states can attach "terms and conditions" upon aliens duly admitted and residing within their jurisdictions. The Supreme Court has grappled with this issue for at least a hundred years, attempting with varying degrees of success to reconcile state legislation with two constitutional provisions—the equal protection clause of the Fourteenth Amendment and the supremacy clause in Article VI.

In 1868, Congress ratified the Fourteenth Amendment, the first clause of which provides that "no state shall deny to any person within its jurisdiction the equal protection of the laws."[65] On the basis of this "equal protection clause," in *Yick Wo v. Hopkins*,[66] the Supreme Court in 1886 granted relief to a Chinese alien who demonstrated that a San Francisco ordinance was selectively enforced against Chinese nationals to prevent them from operating laundries.

Yick Wo v. Hopkins was the exception. Despite the sweeping language of the Fourteenth Amendment, for more than a century after its ratification the Supreme Court continued to sustain most state laws that discriminated against noncitizens.[67] It managed this by applying the so-called "rational relationship" test to legislation that classified on the basis of alienage. According to this test, a state can indeed differentiate between groups in society as long as its statutory schemes bear a rational relationship to a legitimate state end, such as public health or welfare.[68]

Article VI, on the other hand, provides that federal enactments shall be "the supreme law of the land."[69] As a consequence, the Supreme Court has formulated the so-called "preemption doctrine," which stipulates that federal law or policy "preempts" any state legislation that conflicts with, or impedes, its operation.[70] The preemption doctrine is relevant to issues involving noncitizens because the Constitution vests

Congress with exclusive power to make "a uniform rule of Naturalization," and, by judicial extension, with exclusive power to regulate the admission and exclusion of aliens and the conditions governing their residence in this country. At least in principle, related state efforts are consequently foreclosed.

In a 1915 case, *Truax v. Raich*,[71] the Supreme Court held that an Arkansas statute limiting the number of aliens an employer could hire was invalid, not only on equal protection grounds, but also because it was preempted by federal law. The Court reasoned that Arkansas could not limit employment in the "common occupations of the community" to citizens because it would thereby restrict aliens from "the full scope of the privileges conferred" by admission to the country.[72] The Court emphasized, however, that a state retained the right to disqualify aliens from any occupation relating to "the public domain" without, apparently, contravening either the equal protection clause or trespassing on exclusive federal power over immigration.

In cases postdating *Truax* the Court justified many state restrictions by invoking either the "public domain" doctrine, or its corollary, which holds that states, by virtue of their police powers, might limit to citizens those occupations "affected with a public interest."[73] A state court in 1924 accordingly held that Rhode Island could prohibit noncitizens from driving motorbuses because "aliens as a class are naturally less interested in the state, the safety of its citizens, and the public welfare."[74] Ostensibly to promote the public interest, other states enacted similar restrictions, which in time became ludicrous in their scope and variety. In commenting on the occupations forbidden to aliens, Simona Rosales observed that states "do not trust aliens with animals, a corpse, or even a person's hair or beard."[75] The Supreme Court invalidated neither these nor a rash of kindred laws that prohibited aliens from engaging in many licensed, lucrative, or otherwise desirable professions.

Until recently the judiciary also sustained most laws that handicapped noncitizens in areas unrelated to employment,[76] including legislation predicated on invidious grounds. The Supreme Court first questioned the legitimacy of these laws in 1948, invalidating in *Takahashi v. Fish & Game Commission*[77] a California statute that denied commercial fishing licenses to those ineligible for citizenship. California justified the prohibition on the ground that it had a "special public interest" in regulating its fish population.[78] The Court, however, recognized it as a flagrant piece of racial discrimination since, according to federal law, only Japanese immigrants were ineligible for citizenship.[79] It thus invalidated the law on both equal protection and preemption grounds. While the Court conceded that states might apply some laws "exclusively to its alien inhabitants as a class," it declared that such power "is confined within narrow limits."[80]

The Court in *Takahashi* registered its intention to protect resident aliens from state legislation that was patently unjust, but it did not henceforth become their active champion. In fact, another twenty-three years passed before the Supreme Court again upset a state policy that discriminated on the basis of alienage. In 1971, in *Graham v. Richardson*,[81] it invalidated state restrictions conditioning welfare payments on citizenship or lengthy residence.[82] According to the Court, such restrictions conflicted with national policy in an area constitutionally entrusted to the federal government;[83] more important, however, they contravened the Fourteenth Amendment's equal protection clause because states could have no "special public interest" in limiting to citizens the benefits of tax revenues to which aliens had contributed.[84]

Graham's importance rests less in its specific ruling than in the declaration of policy that accompanied this ruling. As the Supreme Court pointed out, prior to the time they are eligible for citizenship, aliens are excluded from the political process, and thus as a class they represent "a prime example of a 'discrete and insular minority . . . for whom heightened judicial solicitude is appropriate.' "[85]

Resident aliens thus comprise what the judiciary calls a "suspect" class—a designation also bestowed upon racial and ethnic minorities.[86] Accordingly, when examining state policy that discriminates against them, the Court would hereafter employ the rigorous "strict scrutiny," rather than the lenient "rational relationship," test. When legislation must satisfy the more exacting standard, it can survive challenge on equal protection grounds only if it promotes compelling ends that cannot be achieved through nondiscriminatory means or by more carefully tailored language.[87]

Graham caught the legal community unprepared. Ordinarily the Supreme Court does not declare bold new policy without preparing for it through incremental rulings. By the time it outlawed dual public school systems in *Brown v. Board of Education*[88] for instance, it had already effectively outlawed segregated post-graduate institutions.[89] No such preparatory action foreshadowed *Graham*.[90] Moreover, there had been little organized movement by or on behalf of resident aliens. *Graham* was decided during a "liberal" era, however, during which both the judiciary and the political branches were particularly sensitive to the rights of many different minority groups, and perhaps aliens were simply the beneficiaries of the time.[91]

On the authority of *Graham v. Richardson*, courts have continued to invalidate many state policies that discriminate against resident aliens—such as ones prohibiting them from practicing law,[92] serving as civil engineers,[93] or receiving public assistance to attend educational institutions.[94] *Graham* thus provided a vulnerable class of people with an historically unprecedented degree of protection, and remains the single most important case involving the rights of resident aliens. Its impact, however, should not be overestimated for three reasons: (1) its holding applies only to permanent residents, who comprise a comparatively small percentage of those foreigners admitted to the United States; (2) and more significantly, *Graham* applies only to state, as opposed to federal, legislation;[95] (3) *Graham's* impact has been considerably diluted by the subsequent evolution of the "political community" doctrine, which was first suggested as dictum in a 1973 case, *Sugarman v. Dougall*.[96]

In *Sugarman v. Dougall*, the Supreme Court invalidated a New York statute that restricted to citizens employment in the state's competitive civil service.[97] New York justified the statute on the ground that a state has a substantial interest in the loyalty and trustworthiness of its civil servants, who must be "free of competing obligations to another sovereign."[98] The Court invalidated the statute, however, essentially because its classificatory scheme was not tailored with precision—it required citizenship for any one occupying low-level civil service positions, yet exempted from the citizenship requirement those persons holding elective and high appointive office.[99] The Court emphasized, however, that a state, by virtue of its sovereign obligations "to preserve the basic conception of a political community," could require citizenship of those persons holding important nonelective positions that involve the formation, execution, or review of broad public policy.[100]

The *Sugarman* opinion was rife with uncertainties: What were the dimensions of this "political community" from which aliens might be excluded? What specific activities, other than public office or suffrage, fell within its ambit? In a series of subsequent cases the Court soon indicated that the "political community" subsumes activities related only peripherally to the formation or execution of high-level policy.

In a 1978 case, *Foley v. Connelie*,[101] the Supreme Court upheld a New York statute that prohibited noncitizens from serving as state troopers.[102] Speaking for the majority, Chief Justice Warren Burger validated the law because, he explained, troopers perform basic governmental functions: Their presence is pervasive in modern society, and "while they do not formulate policy, per se, they exercise an almost infinite variety of discretionary powers."[103] Consequently, it is not surprising that most states insist that their political officers be citizens, "whom the State may reasonably presume to be more familiar with and sympathetic to American traditions,"[104] and who presumably accept and bear allegiance to the Constitution.[105]

Justice Thurgood Marshall submitted a dissenting opinion in which he maintained that the Court's willingness to ascribe high-level policy-making functions to police officers merely demonstrates that the "political community" exception, read without reference to its content, "would swallow the rule."[106] Justice John Paul Stevens also dissented, primarily because he believed the New York law was founded on an unwarranted assumption— that aliens as a class are presumptively disloyal and untrustworthy.[107]

In a 1979 case, *Ambach v. Norwick*,[108] the Supreme Court sustained another New York law that prohibits from serving as a public school teacher any alien who does not become a citizen when eligible.[109] Justice Harry Blackmun made a strong argument that the law, in common with most of the state's other citizen-restrictive statutes, had its "origin in the frantic and overreactive days of the First World War when attitudes of parochialism and fear of the foreigner were the order of the day."[110] The majority, however, apparently accepted New York's contention that in 1938 it first restricted teacher eligibility to citizens out of a concern for the strong nexus between teaching and the needs of the political community. Indeed, in his majority opinion Justice Lewis Powell emphasized the indispensable role teachers play in this community, both as agents of political socialization and as transmitters of civic values.[111]

In January 1982, the Supreme Court decided *Cabell v. Jose Chavez Salido*,[112] its most recent case concerning the employment rights of resident aliens. The case involved a California statute that requires all those categorized as "peace officers" to be citizens.[113] The category is a broad one, embracing myriad high- and low-level occupations. The district court consequently invalidated the law on equal protection grounds, reasoning that some of these occupations could not affect the political community, no matter how "liberally" it is viewed.[114]

The Supreme Court disagreed, and sustained the statute. Justice Byron White, speaking for the majority, explained that the appellees were applying for jobs as probation officers, for which citizenship is a legitimate prerequisite because such officers must inevitably exercise discretion in the course of their duties. In their official capacities, moreover, they symbolize the political community's control over those who have flaunted the norms of the social order.[115] Justice White pointed out that noncitizens seeking positions other than as probation officers could still challenge the statute as it applied to them. He also noted that the Court would continue to disfavor state policies that discriminate against noncitizens on economic, as opposed to political, grounds. He admitted in a footnote, however, that by virtue of the Court's logic, almost every public employee can be understood to affect the political community.[116]

Notwithstanding the Court's decisions in *Foley*, *Ambach*, and *Cabell*, aliens still benefit from significantly greater judicial protection than they did before *Graham v. Richardson* was decided.

As Justice White noted in *Cabell*, presumably the judiciary will continue to disfavor state policies that either discriminate against noncitizens on strictly economic, as opposed to political, grounds, or that deny them a variety of public services, such as welfare and unemployment compensation.[117] Nevertheless, the Court has progressively constricted its holding in *Graham*, which proclaimed that resident aliens constitute a suspect class, entitled to protection under the exacting strict scrutiny test.

Perhaps the Court issued *Graham* without understanding its full implications, for on the basis of this decision thousands of state statutes that discriminate against aliens became constitutionally infirm. At any rate, the prospect of nullifying such legislation on a wholesale basis eventually became unacceptable to a majority of the Court. It thus sought a means by which to carve out an exception to *Graham's* broad ruling, and thereby rescue some state provisions. The "means" appeared in the form of the so-called "political community" doctrine.

The Supreme Court may have served its immediate needs by developing this doctrine, but from a long-term perspective its strategy is unfortunate. By virtue of the "political community" doctrine, aliens are excluded from participation in an increasing number of occupations. Yet the Court has never established the dimensions of this abstract entity, the "political community," nor explained the constitutional basis for its exclusive nature. In the process of ennobling this community, moreover, the Court has revitalized old stereotypes by implying that aliens, as a class, are unworthy participants in a public sphere where trustworthiness and allegiance are essential.

Finally, throughout its opinions in *Sugarman, Foley, Ambach,* and *Cabell*, the Court reiterates that noncitizens can be excluded from the political community because of the important—indeed, crucial—role citizenship plays in the American republic. The Court thereby suggests that citizenship is intended to be a status of such moment that it is a proper prerequisite for any position affecting the public welfare.

Quite the contrary is true. Citizenship was not even defined in the original Constitution, nor was it granted more than a minimal and vague role in subsequent amendments.[118] Moreover, due process and equal protection—those crucial rights guaranteed in the Fourteenth Amendment—are explicitly granted to "all persons" within a state's jurisdiction.[119] Thus, by extolling the virtues and emphasizing the exclusivity of this political community, the Court vests citizenship with a significance that is at variance with the language and history of the Constitution. In so doing, as the late Professor Alexander Bickel observed, it jeopardizes a benign tradition in which fundamental rights have been accorded all human beings within the polity irrespective of their citizenship.[120]

FEDERAL DISCRIMINATION AGAINST ALIENS

Although states may bar noncitizens from the myriad positions that affect the political community, this might not be critical if aliens were guaranteed access to the occupations that remain. This access is not assured, however, since the Supreme Court has indicated that both private employers and the federal government may discriminate against applicants on the basis of their citizenship.

In 1964, Congress passed the Civil Rights Act, Title VII of which prohibits an employer from discriminating against workers on the basis of race, color, sex, religion, or national origin.[121] Although the act does not specifically mention alienage, the Equal Employment Opportunity Commission, which enforces the act, issued guidelines in 1972 providing that

[b]ecause discrimination on the basis of citizenship has the effect of discrimination on the basis of national origin, a lawfully immigrant alien who is domiciled or residing in this country may not be discriminated against on the basis of citizenship.[122]

The Supreme Court found the commission's reasoning unpersuasive. In 1972, in *Espinoza v. Farah Manufacturing Company*,[123] it held that discrimination on the basis of alienage is not equivalent to discrimination on the basis of national origin. Thus Farah's decision to hire only citizens is not in itself illegal. Alienage is frequently a proxy for national origin, the Court explained, but this is not inevitable—certainly not in this instance, where 96 percent of the company's employees were, like the petitioner, of Mexican descent.[124] The Court also reasoned that since Congress has long discriminated against aliens in federal employment, it could not have intended to prohibit private employees from exercising the same option.[125]

Three years after *Espinoza*, the Supreme Court indicated that the federal government continues to be as free as private employers to discriminate on the basis of alienage. In 1976, the Court decided two cases on the same day confirming this fact— *Mathews v. Diaz*[126] and *Hampton v. Mow Sun Wong*.[127] In both cases the Court examined policies that closely parallel the state legislation invalidated in *Graham v. Richardson* and *Sugarman v. Dougall*, and plaintiffs argued that the federal government should not be allowed to discriminate against aliens in ways foreclosed to the states. If discriminatory state laws contravened the equal protection clause of the Fourteenth Amendment, then analogous federal restrictions contravene the equal protection component of the Fifth Amendment.[128]

The Court disagreed, predictably, since it has repeatedly sustained federal legislation that discriminates against aliens, even when it has readily quashed its state counterpart. The Court justifies this double standard primarily on the ground that the political branches, unlike the states, possess what amounts to plenary power over noncitizens. This power arises both as an adjunct of sovereignty, and from the language of the Constitution, which vests Congress with authority to regulate naturalization, and the president with principal control over foreign relations.[129] The Court's deference extends only to situations in which federal policies are challenged on substantive grounds, however. As its resolution of *Hampton v. Mow Sun Wong*[130] illustrates, it is significantly less acquiescent when these same policies are attacked on procedural grounds—that is, on the grounds that in enacting or applying a law or regulation the government failed to observe standards of fairness.

In *Hampton* the majority overturned a regulation promulgated by the Civil Service Commission that prohibits aliens from serving in the federal civil service.[131] The court implied, however, that it would sanction the same regulation if it were authorized either by Congress or the President.[132] Justice John Paul Stevens, on behalf of the majority, noted that aliens, as a class, labor under disadvantages from which the general public is spared. As a consequence,

> [w]henever the Federal Government asserts an overriding national interest as justification for a discriminatory rule which would violate the equal protection clause if adopted by a State, due process requires that there be a legitimate basis for presuming the rule was actually intended to serve that interest.[133]

Justice Stevens reasoned that three interests might be promoted by a policy that prohibits aliens from serving in the civil service: providing the President with a "bargaining chip" with which to secure reciprocal concessions for American citizens residing in foreign countries; maintaining a motivation for resident aliens to obtain naturalization; facilitating administrative convenience by obviating the need to determine the loyalty of alien job applicants on a case-by-case basis. If either Congress or the Executive had expressly formulated the disputed policy, the Court would presume it did so in order to further one of these "overriding national interests."[134] The same presumption could not be extended to a rule issued by the Civil Service Commission, however, whose sole concern is the furtherance of an efficient federal service.

The Court's logic is curious, since by its own admission both Congress and the executive branch knew of, and acceded to, the commission's policy since it was first instituted in 1883.[135] Perhaps this logic served to masquerade the Court's actual motive, however, which was to discourage federal agencies from casually initiating or perpetuating policies that discriminate against noncitizens. Bureaucrats frequently establish such policies out of habit or political expediency, and without the benefit of public debate. Elected officials may be no less influenced by custom and expediency, but unlike administrative agents they presumably must discuss the merits of particular regulations and assume political accountability for them. (President Ford was apparently no more eager than officials at the Civil Service Commission to submit the regulation to public debate, however; immediately after the Court's opinion in *Mow Sun Wong*, he issued an executive order barring aliens from Civil Service

employment under most circumstances—regardless of their
length of residence in this country or the degree of sensitivity
inhering in a given position.[136] In his letter accompanying the
order, the President explained that it was in the "national interest" to preserve the governmental prohibition against the
employment of aliens, although he never explained how this
interest was thereby promoted.)[137]

In the companion case, *Mathews v. Diaz*,[138] a unanimous Court
upheld a federal provision that excludes aliens from the Medicare Supplemental Insurance Program unless they have resided
in the country at least five years.[139] The Court sustained the
provision, although it conceded that its durational requirement
was "longer than necessary to protect the fiscal integrity of the
program."[140] The Court explained, however, that it would sustain the Medicare policy since it was not "wholly irrational": It
might encourage aliens to seek naturalization, and it reflects the
fact that as an alien's attachment to the country grows stronger,
so does the strength of his or her claim to an equal share of its
bounty.[141]

Despite the Court's claim to the contrary, the disputed policy
is, in fact, "wholly irrational." The Court never explains how
aliens' affinity to the country bears any relationship to their rights
to participate in an insurance program, particularly one to which
they contribute no less than a citizen. Additionally, far from
encouraging naturalization, the policy has the perverse effect
of penalizing only those aliens who have resided in the country
less than five years—the very people ineligible for citizenship—
while rewarding those who have deliberately elected to forgo
naturalization.

But what if the policy did encourage naturalization? The same
rationale could justify all manner of discriminatory policies
against aliens. What if the policy's real purpose is to provide
citizens with an economic advantage? As far back as 1915, the
Court held in *Truax v. Raich* that by denying benefits to an alien
in order to promote its own economic position, a state makes
discrimination "an end in itself."[142] The federal government's
action in *Mathews v. Diaz* merits the same indictment.

In a third case, *Fiallo v. Bell*,[143] plaintiffs challenged a provision of the INA that excludes the relationship between an ille-

gitimate child and his or her natural father from the preferential treatment otherwise accorded the child or parent of a United States citizen under the existing immigration quota system.[144] Petitioners argued that the provision subverts the intent of family reunification that underlies the entire immigration scheme. Moreover, they asserted, it represents "double-barreled" discrimination on the basis of sex and illegitimacy—classifications ordinarily impermissible when applied to citizens—since only the relationship between an illegitimate child and its natural mother was accorded preference.

The Court found these arguments unpersuasive. It cited both its limited role when reviewing congressional policy choices, particularly in the area of immigration, and the leeway vested in Congress to treat aliens in ways it could not possibly treat citizens.[145] Justice Marshall dissented, however, precisely because he believed the disputed policy impermissibly discriminates against United States citizens:

Until today, I thought it clear that when Congress grants benefits to some citizens but not to others, it is our duty to insure that the decision comports with the Fifth Amendment principles of due process and equal protection. Today, however, the Court appears to hold that discrimination among citizens, however invidious and irrational, must be tolerated if it appears in the context of the immigration laws.[146]

RESIDENT ALIENS: A "SUSPECT" GROUP?

Justice Marshall is correct: The Supreme Court will indeed tolerate discriminatory legislation if it "appears in the context of the immigration laws" and, by extension, if it relates to the admission, exclusion, or treatment of noncitizens. Precisely for this reason, resident aliens should be considered a "suspect class," as the Supreme Court acknowledged in *Graham v. Richardson*. Categorizing a group as "suspect" has enormous legal ramifications. Any legislation that discriminates against such a group is almost invariably foredoomed because the Court will subject it to the strictest scrutiny, and will spare only that which promotes compelling state ends.

Society is comprised of myriad discrete groups or classes that seek judicial protection—the handicapped, poor, and elderly, for instance, or the young and the institutionalized. If the Court declared all of them "suspect" then legislators would be effectively immobilized.[147] Instead, the Court has reserved this designation only for those whose history of discrimination, on the one hand, and whose minimal political clout, on the other, have rendered them particularly defenseless.[148]

When a group has been subjected to "a history of purposeful unequal treatment,"[149] the Court more readily than otherwise assumes that statutory schemes discriminating against it are prompted more by habit or malice than by a legitimate motive. These statutory schemes ordinarily carry with them a stigma as well, suggesting that members of the target class are inherently less worthy than members of the general community.[150]

Members of a suspect class are also systematically disadvantaged in their efforts to compete in, or at least wrest concessions from, the majoritarian political process, and this above all accounts for the judiciary's vigilance. These members comprise what the Court calls a "discrete and insular minority."[151] This oft-repeated phrase is borrowed from a footnote written in 1938 by Justice Harlan Stone, who suggested in *United States v. Carolene Products*[152] that, under certain circumstances, the judiciary should suspend its customary "presumption of constitutionality" when reviewing statutory schemes:

prejudice against discrete and insular minorities . . . may curtail the operation of those political processes ordinarily to be relied upon to protect minorities, and . . . may call for a correspondingly more searching judicial inquiry.[153]

Guided by these traditional indicia, the Supreme Court earlier had labeled as "suspect" classifications based on race and national origin.[154] In 1971 the Burger Court added "alienage" to the list,[155] recognizing that resident aliens satisfy the preconditions necessary for suspect status. Historically they have been subject to substantial legal discrimination, often prevented from participating in community functions, owning land, or engaging in any occupation that affected the "public interest," however loosely construed. Measures that discriminate between citizens and aliens frequently carry with them a stigma, as well: They suggest the popular and official conviction that aliens are somehow inferior, their loyalty questionable and their allegiance divided. Indeed, the very word "alien" conjures up images of someone who is peculiar and out of place.

Aliens are, above all, a politically powerless segment of society.[156] They have virtually no opportunity to assert their interests in the public forum, where they are not only *underre*presented, but altogether *un*represented. Neither do they possess "the right preservative of all rights," the franchise.[157] Unlike nonresident aliens, moreover, they can rarely enlist the assistance of their native country when they seek to redress their grievances. Legislators, as a consequence, can ignore or even imperil their interests with little fear of retaliation.

Resident aliens thus require and fully merit the "suspect" status they were accorded in *Graham*. As the Supreme Court has progressively narrowed its holding in *Graham*, however, this status has become correspondingly less secure. Presumably aliens are still a suspect class, but only when state—as opposed to either federal or private—action is involved, and even then only when state legislation does not affect the political community. This development is unfortunate because aliens receive adequate judicial protection only in contexts where their "suspect" status is acknowledged.

3

Nonimmigrant Aliens

Nonimmigrant aliens are those who visit or reside in the United States for a temporary period. Unlike resident aliens, who are admitted on a permanent basis and placed on a citizenship track, nonimmigrants come to this country for a specific purpose, presumably with the intention of returning to their homeland.[1] They include students, tourists, diplomats, the Japanese businessman negotiating a deal with General Motors and the Washington correspondent for the *London Times*.

An alien has no constitutional right to enter the United States. The Supreme Court has emphasized time and again that Congress has plenary authority to determine who may enter, for how long, and under what conditions: "[o]ver no conceivable subject is the legislative power of Congress more complete than it is over [the admission of aliens]."[2] Moreover, unless governmental officials disregard statutory or administrative regulations, aliens denied permission to enter the United States ordinarily lack standing even to challenge their exclusion, let alone any claim to the substantive rights accorded duly-admitted immigrants.[3] Once aliens are within the territorial jurisdiction of the United States, however, the situation changes dramatically: They are then entitled to most of the rights guaranteed in the Constitution.[4]

The importance of "territorial presence" is thus overriding, but it is not what it seems. Among the legal fictions that abound in the area of immigration law, few are more problematic than the one governing "territorial presence." According to this fiction, while an alien may be physically present in the United States—indeed, may have spent half a lifetime in its heartland—in a legal sense he or she may never have "entered" the country. Aliens seeking legal permission to enter are theoretically "on the threshold" until they have been officially admitted, and before that point they are legally indistinguishable from aliens who have never set foot in the United States.[5]

Aliens "on the threshold" include those who may have received a visa, but not final approval to enter from immigration officers stationed at ports of entry; resident aliens returning from a trip abroad who are refused readmission on "security" or other grounds, and foreigners temporarily paroled into the United States for humanitarian reasons.[6]

This legal myth creates situations that turn logic on its head. Aliens who overstay their visas, or who slip across the border "without inspection," are considered to be within the country's territorial jurisdiction, and cannot be involuntarily expelled without a full deportation proceeding.[7] Resident aliens, on the other hand, may be denied readmission to the country and excluded without even a perfunctory hearing.[8] This is not common practice, but it does occur, especially when an alien is considered a security risk. The plight of Ignatz Mezei is illustrative.

Mezei was destined for a life, as Justice Robert Jackson described it, of "unrelieved insignificance"[9] until he ran afoul of the United States Immigration Service. Mezei entered the country in 1923 as a resident alien. He spent the next twenty-five years in Buffalo, New York, where he married and raised a family, although he never applied for citizenship. In 1948 he left the country for the first time in order to visit his dying mother in Rumania. Once in Eastern Europe, however, Mezei spent nineteen months in an ultimately futile attempt to gain admission to Rumania, and thus the reunion with his mother never occurred. He returned to the United States in February 1950, at which time an immigration inspector ordered him temporarily excluded, and he was confined to Ellis Island. Three months later, upon the Attorney General's command, the exclusion order was made permanent. Mezei's request for a hearing was denied on the ground that the order was based on confidential information, the disclosure of which would be prejudicial to the security interests of the United States, and he was ordered to leave the country. Thus began Mezei's fervent, but ultimately futile, attempt to gain admission to some other country. He was deported on two separate occasions, to France and Great Britain, but both countries rejected him. Despite negotiations conducted by the United States Department of State, Hungary similarly refused to admit him. Mezei on his own initiative applied, unsuccessfully, for entry to twelve Latin American countries.

Finally, on November 15, 1951, after Mezei had spent almost two years on Ellis Island, a federal district court held that his confinement was unlawful and ordered his release.[10] In March 1953, the Supreme Court reversed this order, declaring that the federal judiciary was not authorized to interfere in exclusion proceedings that were based on danger to the national security.[11] Justice Tom Clark, speaking for the majority, explained that since Mezei was being excluded, rather than deported, Congress could effect this procedure any way it saw fit.[12]

Justice Robert Jackson, in dissent, scoffed at the "legal fiction" by which Mezei's exile was labeled an exclusion proceeding.[13] He castigated his colleagues for disregarding the fundamental procedural rights embodied in the concept of due process. Jackson agreed that Congress could determine whom to admit to this country, and the conditions of their admission, but he denied that it could authorize United States officers to deprive anyone who comes within the country's jurisdiction of life, liberty, or property without providing them with notice of the charges against them and a fair hearing.

In conclusion, Jackson noted that Mezei was free to leave the country "if only he were an amphibian."[14] He was not an amphibian, however, and as it was, no other country would take him:

Since we proclaimed him a Hercules who might pull down the pillars of our temple, we should not be surprised if peoples less prosperous, less strongly established and less stable feared to take him off our timorous hands.[15]

Jackson failed to secure the one additional vote needed for a majority. As a consequence, Mezei was hustled back to Ellis Island, where he faced the likelihood of spending the rest of his life in confinement.[16]

Ellen Knauff's situation was different from Mezei's, insofar as she was not a returning resident alien, but the wife of an American citizen seeking to enter the United States for the first time. Her ordeal resembles Mezei's, however, in that she also experienced the trials to which excludable aliens may be subject. Mrs. Knauff fled Germany in 1939 during the Hitler regime, going first to Czechoslovakia and then to England, where she served in the Royal Air Force. In 1946, she returned to Germany and worked as a civilian employee for the United States War Department. There she married Kurt Knauff, a naturalized United States citizen, and an honorably discharged United States Army veteran who was now serving as a civilian employee of the army.

Knauff attempted to bring his wife to the United States in 1948 under the War Brides Act.[17] This statute was intended to benefit those who had served in the armed forces by facilitating the admission of their spouses—providing they were "otherwise admissible." The attorney general, however, ordered Mrs. Knauff excluded from the country without a hearing. The Supreme Court upheld his action in *Knauff v. Shaughnessy.*[18]

Justice Sherman Minton, speaking for the majority, explained that no one has a right to enter the country; rather, admission is a privilege, granted by the sovereign, and Congress is entitled to condition entry any way it chooses: "[W]hatever the procedure authorized by Congress is, that is due process as far as the alien denied entry is concerned."[19] Accordingly, the Court will not examine determinations made by the Executive unless there is express statutory authorization for judicial review.[20]

Many chapters remained in Mrs. Knauff's bizarre tale. Following the Supreme Court's decision, she was granted a hearing for the first time in March 1950—eighteen months after she had been detained on Ellis Island.[21] At this hearing she learned the nature of the charges against her: Three witnesses accused her of spying for a Czechoslovakian mission in Frankfurt. Mrs. Knauff denied these charges, but the Immigration Appeals Board found her protestations unconvincing, and ordered her deported.

In the meanwhile, her plight had captured national attention. The House of Representatives passed a bill permitting her to remain in the United States, and the Chairman of the House Judiciary Committee warned the attorney general that any attempt to deport Mrs. Knauff while action was pending would be considered "contemptuous of the House." The attorney general nevertheless continued his efforts to expel her, and was close to success when Justice Jackson, on May 17, stayed the deportation—twenty minutes before her plane was due to take off for Germany. Months later, in an unexpected turnabout, the Appeals Board reversed its earlier decision.[22] After the attorney general gave his approval, Mrs. Knauff finally left Ellis Island, which had been her home almost continuously since August 1948.[23]

To Ellen Knauff's and Ignatz Mezei's misfortune, the Supreme Court determined their fate in the early 1950s, during Joseph McCarthy's grim reign.[24] The Knauff-Mezei Doctrine, however, which holds that Congress can treat excludable aliens virtually any way it sees fit, did not retain its vitality much longer than the Wisconsin demagogue. Since the late 1950s, judges have been "overlooking" the doctrine, or with remarkable dexterity distinguishing the factual circumstances in *Knauff* and *Mezei* from those in the cases they are adjudicating.[25] For the last quarter century the judiciary has also presided over a revolution in due process jurisprudence,[26] and today judges not only require the government to accord excludable aliens all of the rights to which they are statutorily and administratively entitled, but occasionally even require it to extend rights beyond those mandated by law.[27] In a 1982 case, moreover, the Supreme Court—while disclaiming any attempt to decide "the scope of *Mezei*"—held that resident aliens ordinarily do not forfeit their legal status by traveling abroad, unless by their actions they indicate an affirmative intent to abandon it.[28]

Notwithstanding these encouraging developments, however, under some circumstances excludable aliens remain subject to peremptory treatment. They can still be banned from the country without a hearing, on the basis of confidential information that is "not disclosable without prejudice to the public interest, safety, or security."[29] Moreover, the Knauff-Mezei doctrine has only been enfeebled, not interred. A few courts still cite it approvingly on occasion.[30] The doctrine could even regain its vigor: Congress, alarmed by the increasing number of aliens who arrive at ports of entry without proper documentation, is considering several prophylactic measures.[31] One provides for the summary exclusion of some classes of aliens "still on the threshold," and others restrict their access to administrative and judicial review.[32] If these proposals become law, the Supreme Court would probably uphold them—invoking as precedent *Shaughnessy v. Mezei* and *Knauff v. Shaughnessy*.

Once nonimmigrants are legally within the country's territorial jurisdiction, they are entitled to procedural due process and many of the Constitution's substantive protections. Nevertheless, during their sojourn in the United States they are subject to restrictions from which citizens and resident aliens are exempt. States may limit the amount or type of property nonimmigrants may own,[33] or impose other reasonable and nondiscriminatory conditions. The judiciary tolerates many of these conditions on the assumption that temporary residents owe no allegiance to the United States, bear few of the obligations of citizenship, and can rely for protection on their native country. Moreover, whereas the federal government "invites" immigrant aliens to enter the United States as permanent residents basically "on an equality of legal privileges with all citizens,"[34] nonimmigrants enter with no such expectations.

The judiciary is less tolerant of state restrictions that trespass on areas within the federal domain. States, therefore, cannot subject aliens to loyalty tests[35] or, without leave from Washington, levy property taxes against foreign diplomats residing within their borders.[36] The federal government, by contrast, labors under few restraints: It may forbid nonimmigrants to work while in the country,[37] or limit the geographical area in which they may travel.[38] If the United States is warring with their homeland, it could even confiscate their property or freeze their assets.[39] Congress and the Executive rarely take this action, and they seldom deport or otherwise penalize aliens for insubstantial or arbitrary reasons. They are constrained less by constitutional or statutory restrictions, however, than by a desire both to maintain friendly relations with other countries, and to discourage them from taking retaliatory action against Americans.

They are also restrained, to some indeterminate extent, by the dictates of international law.

THE ALIEN UNDER INTERNATIONAL LAW

Principles of international law are reflected in treaties, the decisions of international tribunals, charters of multinational organizations such as the United Nations and the Organization of American States and, to a diminishing extent, the uncodified practices that obtain between nations. Without a system of international law, the relationship between sovereign states would be characterized at best by chaos, at worst by chaos and barbarity. Certainly, without such a system individuals could not venture beyond their homeland without jeopardizing their personal security. That international law is indispensable, however, is not to say that it is adequately respected or effective. Principles of international law are neither unambiguous, universally accepted, nor self-enforcing. They frequently embody lofty ideals that provide countries with a valuable norm, but these ideals are readily sacrificed to the demands of political expediency.

Despite the controversy that colors much of international law, certain broad principles are generally accepted. Nations agree, for instance, that certain correlative rights and duties obtain between aliens and their host state. Aliens have no "right" to enter another state, but when they are granted permission to do so they are obliged to honor its laws, to refrain from conduct detrimental to its welfare, and to accord it "temporary allegiance" during their residence. If they fail to observe these conditions, they may be punished or expelled.[40]

A state, for its part, might distinguish between citizens and aliens, as long as the distinctions bear a rational relationship to the different obligations and loyalties that a state might expect from its nationals, on the one hand, and from its guests, on the other.[41] A state might also distinguish between various classes of aliens—a practice that comports with international law as long as the distinctions are reasonable and consistent with applicable treaty provisions.[42] In the United States, for instance, while all people within its territorial jurisdiction are protected from the arbitrary deprivation of life, liberty, and property, there remains a wide spectrum of rights and government services to which individuals become progressively entitled as they approach citizenship. While international law mandates that states treat their alien inhabitants decently, this just begins the inquiry: What constitutes decent treatment? By what measure is a nation's conduct to be judged? Two standards have vied for ascendancy in a contest that is still heated and often acrimonious. Developing nations and socialist states generally subscribe to the so-called "equality of treatment" standard, which stipulates that a state is obliged to treat its alien inhabitants on a parity with its own citizens—no better and no worse.[43] Thus, Mexico may duly convict a United States citizen for violating its narcotic laws and incarcerate him in a prison that by American standards "shocks the conscience." Those adhering to the "equality of treatment" norm would maintain that the United States has no right to seek redress under international law as long as Mexican nationals receive the same treatment.

By contrast, the older and economically developed countries, such as the United States, ordinarily support the "international minimum" standard. According to this standard, a state is obliged to observe "universal principles of justice" in the treatment of aliens and their property, regardless of whether it bestows the same benefits on its own nationals, or even whether such treatment is consistent with its own laws.[44] Partisans of this standard would contend, then, that even if Mexico prevents its own citizens from appealing a criminal conviction, it must provide foreign nationals with at least one appellate review.

A majority of states have adopted the international minimum standard.[45] Its proponents enjoy a somewhat sullied victory, however, because no one is sure what the "international minimum standard" means, what conduct it prescribes, and what it prohibits. Most authorities at least agree that in order to comply with the standard a state must grant aliens access to its courts in order to defend those rights to which they are entitled under international law, treat them in accordance with generally accepted standards of both substantive and procedural law, and compensate them sufficiently for injuries for which it bears international responsibility.[46] Finally, a state must treat aliens with general even-handedness, meaning it is derelict if it differentiates without reasonable ground either between aliens and nationals, or between aliens of different nationalities.[47]

Under both the international minimum and the equality of treatment standard, aliens are ordinarily not entitled to the interposition of their government until they have availed themselves of all local remedies. Assuming their government intercedes at this point, the controversy then becomes one between the two states involved. The sovereign in whose territory the injury occurred is obliged to make reparations to the state whose national was injured. This practice reflects a long-standing theory, or legal fiction, that an unredressed injury to an alien represents an injury to his or her state.[48]

The United States has been reluctant, in recent years, to single out specific classes of aliens for favorable treatment, although until 1965 it did so routinely.[49] Present distinctions are few, and the ones either in effect or being contemplated are generally reasonable. For instance, there have been many proposals to double the immigration quota for Mexico and Canada in recognition of their "special relationship" to this country, although by so doing the United States will be favoring their nationals over ones from noncontiguous nations.[50] The government will also impose sanctions on a selective basis against nonimmigrants in order to accrue "bargaining chips" for diplomatic negotiations. In 1979, for example, after angry students seized the American Embassy in Teheran and held its staff captive, President Carter responded by issuing regulations that were applicable only to Iranian students residing in the United States.[51]

If the United States faithfully abided by international law, it could no longer treat noncitizens with the license it now employs. The United States pays verbal homage to international law, and inveighs against those who flout its dictates, but like most other countries it values above all its sovereign prerogatives. Among these prerogatives it values none more highly than its asserted right to exercise absolute control over those whom it allows into the country, and accordingly to determine without external restraint the number of entries, their composition, even their sexual preferences and ideological predilections. Thus, while policy-makers have tempered most areas of American law, the statutes governing the admission and exclusion of nonciti-zens remain severe.

EXCLUDABLE ALIENS: MARIJUANA VIOLATORS AND HOMOSEXUALS

The severity of immigration laws is nowhere more evident than in their treatment of marijuana violators, who are excluded from the country with less opportunity for appeals or waivers than individuals convicted of murder or other heinous crimes.[52] For instance, a conviction for most serious offenses involving moral turpitude may be waived if the miscreant is a relative of a United States citizen or resident alien. No waiver is available for the person convicted of a narcotic violation, regardless of the attendant circumstances.[53]

Before 1960, immigration laws providing for the automatic exclusion of those who committed narcotic-related offenses did not include marijuana violations. By the Act of July 14, 1960, however, Congress expressly added the trafficking in or pos-session of marijuana.[54] According to the legislative history of the 1960 act, this provision was included because some author-ities believed the substance led to violence and served as a pre-cursor to more dangerous drugs.[55] Although the National Commission on Marijuana and Drug Abuse discredited this be-lief,[56] the law has nevertheless remained intact.

The judiciary and, on occasion, even the Immigration and Naturalization Service (INS), seek ways to relieve the harsh-ness of the immigration laws. In cases involving nonimmigrant as well as resident aliens, they will accordingly stretch statu-tory language or convolute the facts in a particular case in or-der to yield an equitable result. *Lennon v. INS*[57] is illustrative. John Lennon, the musician, had been convicted in Britain for the possession of hashish, and was therefore an excludable al-ien at the time he entered the United States. British law, how-ever, allows an individual to be convicted without proof that he or she knowingly possessed the drug, and this lack of *scien-ter* provided the Second Circuit Court of Appeals with the necessary pretext: It concluded that absent such proof the singer's prior conviction in Britain did not constitute sufficient ground for deportation.[58]

By imposing severe penalties for the possession of small amounts of marijuana, the government encourages a general disregard for the law. Indeed, even those charged with enforcing it struggle to evade its dictates. Such laws are also fundamentally unfair because they reflect no sense of proportion: They penalize those found guilty of possessing one marijuana cigarette as readily as the confirmed drug trafficker; the individual whose offense occurred years or even decades ago as readily as the person who currently profiteers.

Even less defensible than the INA provision mandating the automatic exclusion of marijuana violators is the one barring homosexuals.[59] Notwithstanding individual family relationships, the length of time they may have lived in the United States, their creative or professional accomplishments, by virtue of §212(a)(14) of the INA, homosexuals are prohibited either from entering the country in the first place or, if they are resident aliens, from reentering once they have traveled abroad.

Legislators have been intent upon excluding homosexuals, but they have balked at the prospect of incorporating the term itself into a statute. Before 1952, therefore, the immigration laws provided for the exclusion of those aliens with a "constitutional psychopathic disorder."[60] In deference to lawmakers who considered this term ambiguous, however, in 1952 Congress amended the provision; thereafter no one could enter the country who was "afflicted with a psychopathic personality, or sexual deviation, or mental defect."[61] This new term was intended to embrace "homosexuals and other sex perverts,"[62] but it too was criticized for vagueness. Finally, in 1965, Congress expressly provided that "sexual deviants" were included among those possessing a "psychopathic personality."[63]

The matter did not end there, however. In 1965 the INS ordered Clive Boutillier, a Canadian national, deported after medical officers certified that he had been a "psychopathic personality" at the time of his admission to the United States. Boutillier appealed his deportation order, primarily on the gound that the immigration laws mandating the exclusion of "psychopathic personalities" did not include homosexuals. Boutillier thus provided the Supreme Court with an opportunity to examine this particular provision of the INA.

After examining the legislative history of the disputed provision, the Court concluded that "beyond a shadow of a doubt . . . Congress intended the phrase 'psychopathic personality' to include homosexuals."[64] The term is not to be understood in its clinical sense, the Court continued, or according to what "different psychiatrists may think";[65] rather, it is to be understood as a legal term of art intended to exclude "all homosexuals and other sex perverts."[66]

Even the Court's unequivocal ruling did not settle the issue, because action by the Public Health Service (PHS) occasioned a new round of troubles. According to the INA, §212(a)(4) is to be enforced by both the INS and the PHS.[67] Whenever an immigration officer at a port of entry suspects that an entering alien may suffer from a physical or mental defect, the alien is assigned to a PHS medical officer who, upon examining the alien for any health defects, reports his findings to the INS. This system proceeded smoothly until August 1979, when the surgeon general issued a memorandum declaring that henceforth PHS medical officers would no longer consider homosexuality a "mental disease or defect."[68] The service explained that medical diagnostic procedure is unable to determine the presence or absence of homosexuality. Moreover, its action reflected current medical opinion since the American Psychiatric Association no longer considers homosexuality a mental disorder.[69]

The INS was in a quandary. The Department of Justice's Office of Legal Counsel concluded that the service was statutorily required to exclude homosexuals even without assistance from the PHS.[70] Without the PHS medical examination and certification, however, the agency had no way of effecting this requirement. Eventually the INS solved its dilemma in an ingenious manner. It promulgated a new policy denying immediate entry to an alien who offers "an unsolicited, unambiguous admission of homosexuality" to an INS inspector, or who has been identified as a homosexual by a "third party who has arrived at the same time."[71] These individuals will then be subjected to a "secondary inspection," where they will be asked whether or not they are homosexuals. Those answering "no" are admitted to the country; those answering "yes" may either leave the United States voluntarily or request a formal exclusion hearing.[72]

By providing for the automatic exclusion of homosexuals, Congress demeans both those who enforce the policy and those it affects. Immigration officials are required to pry into, or speculate, about intimate aspects of another person's life. Homosexuals, in turn, are categorized as "perverse" on the basis of a sexual preference that increasing numbers of medical and psychiatric authorities no longer consider aberrant. Finally, in order to gain admission to the country homosexuals must deny their orientation and thereby collude in a farcical transaction.

EXCLUDABLE ALIENS: CONSTITUTIONAL CONSIDERATIONS

By excluding marijuana offenders or homosexuals, legislators honor the biases held by many of their influential constituents. In the domestic context, however, there are concessions a legislator cannot permissibly make, even to satisfy a clamorous public. Minority rights must also be respected. Indeed, the Bill of Rights and the Fourteenth Amendment, in particular, are dedicated to the proposition that even members of vilified minorities are entitled to worship as they please, to associate with people of their choice, and to benefit from laws that apply evenhandedly. These constitutional provisions, however, are applicable only to permanent residents.[73] Their protective armor does not shield those who lack this status. As a result, Congress can discriminate against all but resident aliens on the basis of their political or religious beliefs or even—as Iranians studying in the United States discovered—on the basis of their national origin.

The 50,000[74] or so nonimmigrant students who are enrolled in educational institutions in this country enjoy many of the rights possessed by citizens and resident aliens, although there are some significant exceptions. Ordinarily, they are not permitted to work while attending school;[75] they are subject to ongoing supervision by the INS;[76] and, as America's recent brouhaha with its Iranian students demonstrates, they may be penalized for the expression of unpopular views.

In November 1979, a throng of Iranian students—with the complicity of their government—seized the American Embassy in Teheran and held as hostage sixty-five United States citizens who were employed there. The American public responded with anger. When a number of Iranian students in the United States thereafter demonstrated in support of their country, this anger ballooned into outrage. Soon afterwards the United States undertook reprisals against both the Iranian students and their home country.

Within ten days after the Embassy was seized, President Carter imposed an embargo on oil imports from Iran and ordered all of its assets in the United States frozen.[77] In addition, he directed the attorney general to initiate deportation proceedings against any Iranian students in the United States who were not in compliance with their entry visas. Attorney General Benjamin Civiletti accordingly issued a regulation ordering all nonimmigrant Iranian students in post-secondary schools to report to the INS by December 14, 1979, in order to document their residence and student status.[78] The INS would then determine whether the students had abided by the terms of their visas, and would institute deportation proceedings against those who had not. Immigration officials were further instructed to take "discretionary" measures against the Iranians, including rescinding all directives deferring the departure or deportation of those who were excludable, and revoking all authorizations for either temporary stays or employment.[79]

The attorney general's action prompted Mr. Narenjii, a student from Iran, and the Iranian Student Association to file suit.[80] Ultimately the district and circuit courts focused on two of the several issues raised in their complaint: One, did Congress empower the Executive to discriminate among classes of aliens in order to promote foreign policy objectives? Two, even if authorized by Congress, does this action nevertheless violate the equal protection component of the Fifth Amendment?

Speaking for the district court, Judge Joyce Hens Green answered both questions in the negative. While the INA empowered Congress to delegate broad authority to the Executive, this grant did not contemplate the power to classify aliens on the basis of their nationality. By singling out the Iranians for discretionary treatment, the attorney general consequently exceeded his authority and, absent a showing that his action served overriding national interests, contravened the Constitution's Fifth Amendment.[81]

Although the judiciary assumes substantial risks whenever it acts to "inhibit the flexibility of the political branches of government to respond to changing world conditions,"[82] Judge Green acknowledged, it must nevertheless insist that executive action respect constitutional limitations. She concluded that

[c]onstitutional submission to the wash of emotions would eliminate the fair play and equality that is [sic] the quintessence of the American way, and it is cardinal that the diminishment of the rights of those most vulnerable diminishes in the end the rights of all others.[83]

Judge Green's pronouncements provoked an admonishment from the appellate court.[84] Judge Roger Robb, speaking for a majority on the Court of Appeals for the District of Columbia, upbraided the lower tribunal for forgetting that whenever the judiciary confronts political issues—particularly ones affecting foreign policy—its role is extremely limited.[85] The judiciary, Judge Robb explained, has limited competence in this area, being neither authorities in international relations nor privy to confidential data. The President, by contrast, is vested with broad and indeed nearly unfettered discretion to act in the area of foreign affairs, because he alone is in a position to appreciate prevailing conditions and to receive classified information.

Consequently, courts should uphold the Executive's actions in the area of foreign affairs whenever they are not "clearly in excess" of his authority, and whenever the means employed are not "wholly irrational."[86] The disputed action was clearly within the President's authority, involving as it did foreign relations. Classifying Iranian students on the basis of their nationality was "reasonable," moreover, since the classificatory scheme represents appropriate reciprocity for the treatment of Americans in Iran.[87]

Four judges explained, in dissent, why they believed this case should be reheard:

It may be that the President, in these troubled days, has the power to decide that our deep aversion to selective law enforcement against a group solely on the basis of their country of origin must give way to some other imperative.[88]

Before reaching this conclusion, however, the court should first scrutinize the issue carefully and reflect upon "fine and often difficult questions of value," because in a time "when the rule of law [was] being compromised by expediency in many places of the world, it [was] crucial . . . to make certain that the United States did not retaliate in kind."[89]

Very few, if any, Iranian students were deported as a result of President Carter's directive, mainly because the INS was unable to determine even the rough numbers or identities of the Iranians studying in the United States, let alone the extent to which they were complying with their visas.[90] The court's resolution of *Narenjii v. Civiletti* thus occasioned little direct harm. Its resolution occasioned substantial indirect harm, however, by reassuring the political branches that whenever they abridge the rights of noncitizens the judiciary will be reliably deferential.

The judiciary should, of course, proceed with caution in any case where, as in *Narenjii*, the government's foreign policy interests are at least arguably at stake. Caution, however, need not imply obsequiousness. The judiciary lacks the expertise and, ordinarily, even the constitutional authority to assess the government's foreign policy objectives. It nevertheless still possesses the capacity and, indeed, the obligation, to insist that the government tread upon the rights of individuals no more than necessary in promoting these ends. The court should accordingly insist that the government demonstrate the need for its action by providing reasonable assurance that its objectives cannot be achieved through less onerous means, or through processes that are more carefully tailored.

When the government advances justification for its discretionary action, moreover, the judiciary should at least make sure these justifications represent more than a mere pretext for penalizing unpopular classes of people. In *Narenjii v. Civiletti* the circuit court never questioned whether, in discriminating against Iranian students, the government promoted any legitimate—let alone "overriding"—national interests, or whether these interests could have been served by alternate means. Rather, the court suggested that it would sustain any action involving noncitizens in the area of foreign policy, providing only that it is not "wholly irrational."[91]

Perhaps the government's conduct was not "wholly irrational"—indeed, few undertakings are. Since the government's action impinged on a vulnerable class of people, however, the court should have inquired further: Was the action designed to promote legitimate ends? In this case, individual students were penalized on the basis of "gross generalizations" about members of their class, which suggests that the government wished to appease a vengeful public, rather than promote legitimate foreign policy objectives. Moreover, the students were penalized in response to international conditions beyond their control, despite the court's proclamation in an earlier case that

[d]iscrimination against a class of aliens in this country because of activity being undertaken by their homeland is the type of action that is odious to a free people whose institutions are founded upon the doctrine of equality.[92]

The American hostages are now free and presumably the Iranian students are pursuing their activities unmolested by the immigration authorities. Meanwhile, *Narenjii v. Civiletti* remains controlling. The Executive is thus free to exercise discretion in ways heretofore considered beyond his authority. While the President has always had power to expel "undesirable aliens," until this case the judiciary has insisted that he do so only upon a specific claim that a given alien acted in a way inimical to the country's welfare.[93] The District of Columbia Circuit suggests, however, that the government can levy penalties against whole classes of people on the basis of their national origin. The consequences are serious. Whenever citizens of other countries reside in the United States they remain in danger, as Judge Green warned, of "[b]eing singled out, selectively corralled, and required to perform certain actions to develop affirmatively that they are blameless despite the actions of their government."[94]

The dissent in *Narenjii* was disturbed not only because the President ordered the Immigration Service to discriminate against Iranian students on the basis of their national origin, but also because he undertook this serious action without express congressional authorization.[95] Courts ordinarily hold that while the President, or his delegates, may exercise considerable discretionary power, they cannot implicate the fundamental rights of American citizens without express authorization from Congress.[96] The judiciary thereby contributes to the preservation of the balance of power, and also insures that legislators will engage in at least minimal public debate before they invest bureaucrats with new and potentially dangerous powers. When Congress's action affects noncitizens, however, the judiciary is willing to tolerate almost open-ended delegation. It evidenced this tolerance in *Narenjii*, and in another recent case, *Unification Church v. Attorney General*.[97]

The Immigration Service refused to grant "trainee" visas to several hundred foreign members of Reverend Sun Yung Moon's Unification Church. The INA provides for the admission of aliens as temporary "trainees" if the service approves the training program.[98] In this instance, an INS district director refused to certify a program sponsored by Reverend Moon because the religious leader intended to use the newcomers partly for fund raising, a condition of employment not ordinarily associated with bona fide training programs. The district director's decision was subsequently affirmed by the regional commissioner.[99]

In challenging this decision plaintiffs alleged that by inquiring into the need, effectiveness and utility of the church's training program, the service thereby abridged their First Amendment right to the free exercise of religion. They further argued that since Congress had never vested agency officials with the power to discriminate among visa applicants on the basis of their religious beliefs, they were consequently exceeding their jurisdiction.[100] The Court of Appeals for the District of Columbia Circuit upheld the Immigration Service, however, on the ground that the district director was fully authorized to deny training visas whenever he determined that a program was not primarily intended to train.[101] Since the district director acted within his discretion, that ended the matter: It was not necessary to examine the merits of the plaintiff's First Amendment claims. This is an unfortunate decision. By not insisting that administrators receive express congressional authority before they decide issues affecting the fundamental rights of aliens and, by extension, their citizen-sponsors, courts allow bureaucrats to exercise undue discretion. The district director's refusal to certify the Unification Church's trainee program may have been based on nondiscriminatory standards applied across-the-board. Yet his decision should nonetheless be subject to judicial review. The director may have been influenced by the public's widespread aversion to the Unification Church; perhaps unwittingly he might also have penalized those religions whose practices or recruitment policies do not conform to familiar western standards. Ultimately, therefore, it is the responsibility of the judiciary and not the bureaucracy to determine what does and does not qualify for constitutional protection.

Unification Church v. Attorney General and *Narenjii v. Civiletti* suggest that administrators can expect little interference from the judiciary whenever they discriminate against noncitizens on the basis of their religious beliefs or national origin. Recent court action suggests that administrators operate with similar license whenever they exclude aliens on the basis of their political affiliations.

POLITICAL GROUNDS FOR EXCLUSION

Congress began barring people from the country in 1875, and thereafter it has continuously added to the categories of inadmissible aliens.[102] Its first prohibitions were intended to preserve the country's original racial and ethnic composition. Subsequent bans, such as the Anarchist Act in 1903[103] and the Alien Registration Act of 1940,[104] were designed to protect it from ideological contamination. Notwithstanding these acts, however, exclusionary provisions based on political grounds did not proliferate until the McCarthy Era, when the country was infected with a virulent strain of anti-communism. Congress then passed the Internal Security Act of 1950[105] and, more notably, two years later enacted the McCarran-Walter Act.[106]

The McCarran Act, as amended, remains the country's basic immigration statute. Among its controversial provisions none are more troubling than the ones mandating the deportation or exclusion of reputed subversives;§27 of the act renders ineligible for a visa any alien who the attorney general or a consular official "suspects" might be attempting to enter the country "solely, principally . . . or incidentally to engage in activity which would be prejudicial to the public interest, or endanger the welfare, safety, or security of the United States."[107]

Eight broad categories of aliens who are inadmissible are listed in§28, including those who are presently, or who were at any time in the past, members or affiliates of any Communist or anarchist organization, or who, while not members, nevertheless propagate their beliefs in some way.[108] Finally, §29 renders ineligible any alien who, after entry, "probably would engage in espionage, sabotage, public disorder or other activity subversive to the national interest."[109] These provisions apply not only to aliens who wish to make the United States their permanent home, but also to those who wish to visit the country for a limited time, even for the few days necessary to deliver a lecture, attend a conference, or receive an honorary degree.

When international tensions are particularly high, Congress routinely responds by enacting laws that create broad new categories of excludable aliens. Then, upon sober "second thought," it seeks ways to relieve the harshness of these laws. Rather than refine or eliminate any exclusionary categories, however, Congress enacts follow-up provisions granting various forms of discretionary relief. The result is a tortuous system riddled with inconsistencies and loopholes, a system with such amorphous standards and imprecise terminology that it depends on the discretionary judgments of low- and- high-level bureaucrats for its interpretation and application.

The McCarran Act's exclusionary provisions are written in language that is completely open-ended. The act stipulates, for instance, that aliens may be denied a visa if their conduct could be "prejudicial" to the "best interest" of the United States, or if, upon entry, they "probably would" engage in "public disorder." Sam Bernsen, former general counsel of the INS, points out that after three decades even the most experienced officials in the Department of State and the INS are still "perplexed" over the meaning of such terms.[110] These terms possess such inherent elasticity that conceivably any one associated with unorthodox thinking could be barred from the country.

The United States occasionally denies a visa to aliens identified with conservative ideologies, such as the Reverend Ian Paisley, a Northern-Ireland spokesman for the extreme Protestant movement. As a rule, however, the government invokes the McCarran Act when visa applicants are considered "left wing," or radical. In 1975, for instance, the administration excluded an Italian Communist shortly after the leader of Italy's neo-Fascist Party had been granted a visa. By excluding controversial figures, whatever their political leanings, the government may be violating the Helsinki Final Act of 1975,[111] which calls upon the United States and each of the thirty-four other signatories to "gradually simplify . . . and administer flexibly the procedures for exit and entry," and "to ease regulations concerning movement of citizens from other participating States in their territory, with due regard to security requirements."[112]

In 1977, Congress passed the McGovern Act[113] in order to bring United States law into conformity with the freedom-to-travel provisions of the Helsinki Accords. This act streamlines the application process for an alien who would be otherwise inadmissible because of membership in a proscribed organization. It stipulates that such an alien is presumed eligible for a visa unless the Secretary of State, within thirty days after the alien applies for admission, certifies to appropriate members of Congress that the country's security interests would be adversely affected by the applicant's entry.[114]

The act, however, does not apply to "applicants ineligible on grounds other than, or in addition to, mere organization membership."[115] Moreover, by virtue of its subsequent emendation, the Secretary of State may recommend that a waiver be denied aliens from signatory countries that are not in substantial compliance with the Helsinki Final Act.[116] These two caveats enable the government to exclude aliens almost as effectively as it did before the McGovern Act became law, and thus to circumvent the spirit, if not the letter, of the Helsinki Accords.

Individuals whose political activities are considered objectionable to the administration continue to be excluded from the United States, regardless of whether they ever acted, or proposed to act, in a manner inimical to the security interests of the country. As a result, many foreigners regard Americans as "hypocrites" who espouse political freedom and the open exchange of ideas, who inveigh against the dearth of First Amendment freedoms characteristic of closed societies, yet who still guard their own doors with vigilance—who "station nannies at the gate,"[117] as a *New York Times* editorialist phrased it—lest anyone slip in bearing incendiary ideas.

According to Laurie Sapper, general secretary of the British Association of University Teachers, §28 of the McCarran Act serves as a significant deterrent to the association's membership:

The record of actual refusals is small, not because of the liberal attitudes of the United States government, but because many of our members, as a matter of principle, consider it anathema to have to attest to their political views and affiliations.[118]

As a result, many British academics refuse to apply for a visa.

Professor Dwight Simpson is among the many Americans who are also offended by the government's officiousness. In 1982, he invited Iran's United Nations representative to speak on contemporary political conditions in Iran to his students and colleagues at San Francisco State College. The representative never delivered his lecture, however, because Jeane Kirkpatrick, America's ambassador to the United Nations, judged his visit "contrary to the United States interest," and refused him permission to travel.[119] (About the time Ambassador Kirkpatrick denied the Iranian permission to speak, her own attempts to address students at the University of California at Berkeley and the University of Minnesota were thwarted by student hecklers. Professor Simpson noted that, while the ambassador publicly and repeatedly decried this assault on her First

Amendment rights, she evinced no comparable solicitude for the rights of the San Francisco community.)[120]

Through its exclusionary practices, the government often disadvantages the American public as a whole, depriving it of many opportunities for cultural enrichment and intellectual stimulation. Americans have been denied the opportunity to converse with such internationally acclaimed writers as Carlos Fuentes, Regis Debray, and Colombian novelist and Nobel prize winner Gabriel Garcia-Marquez. They have missed the chance to exchange views with Bernadette Devlin McAliskey, an outspoken member of Britain's Parliament, and Mrs. Salvatore Allende, whose husband, the former president of Chile, was assassinated in 1971.[121]

The United States is deeply enmeshed in military struggles in El Salvador and Nicaragua, where it is pursuing objectives that many consider confusing or misguided. Yet the State Department recently denied visas to Roberto d'Aubisson, then president of the Salvadoran Constituent Assembly, and Tomas Borge, Nicaragua's Interior Minister. It thereby deprived the American public of a valuable opportunity to acquire knowledge from key non-administration sources, without which they cannot intelligently evaluate their country's foreign policies.[122]

In 1980 Dario Fo, a prominent Italian playwright, and his actress-wife, Franca Rame, sought a temporary visa in order to participate in an Italian festival in the United States. Their visas were denied, apparently because of the couple's active role in a group called Soccorso Rosso, or Red Aid, which the American ambassador in Italy maintained was "sympathetic to the terrorist movement."[123] In fact, the organization helps individuals imprisoned for politically-motivated crimes. The state department conceded that Fo had aggressively denounced political violence. According to a department spokesman, however, "Fo's record of performance with regard to the United States is not good. Dario Fo has never had a good word to say about [the United States]."[124]

While the government indisputably has the right to exclude those who pose a threat to its welfare or security, its handling of Dario Fo raises another question: May the government also bar those whose only threat is to the country's ideological complacency? Apparently so, for in a 1973 case, *Kleindienst v. Mandel*,[125] the Supreme Court suggested that Congress or the attorney general might deny visas to anyone whom they find politically objectionable.

In 1969 Ernest Mandel, a Belgian journalist and a well known Marxist theoretician, although not a member of the Communist party, was invited by Stanford and a number of other universities to deliver a series of lectures. The justice department, however, refused to grant Dr. Mandel a nonimmigrant visa, citing as authority for its action §28 of the McCarran Act. Although the attorney general routinely grants waivers to excludable aliens, he explained that a dispensation would be withheld in this case because the applicant had failed to observe strict limitations placed upon him during previous visits to the United States. The Supreme Court readily accepted this explanation, notwithstanding the fact that Dr. Mandel had never been notified of such limitations.[126]

The Belgian's intended hosts brought suit, alleging that the attorney general's action was unconstitutional because it interfered with their First Amendment "right to hear." They claimed, moreover, that the attorney general exercised his discretion capriciously, since he granted or withheld waivers on the basis of no ascertainable standards. The district court agreed with the plaintiffs, holding that by virtue of the First Amendment they had a right to hear, speak, and debate with the professor in person.[127]

The Supreme Court disagreed. On behalf of the majority, Justice Harry Blackmun explained that Congress, and by fair delegation the attorney general, possess essentially plenary power to determine who shall and shall not be admitted to the country.[128] To bolster this pronouncement, he cited *The Chinese Exclusion Case*.[129] Since these decisions are primarily political in nature, and constitutionally entrusted to the legislative and executive branches, the Court's role is limited. If the attorney general has made a determination that appears "facially legitimate and bona fide," the Court will inquire no further.[130]

This language is astounding. The Court is suggesting that Congress and the attorney general possess unfettered authority to deny visas to anyone whose political views they dislike, providing only that they have a "facially legitimate and bona fide reason" for so doing. The Court will look no further. It will not examine this reason to determine whether it rests on legitimate or concocted grounds; it will not inquire whether the alien denied entry is an active Communist, one who poses a potential threat to the country's security, or merely an academic proponent of Marxism. Finally, while conceding that the right of free speech includes the right "to receive information and ideas,"[131] it will not balance the government's asserted needs against the First Amendment rights of those citizens who wish to communicate with the excluded speaker.

A federal district court in New York City was similarly disinclined to balance competing values when it supported the government in another recent incident. In June 1982, on the authority of §28 of the McCarran Act, immigration authorities denied visas to nearly 500 foreigners who hoped to attend activities associated with a United Nations conference on nuclear disarmament. The Immigration Service subsequently permitted some of them to enter the country, providing they were officially invited by the United Nations, but forbade them to travel more than twenty-five miles beyond New York City's Columbus Circle. The remaining 350 aliens who lacked an official invitation were barred, the state department explained, because of their connection either with a Japanese disarmament group, or with the World Peace Conference, both described by the administration as "Soviet fronts."[132]

The New York and American Civil Liberties Unions challenged the government's action in federal court, seeking an order requiring the state department to issue visitors' visas to those unable to obtain them. According to a spokesman for the New York Civil Liberties Union, the suit was "on behalf of Americans who have been denied the right to meet, converse and exchange ideas with international representatives of the disarmament movement."[133] Lawyers for the Civil Liberties Union also accused the government of flouting both the Helsinki Accords and the McGovern Act.

The lawyers pointed out that the government had no proof that any of the excluded aliens actually belonged to an organization advocating world communism, or even subscribed to

Marxist tenets. Rather, this was a classic case of guilt by association: "Most of the barred Japanese" belong to an organization with "indirect" ties to an organization "supposedly" linked to communism.[134]

The government's defense was simple, but sufficient to persuade the district court: "It is the sovereign power of the United States to determine who may enter."[135] Yes, it is a sovereign power, but presumably not one that can be exercised with total license. The United States is also dedicated to the proposition, embodied in the First Amendment, that a populace is rendered strong and free by exposure to ideas of all sorts, even those that are uncomfortable or offensive. That government bureaucrats should pose as gatekeepers, determining to whom the public can be safely exposed, is an assault on the First Amendment and an insult to those Americans who prefer to make such decisions for themselves.

4

Undocumented Aliens

During the last fifteen years the United States has absorbed an unprecedented number of undocumented migrants, who may be contributing as many as 500,000 people to its population each year.[1] Newspapers feature accounts of the "swarming multitudes" who wade across the Rio Grande or beach on the Miami coast. Other articles describe those wayfarers who never make it at all: The thirteen Salvadorans who died on an unfamiliar desert terrain after being abandoned by their guide, and the Haitian families whose leaky boat capsized within sight of the Florida shore.

Undocumented or illegal migrants—those who either enter the country "without inspection" by the INS, or who enter lawfully, but thereafter violate the terms of their visas[2]—have been a part of the American landscape ever since the United States first enacted restrictive immigration laws. This past decade, however, when unemployment has stood at rates unequaled since the Great Depression, the customary indifference with which the public has viewed their presence has been replaced by alarm and even outrage.[3]

Public awareness has been magnified by media exposés, and by outcries from public officials. Early in the 1970s, then commissioner of the INS, General Leonard Chapman, announced that the United States was "under seige," and he launched a public relations campaign to convince the citizenry that the problems occasioned by undocumented migrants were staggering in their dimensions.[4] A few years later, Attorney General

Griffin Bell declared that the issue of illegal aliens "looms like a giant cloud" over the country.[5] Other officials characterized the influx as an "invasion," a "national disaster."[6]

Undocumented migrants have been blamed for everything from unemployment to the country's deteriorating quality of life; such allegations are grounded mainly on conjecture, however, because there is a dearth of verifiable data with which to determine the social and economic impact, geographic dispersion, or long-term consequences of undocumented migration, or even the most fundamental fact: the number of such migrants.[7] Trustworthy data are so scarce, in fact, that authorities are not certain whether, on balance, undocumented aliens represent a net gain or loss for this country.

Public alarm is nevertheless not inappropriate because the institutional health of a nation is imperiled whenever sizeable communities live outside the law; indeed, a large contingent of undocumented migrants challenges the very notion that the United States is a country under law. The nation's immigration statutes are openly and flagrantly violated, in part because the INS, the agency entrusted with enforcing these laws, is so understaffed and ill-equipped, so mismanaged and demoralized by official inattention that, to the extent it functions at all, it does so in only the most capricious and haphazard fashion. According to an official report issued by the United States General Accounting Office, any unauthorized person, once here, "has little chance of being located and deported."[8] As a result, the United States has what the Select Commission on Immigration and Refugee Policy calls a "half-open door policy": While the country officially forbids illegal entry, it effectively condones it through lax enforcement.[9]

The judiciary has commented on this phenomenon. In a recent case involving undocumented aliens, federal district court judge William Wayne Justice observed that "(an immigration) quota is set without much deliberation because all know it will be disregarded";[10] circuit court judge Frank Johnson similarly commented that undocumented aliens have so little chance of being apprehended that a "de facto amnesty" prevails.[11] He also noted that "a large part of the controversy surrounding illegal immigration stems from the resentment that the federal government is not enforcing its immigration laws."[12]

When immigration statutes are flouted, law-abiding applicants suffer, particularly those who wait years for a visa; ultimately, however, everyone suffers because lawlessness feeds on itself and contributes to the deterioration of the entire legal system. This deterioration is already evidenced by the many otherwise "upstanding" citizens who hire undocumented aliens to work "off the books" as housekeepers and gardeners, as babysitters and chauffeurs; by the extent to which those employing undocumented workers spurn minimum wage and occupational safety laws; and, finally, by the entire underground subculture that has emerged to service these migrants. Smugglers, or "cayotes," offer transport to the United States, and constitute what a California border patrol agent referred to as "perhaps the biggest industry on the [Mexican] border", one which is "if not a modern-day slave trade, the next closest thing to it."[13] A second flourishing industry specializes in fraudulent documents, as illustrated by the resourceful alien who was apprehended with 900 phony social security cards clutched in his hands.[14] Recent news accounts describe the growing number of corrupt INS and consular officials who "sell" visas. According to one estimate, between 20,000 and 50,000 visas are sold by American diplomats or local employees every year.[15]

Given this flaccid enforcement, the American public understandably perceives immigration to be "out of control." Its consequent anxiety has been compounded by the demographic changes wrought by this immigration. During the 1970s, for the first time in American history, the majority of its immigrants were not white; ten years later more than 70 percent were from either Latin America or Asia.[16] During this period, moreover, at least 50 percent of the entrants spoke a single foreign language, Spanish.[17] Thus, not only the perceived number, but also the composition of these newcomers has provoked a backlash, evidenced by mounting opposition to "foreigners" and, indeed, to cultural pluralism in general.

In a recent Roper opinion poll, 91 percent of those questioned believed the United States should make "an all out effort" to stop illegal immigration,[18] and a substantial percentage wanted to curtail legal immigration as well. Public opinion is also reflected in the plethora of state and federal statutes that impose restrictions—many gratuitous and of dubious legality—on undocumented residents,[19] and in efforts by the citizenry to discourage public recognition of non-Anglo languages and cultures.

In 1980 voters in Dade County, Florida, by a three-to-one margin, passed an ordinance establishing that "expenditures of county funds for the purpose of utilizing any language other than English, or promoting any culture other than that of the United States, is prohibited."[20] Similar measures have been passed throughout the country.[21] A number of state and federal courts have refused to enjoin the publication of government documents, such as social security guidelines, printed only in English.[22] These manifestations of Anglo chauvinism reinforce the alienation experienced by many Hispanic Americans, who consider them rearguard assaults on the Latin language and culture. In fact, for the 15 million Hispanics living lawfully in the United States, these measures merely supplement a catalogue of indignities which they suffer as victims of the so-called "wetback syndrome," what one commentator described as preoccupation with Hispanic, and especially Mexican people, who are assumed to be not only illegal aliens, but also threats to this country's demographic and cultural integrity.[23]

This official "preoccupation" is amply demonstrated. For instance, in its effort to apprehend unlawful migrants, the Immigration Service disproportionately singles out Hispanics for surveillance and interrogation.[24] The service concentrates the bulk of its enforcement efforts along the United States-Mexican border, thereby neglecting those remaining ports of entry through which nationals of other countries typically enter. Whereas along the Mexican border authorities have installed radar devices and sensor equipment, for many years the only official presence along the Canadian border was often a road sign requesting those entering the United States to "kindly report" to the nearest INS office.[25] Hispanics maintain that the Immigration Service engages in selective enforcement. In its eagerness to corral Spanish-speaking aliens it neglects the "better off," "whiter" students, tourists, businessmen, and visitors who are categorized as "visa abusers," and who contribute roughly 300,000 people to the country's illegal population each year.[26]

When immigration laws are poorly or capriciously enforced, not only Hispanics, but every unauthorized resident, suffers. In a recent case involving undocumented aliens Judge William Wayne Justice explained that "the confluence of governmental policies has resulted in the existence of a large number of employed illegal aliens . . . whose presence is tolerated, whose employment is perhaps even welcomed, but who are virtually defenseless against any abuse, exploitation, or callous neglect to which the state or the state's natural citizens and business organizations may wish to subject them."[27] As the plaintiffs noted in the same case, the result is that "the historical treatment of undocumented aliens is an unbroken history of exploitation by government and citizens alike."[28]

UNDOCUMENTED ALIENS: AN HISTORICAL PERSPECTIVE

That undocumented aliens have suffered "an unbroken history of exploitation" by the government, as distinct from private citizens, is not altogether true: Government officials did launch a concerted, if generally ineffective, campaign in the late nineteenth century to deport Chinese aliens, but they regarded other undocumented migrants with relative indifference until after World War I. In fact, between 1900 and 1930 more than a million undocumented Mexican nationals settled in the United States,[29] and Mexicans were actively recruited during the labor shortage occasioned by World War I. Although government officials made a half-hearted attempt to enforce the Alien Contract Labor Law, which prohibited employers from soliciting in foreign countries, they left employers free to hire workers as soon as they crossed the border.[30]

After World War I, undocumented laborers were no longer needed, and the government commenced a "repatriation" operation in which more than 500,000 people of Mexican descent were rounded up in border patrol raids and sent back to Mexico.[31] These repatriates were again welcomed during the 1940s, however, when World War II created another labor shortage. In order to accommodate the needs of United States employers and to reduce the pressures of illegal migration, in 1942 the United States and Mexico initiated the so-called bracero program, under the terms of which domestic employers contracted for temporary Mexican laborers.

The bracero program neither minimized undocumented migration nor enhanced the welfare of the Mexican laborers. During its twenty-two-year existence it actually stimulated illegal migration by attracting labor to the United States in numbers far greater than the program could accommodate. The President's Commission on Migratory Labor concluded in 1950 that "illegal entry" was its dominant feature.[32] Proponents of the bracero program maintained that legally employed Mexicans, with decent living conditions guaranteed, would be spared the exploitation suffered by their undocumented brethren. In operation, however, reports of mistreatment abounded, and contract laborers complained of such abuse that the Mexican government temporarily withdrew its support. The United States officially terminated the program in 1964. By then, however, more than one million Mexican workers had become dependent on the employment it guaranteed, and they continued to work in the Southwest—although in a status that had abruptly become illegal.[33]

In 1954, while the bracero program was still in operation, government officials resolved to rid the country, once and for all, of its undocumented workers. In a campaign much broader in scope, but otherwise reminiscent of the repatriation efforts following World War I, Attorney General Herbert Brownell and INS Commissioner Joseph May Swing launched "Operation Wetback." At the conclusion of this campaign, more than one million Mexicans—one-sixth of the total Mexican population residing in the United States—had been expelled.[34] In its 1955 Annual Report the INS described the operation in terms suggestive of a paramilitary operation:

A "Special Mobile Force Operation" began in California . . . and after the backbone of the wetback invasion was broken [there], shifted to South Texas. Light planes were used in locating illegal aliens and directing ground teams in jeeps to effect apprehensions. Transport planes were used to airlift aliens to staging areas for prompt return to Mexico . . . these activities were followed by mopping up operations in the interior and special mobile force units are continuing to discover illegal aliens who have eluded initial sweeps through such cities as Spokane, Chicago, Kansas City, and St. Louis.[35].

Operation Wetback violated the civil rights of United States residents on a wholesale basis. The older members of the Hispanic community still shrink from the symbols they associate with the 1954 purge—late night sirens, the low-flying aircraft, the special forces, brandishing night sticks and blaring their whistles, that swept through their neighborhoods and places of work.

Since 1954, government officials have launched no expedition equal in magnitude to Operation Wetback. The INS still conducts occasional "dragnet raids," however, and, according to a recent government report, it continues to subject "foreign looking" people to abuses from which other residents are spared.[36] These abuses are less frequent than in the past, however, in part because state and federal courts have begun to extend constitutional protection to all people within the country's jurisdiction, regardless of their immigration status.

THE CONSTITUTIONAL RIGHTS OF
UNDOCUMENTED ALIENS

Within the last few decades, the Supreme Court has concluded that the judiciary is particularly obligated to safeguard the interests of those whom it describes as "suspect classes," a rubric that includes members of racial and ethnic minorities and, at least under some circumstances, resident aliens. Groups considered "suspect," or worthy of particular judicial solicitude, are frequently penalized for "immutable biological traits," such as skin color, over which they have no control and that bear no relationship to their capabilities.[37]

Members of suspect groups have also suffered a history of official discrimination, which suggests that without judicial intervention they will continue to be victimized by a vindictive, or simply thoughtless, public. Finally, suspect classes lack the political clout necessary to protect their interests in the electoral process and this, more than any other factor, has convinced the Court that intercession on their behalf is crucial.[38]

In one sense undocumented aliens constitute a problematic class because their status is ordinarily not immutable. In every other respect, however, they qualify for suspect status: theirs has been a long history of official discrimination. In 1970, in fact, the United States Civil Rights Commission equated the status of the undocumented alien in South Texas with that of the black person in the antebellum South.[39] Moreover, as plaintiffs noted in a recent case, undocumented aliens lack all opportunity to compete in, or at least wrest concessions from, the electoral process:

> While the legal alien is unable to vote, he is at least able "to come out of the closet" to voice his sentiments and seek to persuade others to vote his interest. The undocumented alien is unable to protect himself through even this circular fashion. For the undocumented alien, it is not mere theory that those with power exploit the vulnerable.[40]

Notwithstanding these facts, courts have not accorded undocumented aliens the same rights they have bestowed upon other vulnerable minorities. For one reason, as a district judge explained, undocumented aliens fear deportation, and hence "are reluctant to invoke the benevolent protections of the law."[41] Consequently, until recently the judiciary has had little opportunity to determine either the scope of their rights or the corresponding responsibilities of the states. Many of the lawsuits to date have involved alleged procedural inadequacies in deportation proceedings, which are already underway.

Courts have also hesitated to accord them rights because undocumented aliens are in the United States, after all, by virtue of breaking the law. At one time many jurists subscribed to the so-called "outlaw theory," according to which undocumented aliens are violators of the federal immigration statutes, and thus forfeit any benefits that might accrue from their unauthorized presence.[42] One public interest group recently expressed the philosophy underlying this theory when it urged the Fifth Cir-

cuit Court of Appeals to validate a Texas policy that denied undocumented children free public education: "To give [an undocumented alien] rights due to his unlawful status greater than
those he would have had he not come to this country would be
the worst sort of bootstrapping."[43]

In another case a judge dissented from a majority opinion
which had held that undocumented aliens were "employable"
within the meaning of the National Labor Relations Act, and
therefore eligible to vote in union elections. He argued that "illegals had no right to be here, no right to the jobs, and consequently no right to make determinations binding on the company after their deserved departure."[44] Employing the same
rationale, other tribunals have decreed that because of their
status, even those undocumented aliens who have worked in
the United States for several years may be denied unemployment compensation or even standing to maintain a tort action
for personal injury or to sue for unpaid wages.[45] Recently,
however, many courts have abandoned the outlaw theory, in
part because they recognize the extent to which it benefits those
who would abuse undocumented migrants. An Alaska court
reasoned, for instance, that if an undocumented worker were
not allowed to sue for unpaid wages, employers would be not
only unfairly enriched, but also encouraged to hire an increasing number of unlawful laborers whom they could similarly refuse to pay.[46]

While most judges profess to rule only upon the constitu-
tional/legal issues raised in a case, they are inescapably influenced by extralegal, or "policy" considerations as well, and such
considerations have also encouraged them to abandon the outlaw theory. In particular, they realize that many undocumented aliens are in the United States through official suffer-
ance, if not encouragement. Judge William Wayne Justice noted
in Doe v. Plyler that a tribunal should be skeptical whenever the
state acts independently of the federal exclusionary purposes,
accepts the presence of undocumented aliens, and then subjects them to discriminatory laws.[47]

Thus, many courts now agree with a 1903 Supreme Court
holding that the ancient outlawry doctrine is inapplicable to
undocumented aliens because "[e]ven an unlicensed dog is not

an outlaw and is entitled to some rights."[48] Most tribunals currently hold that undocumented migrants are "legal persons" who possess standing to assert their rights in courts,[49] and to recover for personal injuries and for breach of contract.[50] Undocumented aliens may vote in union-certified elections[51] and maintain tort actions[52] because "[a] person does not become an outlaw and lose all rights by doing an illegal act."[53]

Most courts agree that undocumented migrants are entitled to many statutory rights unrelated to their violation of the immigration laws, but they are less certain whether they merit full constitutional protection. Courts have yet to determine, in particular, the extent to which they are entitled to those rights guaranteed by the Fourth Amendment, which proscribes unreasonable searches and seizures, and by the due process and equal protection clauses of the Fourteenth Amendment.

PLYLER V. DOE

As far back as 1896, the Supreme Court held in *Wong Wing v. United States*[54] that anyone within the territorial jurisdiction of the United States is entitled to the due process of law, as secured by the Constitution's Fifth and Fourteenth Amendments. As a result, before the government can deprive undocumented aliens of fundamental rights it must provide them with a hearing that conforms to prevailing standards of fairness. In 1976, the Supreme Court reaffirmed this message in *Mathews v. Diaz*:[55]

There are literally millions of undocumented aliens within the jurisdiction of the United States. The Fifth Amendment, as well as the Fourteenth Amendment, protects everyone of these persons from deprivation of life, liberty, or property without due process of law. . . . Even one whose presence in this country is unlawful, involuntary, or transitory, is entitled to that constitutional protection.[56]

The Fourteenth Amendment also provides that no state "shall deny to any person within its jurisdiction the equal protection of the laws." Courts have generally interpreted this to mean that when a class of persons merits coverage under this "equal protection clause," a state cannot discriminate against its members on invidious or irrational grounds, but only to further legitimate governmental interests.[57] Intermittently for nearly one hundred years the Supreme Court has debated whether, or to what extent, undocumented aliens deserve protection under this clause.

In the 1896 case noted above, the Court indicated that they did merit protection: "[The Fourteenth Amendment's equal protection clause] is universal in its application . . . without regard to any difference of race, color or nationality."[58] In subsequent cases, however, the Court suggested that undocumented aliens may, in fact, *not* be entitled to coverage. In 1971 when it held in *Graham v. Richardson* that aliens merit "particular judicial solicitude,"[59] it carefully limited its holding to noncitizens legally present in the United States, and five years later, in *Mathews v. Diaz*,[60] the Court emphasized that the rights and benefits accorded by the federal government to legal residents do not necessarily extend to illegal aliens: "[T]he illegal alien can [not] advance even a colorable constitutional claim to a share in the bounty that a conscientious sovereign makes available to its own citizens and some of its guests."[61] The remark was intended as dicta, however, and the Court waited another several years before it decided *Plyler v. Doe*,[62] the only case it has heard to date that squarely involves the equal protection rights of undocumented aliens.

At issue in *Plyler* was the constitutionality of §21.031 of the Texas Education Code, which authorized individual school districts either to prohibit undocumented alien children from attending public schools, or to accomplish the same objective by charging them tuition.[63] The Court's responsibility was to determine whether §21 violated the equal protection clause of the Fourteenth Amendment. In order to answer this, however, the Court was first required to answer an antecedent question: Does the equal protection clause extend to those who are unlawfully present in the United States?

While the Court was called upon to resolve a relatively straightforward constitutional question, the case itself inspired enormous controversy. Those opposing §21.031 claimed that the state's exclusionary policy fostered a "ghetto of ignorance,"[64] which was indefensible even from an economic point of view since Texas is one of the richest states in the union, with a tax surplus in 1980 that exceeded two billion dollars.[65] John Crewdson, writing in *The New York Times*, faulted the state on similar grounds:

> For decades, aliens from Mexico without proper immigration papers have been welcomed in Texas, as they have across the Southwest, as an unending source of cheap, willing, diligent labor. There is something niggardly in [the state's] refusal to educate the children of the workers who have contributed so much of its brushfire growth.[66]

Those supporting the Texas policy were no less adamant. According to Mark White, then the state's attorney general, it was the "height of hypocrisy" for Congress to refuse to finance the education of undocumented children, who were here in the first place because the federal government was unable or unwilling to enforce its immigration laws.[67] An attorney from Brownsville, Texas, berated northern "liberals" for similar hypocrisy, and pointed out that "[d]own in the trenches one must face and prepare for the awesome effects on this side of the Rio Grande of a demographic disaster next door."[68] Proponents of the Texas policy predicted that unless the Supreme Court upheld §21.031, states would thereafter be compelled to grant every public benefit to any alien who "successfully eluded our immigration scheme."[69]

When the Supreme Court eventually issued its opinion in *Plyler v. Doe*, its holding was narrow and carefully circumscribed—perhaps reflecting the Court's reluctance to proceed quickly in an area so laden with controversy. Notwithstanding its circumspection, however, *Plyler* represents the most important case the Supreme Court has heard to date involving the rights of undocumented aliens because the Court unequivocally held for the first time that "the protection of the Fourteenth Amendment extends to anyone, citizen or stranger, who is subject to the laws of the state, and reaches into every corner of a State's territory."[70]

Justice William Brennan, who spoke for the Court, explained that while undocumented aliens deserve protection from the

Court, they do not constitute a suspect class. Unlike racial or ethnic minorities who are penalized for conduct over which they have no control, undocumented aliens are penalized for conduct that is deliberately unlawful. Justice Brennan suggested, however, that at least in some circumstances undocumented immigrants constitute a "sensitive" class, entitled to more than routine judicial protection. As a result of the sheer incapability or lax enforcement of the immigration system, he explained, there exists in this country a "shadow population" of illegal migrants that numbers in the millions:

This situation raises the specter of a permanent caste of undocumented resident aliens, encouraged by some to remain here as a source of cheap labor, but nevertheless denied the benefits our society makes available to citizens and lawful residents.[71]

Undocumented children comprise a particularly sensitive class. Justice Brennan noted that while "a State may withhold its beneficence from those whose very presence within the United States is a product of their own unlawful conduct," such logic falters when the victims are minor children, illegally present in the country through no fault of their own.[72] Justice Brennan also observed that many undocumented children will settle in Texas indefinitely, either from clear entitlement or because they apparently enjoy "an inchoate federal permission to remain."[73] He noted, moreover, that when Attorney General William French Smith recently presented Congress with a package of proposed immigration reforms, he included one that would grant amnesty to undocumented aliens residing in the United States.[74] It is, therefore, "difficult to rationalize"[75] §21.031 of the Texas Education Code since the state is undermining its own institutional integrity by fostering within its border a generation of illiterate, welfare-dependent and crime-prone adults.[76]

Irrespective of its harsh results, Texas insisted that §21.031 was justifiable because undocumented children are "outlaws" whose illegal status in itself justifies special disabilities.[77] The Court conceded that Congress could establish such disabilities, given its plenary authority over immigration; a state, on the contrary, can penalize undocumented residents only if its actions are either consistent with the federal immigration scheme, or serve important state interests.[78] Justice Brennan concluded that the penalty imposed by §21.031 corresponds to no identifiable federal policy,[79] and thus the only question remaining was whether it promoted any substantial state interest.

Texas asserted that §21.031 operated, above all, to preserve the state's "limited resources for the education of its lawful residents."[80] Justice Brennan was unpersuaded: A concern for the preservation of resources in itself could not justify a state policy that singled out a discrete class of children for discrimination.[81] Texas further argued that the disputed provision served as a disincentive for illegal immigration. Justice Brennan pointed out, however, that the dominant "pull" factor was unquestionably the availability of employment, and according to the evidence few, if any, families migrate to the United States in order to benefit from public education.[82] Thus, "[c]harging tuition to undocumented children constitutes a ludicrously ineffectual attempt to stem the tide of illegal immigration," certainly when compared to the alternative of prohibiting the employment of illegal aliens.[83] In reaching this conclusion, Justice Brennan was presumably influenced by the district court record, which points out that Texas has time and again declined to enact an employer sanction law, and in fact has successfully frustrated congressional attempts to establish a federal prohibition.[84]

The Court concluded that §21.031 of the Texas Education Code could not survive, and thereby provided plaintiffs with a substantial victory.[85] The Court's holding in *Plyler v. Doe* is nonetheless limited: It affects only undocumented alien children, and only in the area of public education. It in no way precludes most state efforts to discourage illegal immigration, since the Court emphasizes that these efforts will be sustained as long as they either serve important governmental interests or can claim even tacit congressional approval. Certainly the holding in no way obliges states to provide undocumented aliens with any social services other than education. Finally, it in no way forecloses congressional action—even action that would effectively resurrect §21.031.

The Court suggested throughout *Plyler* that Congress could either forbid undocumented children from attending public schools, or authorize the states to exclude them at will. The Court thereby reaffirmed its longstanding policy of deferring to Congress and the executive branch whenever it examines substantive policy involving noncitizens.[86] Such capitulation is mandated neither by the Constitution nor by reasons of state and it detracts from an otherwise meritorious opinion.

FOURTH AMENDMENT RIGHTS

A few years ago, immigration agents ordered one hundred investigators to surround subway stations in Queens, New York, and, as people emerged from the underground depots, to stop and interrogate those who looked "ethnic."[87] Again in April 1982, the Immigration Service launched "Operation Jobs," during which hundreds of INS inspectors invaded factories and other commercial enterprises just after the workers had started their morning shifts.[88] As one observer noted, "they came in like Jesse James, scaring people half to death."[89] During this week-long blitz, involving nine cities throughout the country, officers rounded up almost 6,000 aliens, many of whom were subsequently discovered to be American citizens or lawfully resident aliens. While these are grim illustrations, they differ only in detail from similar operations conducted routinely by immigration officers any place in the country where they suspect undocumented aliens are clustered.

Immigration authorities admit their officers are at times overzealous, that occasionally they disregard procedural niceties. They point out, however, that their task is scarcely enviable: Woefully underfunded and short-staffed, they are nevertheless expected to process aliens at ports of entry, conduct deportation and exclusion hearings, handle a staggering amount of paper work, and still track down millions of undocumented aliens.

Courts recognize, on the one hand, that immigration agents operate in a nether world, seeking "shadow" people who slip in and out of sight. Concededly the Immigration Service cannot confine itself to "white glove" procedures. Courts realize, on the other hand, that if government officials fail to accord aliens both fairness and the appearance of fairness, they will compound the disaffection that already pervades minority communities. The problem, then, is to reconcile the legitimate needs of the Immigration Service with the commands of the Fourth Amendment, and with those other constitutional provisions that affect aliens as well, particularly the Fifth and Sixth Amendments, which collectively guarantee basic procedural rights to any one whose life, liberty, or property is jeopardized by governmental action.

The Supreme Court has held that the Fourth Amendment applies to all persons in the United States, citizens or aliens, documented or undocumented. This amendment provides that

the right of the people to be secure in their persons, houses, papers and effects against unreasonable searches and seizures shall not be violated, and no warrant shall issue but upon probable cause, supported by oath or affirmation and particularly describing the place to be searched and the persons or things to be seized.[90]

In operation this amendment guarantees neither total privacy nor total security, but it does prohibit unreasonable assaults upon either.

The INA confers vast authority on the Immigration Service to search for, interrogate, and detain those persons believed to be unlawfully present in the United States.[91] This authority, however, must be exercised within the confines of the Fourth Amendment. Since this amendment only prohibits searches or seizures when they are unreasonable, the fundamental question becomes: What is "reasonable"? In traditional law enforcement, a constitutional search or seizure is ordinarily one undertaken under the authority of a warrant, issued by a magistrate only upon a showing of "probable cause" indicating that a named individual has engaged in illegal activity, or that the specified papers or effects to be seized are evidence of crime.

The judiciary has relaxed the traditional strictures of the Fourth Amendment in order to accommodate the fast-paced, "hound-and-hare" world of immigration control, and consequently interprets as "reasonable" much, although by no means all, activity undertaken without a warrant. What constitutes reasonable behavior is then usually determined on a case-by-case basis, in light of the totality of circumstance: the geographic area where the search occurs, the extent to which those questioned or detained might have an "expectation of privacy," the interest that predominates in a balancing test.

The INA grants border patrol officers wide authority to stop vehicles and search for aliens within 100 miles of any external boundary,[92] and in those areas considered "functional equivalents" of the border, that is, those particular locations at which one could not reasonably arrive without having traversed an international boundary.[93] These searches may be conducted without a warrant because, the Court reasons, the government's fundamental interest in regulating those who enter the country outweighs the rights of an individual, who suffers at any rate only a minimal and anticipated invasion of privacy. The government's action, moreover, affects all border crossers and thereby minimizes the possibility of selective enforcement.

The latitude accorded immigration officials in border areas shrinks as they move toward the interior of the country. There they establish checkpoints at fixed places along major highways leading away from the border, primarily near the United States-Mexico line. Although officials stop people at random and without probable cause, they cannot act with total license. In 1976, the Supreme Court held in *United States v. Martinez Fuerte*[94] that checkpoints must be "reasonably located," the stops "routinely conducted," and the interrogations "brief," even if persons are stopped "largely on the basis of apparent Mexican ancestry."[95]

Although the checkpoints at issue in *Martinez Fuerte* were situated as far as ninety miles from the Mexican border, the Court found them reasonable: The intrusions were minimal, and, given the formidable enforcement problems confronting the border patrol, "the need to make routine checkpoints is great."[96] Justice Brennan dissented. He argued that since checkpoints are designed almost exclusively to detect Mexicans illegally in the country, officials left free to stop whomever they choose will inevitably engage in selective enforcement: "The process will then inescapably discriminate against citizens of Mexican ancestry and Mexican aliens lawfully in this country."[97]

Although in interior locations immigration officers cannot ordinarily stop automobiles at random, by virtue of another provision of the INA they may stop vehicles and interrogate their passengers whenever they have "founded" or "reasonable suspicion" to believe that the occupants are aliens.[98] Equipped with this statutory authority, officers thus conduct "roving patrols" in strategic areas throughout the country.[99] In *United States v. Brignoni-Ponce*,[100] the Supreme Court sanctioned the use of these patrols, but held that arresting officers could stop vehicles in order to question their occupants only when they had a reasonable suspicion, based on "specific articulable facts" and reasonable inferences drawn from these facts that the vehicle contained persons unlawfully present in the United States.

Brignoni is a troubling case. Apart from sanctioning roving patrols, which even more than checkpoints result in discriminatory enforcement, it left unresolved two major issues with which the judiciary continues to wrestle: (1) What constitutes "reasonable suspicion" that an individual is undocumented? (2), While *Brignoni* established that officials could stop vehicles only when they suspected that their occupants were illegally present in the United States, the Court noted but deliberately left unanswered a related question: In nonvehicular stops, conducted away from the border, may officials stop and interrogate those whom they merely suspect to be aliens, or must they also have reason to believe these aliens are unlawfully present in the United States?

According to David Carliner, a specialist in immigration law, officials accumulate reasonable suspicion from a motley assortment of subjective impressions:

Typically an alien who is taken into custody is at a place of work, or apprehended while he's walking down the street, and the procedure is for an immigration officer who may or may not have a substantial basis for knowing that the person is an alien other than his impression of what he looks like. He looks Chinese, he looks foreign, he looks Mexican. He wears certain types of clothes. At one time they had an operational . . . guideline of Immigration Service officers in New York whose description stated, "People who wore foreign-looking clothing and carried brown bags," they were assumed to be Spanish-speaking aliens from Spanish-speaking countries, because that combination, in the experience of Immigration Service, reflected [that] a person who

had his lunch in this brown bag and . . . had foreign-cut clothing . . .
was probably not a citizen of the United States [or probably] not even
a permanent resident alien of the United States.[101]

Federal courts have frequently held that officers acted upon
"reasonable suspicion," even when this suspicion was trig-
gered by physical clues as arbitrary as those cited by Carliner.
In a 1972 case, *Cheung Tin Wong v. INS*,[102] the District of Columbia circuit concluded that immigration officers had "reasonable suspicion" before they stopped and questioned two people of Asian ancestry near a Chinese restaurant. One of the two
had signaled a taxi and then spoken to the driver. From this
scene, the officers inferred that the other Asian spoke no English. The foreign appearance of the two men, their proximity
to a Chinese restaurant that reputedly employed undocumented aliens, coupled with the one's assumed inability to speak
English, created sufficient evidence to justify suspicion.

The Second Circuit Court of Appeals also found that immigration officers possessed a "reasonable suspicion" of alienage
when a woman in a bus station in Buffalo pronounced the name
of the city as "Boofalo";[103] a district court in California concluded the same when two men sitting in the back seat of a car
looked at INS officers with "apparent nervousness."[104] Another district court, this one in Chicago, held that "furtive conduct and flight" might legitimately provoke suspicion,[105] and a
federal circuit court held that an individual's failure to produce
identification upon request might also provoke suspicion.[106]

Does one's race alone, or ethnic appearance, give rise to reasonable suspicion? In 1976, an appellate court held that officers
could not permissibly stop and interrogate people based exclusively on their foreign appearance.[107] Other tribunals have held
that while an individual's race or ethnicity may be considered,
officers cannot interrogate these individuals unless there is also
some other clearly definable fact that suggests that they are
aliens.[108] In *Brignoni*, the Supreme Court also fobade immigration authorities to rely upon appearance of "Mexican ancestry"
as the sole factor in determining whether to question an individual, but it conceded that it could be a "relevant factor,"[109]

along with such other indicators as "the character of the area," "obvious attempts to evade officers," "mode of dress and hair cut."[110]

Much of the evidence cited by the courts does indeed suggest that the individuals interrogated might be aliens: They have difficulty with English; they are uncomfortable around authority figures; they wear garb that is ill-fitting and peculiar. These factors, however, do not suggest that they are unlawfully present in the United States, and by condoning interrogations prompted by such factors the judiciary therefore indicates the answer to the second question raised in *United States v. Brignoni-Ponce*: Immigration officials can stop and question anyone whom they believe to be unlawfully present in the United States.

In a 1976 case, *Illinois Migrant Council v. Pilliod*,[111] the Seventh Circuit Court of Appeals attempted to modify this conclusion by holding that immigration agents could approach anyone on the basis of their alienage alone, provided they conducted only casual inquiries into their citizenship and made no attempt to detain them; even a brief detention, however, requires a reasonable suspicion of unlawful presence. In making this ruling, the Seventh Circuit was influenced by a leading Fourth Amendment case, *Terry v. Ohio*,[112] decided by the Supreme Court in 1968. The Court held in *Terry* that the Fourth Amendment's prohibition against unreasonable searches and seizures applies whenever an enforcement officer "seizes" or "forcibly detains" an individual. A seizure occurs whenever the person being questioned becomes aware of the fact that he or she has lost the freedom to walk away. According to the principle established in *Terry*, officers cannot constitutionally make an investigative stop—or "seizure"—unless they have "specific articulable facts" that give rise to a "reasonable suspicion" that a crime has been committed with which the suspect is connected.[113]

Following *Illinois Migrant Council* a number of other tribunals have accordingly established that INS officers must have a reasonable suspicion, based on specific articulable facts, that an alien is unlawfully present in the United States before they can detain that individual for interrogation.[114] On the other hand, these officers may "casually" question a cooperative person when they have reason to believe this person is an alien. Thus, the "cooperativeness" of the respondent becomes crucial when courts determine whether he or she has been detained or simply questioned.

The presence or absence of "cooperativeness" is a workable standard providing that its underlying assumption is sound: that respondents as a class are sufficiently discerning and legally astute to distinguish between a casual inquiry and one that is not, and to appreciate the range of their constitutional rights under either circumstance. In 1977 a New York district court explained in *Marquez v. Kiley*[115] why it believed such an assumption is untenable:

> It is in the nature of an oxymoron to speak of "casual"inquiry between a government official, armed with a badge and a gun and charged with enforcing the nation's immigration laws, and a person suspected of alienage. . . . For a constitutional rule in these matters to depend on the "voluntary cooperation" of the suspect is to impose a gloss upon real life. When it is further considered that refusal to cooperate or an attempt to evade such a "casual encounter," indeed, even the appearance of nervousness, may well be held to provide reasonable grounds to suspect unlawful presence and therefore to authorize forcible detention . . . the rule urged upon us by the government appears unworkable.[116]

Notwithstanding this firm indictment, many federal tribunals continue to distinguish between permissible and impermissible searches on the basis of their supposed "voluntariness." This is unfortunate, not only because the rule is unworkable for all the reasons explained in *Marquez v. Kiley*, but also because it thrusts the alien into a "Catch 22" predicament. As the court noted in *Kiley*, when aliens refuse to cooperate during a "casual encounter," or indeed appear nervous, this in itself might supply the inquiring officer with the reasonable grounds necessary to suspect unlawful presence and thus to subject the alien to forcible detention.[117]

In another case noted above, *Cheung Tin Wong v. INS*,[118] the Circuit Court for the District of Columbia concluded that immigration officials had acted properly when they questioned two individuals upon noting their Asian ancestry, proximity to a

Chinese restaurant, and language difficulties. The court held, however, that while these factors constituted suspicion to question, they did not yet constitute the "reasonable suspicion" necessary to forcibly detain and interrogate them. What would provide this extra ingredient? The majority did not say, but one judge suggested in his concurring opinion that perhaps the inquiring officer needed to ask only one simple question, "Do you have any immigration papers?" When the alien said "no," the agent automatically acquired the "reasonable suspicion" necessary to detain the person for interrogation.[119]

For all the judiciary's feints and forward moves, immigration authorities can still effectively stop and interrogate anyone they meet, wherever and whenever, providing only that the respondent looks foreign. While they cannot in theory question people on the basis of racial or ethnic appearance alone, they in fact do so consistently, and no one familiar with the realities of immigration enforcement would suggest the contrary.

AREA CONTROL OPERATIONS

Immigration officers need not rely solely upon an individual's "foreign appearance" in their pursuit of undocumented aliens. Frequently they are provided with "tips" from either public officials or private parties. They may receive a phone call from the local police, for instance, reporting that they arrested someone who seems to be an "illegal"; or from a welfare administrator, noting that an applicant for assistance has suspicious credentials.

At other times the INS receives an anonymous tip that Sun Moo Kim, or Jose Garcia, works at a certain factory, or drinks beer every afternoon at the Pinewood Tavern. These private informants are typically rival claimants for a job, deserted spouses, credit bureau agents, employers seeking the apprehension of their work force before pay day, or simply grudge bearers. Private tips unquestionably provide the INS with valuable leads, but reliance upon them is questionable from the standpoint of public policy: When neighbor is allowed to incriminate neighbor, a wife her husband, or a worker his colleague, the mutual trust that forms the basis for decent family and community life is eroded.[120]

On the basis of tips, immigration officers conduct INA-authorized dragnet searches—so-called "area control operations (ACOs)," or, in INS parlance, "factory surveys."[121] Sometimes they conduct sweeps of entire neighborhoods, or station themselves at busy street corners, at subway stations or bus stops, wherever they are likely to find undocumented aliens. More frequently, however, officers conduct ACOs at factories and other commercial establishments where a large number of aliens are reputedly employed, and in this way apprehend thousands of unauthorized workers each year.

A typical raid was staged in 1978 at Blackie's House of Beef, a popular restaurant in Washington D.C. In a meticulously planned maneuver, agents surrounded the building, blocked its entryways, and then burst into the premises, brandishing their badges and commanding everyone present to remain where they were. They created pandemonium as terrified people rushed around, bumping into one another and screaming. Agents questioned employees for many hours, and then took several down to INS headquarters for further interrogation.[122]

ACOs would not survive their first confrontation with the Fourth Amendment if the apprehension of undocumented aliens were considered a criminal, rather than civil, operation. In a criminal operation enforcement officers cannot ordinarily conduct a search without first obtaining a warrant, which a magistrate will issue only upon "probable cause," which means the officers must identify the specific person to be searched and adduce credible evidence linking this person to illegal behavior. In civil proceedings, by contrast, government agents only need "administrative warrants," which are issued in accordance with substantially relaxed Fourth Amendment standards.[123]

The Supreme Court has held that in issuing a search warrant in a criminal case a magistrate might properly consider evidence based on tips or hearsay evidence, but only if this evidence is independently corroborated.[124] Until recently, however, the judiciary has sustained the constitutionality of administrative warrants based on unverified tips. In planning and executing their ACOs, in fact, the INS routinely depends on anonymous tips, which by their very nature can rarely be substantiated. Charles Sava, former INS Associate Commissioner for Enforcement, explained agency procedure during testimony before the United States Civil Rights Commission:

> [in ACOs we] would be looking for, let's say, undocumented workers in an area, or seeking them in a place of employment. While we might have some information they were there, it's different from having a case where we are going to interview a particular person by name at a given location.[125]

As a consequence, administrative warrants frequently lack any specificity. Agents are unable to "name" the individuals they seek, or to link them to unlawful behavior on the basis of anything more sturdy than a covert tip. They must accordingly seek the broad-based, or general, search warrant that the Fourth Amendment was intended to prohibit. Such a warrant, moreover, discourages agents from complying with the strictures set forth in *Brignoni-Ponce* and *Illinois Migrant Council*, that no individuals be subjected to detention or interrogation unless investigating agents have founded suspicion that they are unlawfully present in the United States. During dragnet searches, in fact, how can officers distinguish between one unnamed worker and another? They must either interrogate everyone within the targeted area, or single out for questioning only those whose dialect is peculiar or whose skin is brown or yellow.

The difficulty in conducting a limited ACO is evidenced by the circumstances surrounding the search of Blackie's House of Beef. Immigration agents possessed an administrative warrant that had been supported by an affidavit alleging the presence of "known illegal aliens" on the premises. The specific names of these "known" individuals were not provided, however, nor were any other data identifying the persons sought, or even an estimate of their numbers.[126] The United States Court of Appeals for the District of Columbia nevertheless upheld the constitutionality of the search, holding in July 1981, that INS agents could obtain a warrant without satisfying the more rigid standards mandated in criminal law, particularly the one requiring that they specify by name and describe each alien they suspected of being undocumented.[127]

The appeals court emphasized that immigration officers deal with aliens who are "fugitive(s) outside the law,"[128] whose vital statistics are not likely to be on file anywhere in the country.[129] Accordingly, immigration agents can properly utilize administrative search warrants that would not satisfy the probable cause standards demanded by the courts in criminal investigations. Rather, they may obtain an administrative warrant upon a showing that there is "sufficient specificity and reliability to prevent the exercise of unbridled discretion by law enforcement officers."[130] Under the circumstances that prevailed in Blackie's, the search warrant sought by immigration authorities was "as descriptive as reasonably possible."[131]

A year later, however, in *International Ladies Garment Workers v. Sureck*,[132] the Court of Appeals for the Ninth Circuit held the INS to stricter Fourth Amendment standards. *Sureck*, which focused on the same questions raised in *Blackie's House of Beef*, grew out of three raids that the INS conducted in 1977 on two garment factories in Los Angeles. According to the Ninth Circuit, by positioning individuals at the factory exits to prevent any one from escaping, the government effectively "seized" the entire work force. This was permissible only if it had reason to believe that every individual detained was illegally present in the United States.

In April 1984, the Supreme Court resolved the dispute between the lower tribunals by unequivocally upholding the constitutionality of broad-sweeping ACOs. Hearing *Sureck* on appeal, in a case now called *INS v. Delgado*,[133] the Court held that the entry and behavior of immigration agents did not constitute a "seizure" of the entire work force because factory workers were at least theoretically free to leave the premises at any time. Although those who left would have been questioned, they would have been allowed to go as long as their answers satisfied immigration agents. "Mere questioning," the Court concluded, "does not constitute a seizure." Moreover, while the Court conceded that actual detentions required at least "some minimal level of objective justification" under the Fourth Amendment, it maintained that the brief and limited questioning to which most workers were subjected was simply "classic consensual encounters" that raised no issue under the Fourth Amendment.[134]

The government will find the disposition of *Delgado* heartening, since the Justice Department had argued in its Supreme Court brief that if the Court interpreted the Fourth Amendment to outlaw area control operations, this would "almost completely destro[y] the utility of an important and effective tool in apprehending aliens who are illegally present in the country."[135] The Justice Department is correct: It is difficult for the Immigration Service to identify specific undocumented aliens prior to a raid, or otherwise to conduct these surveys in conformity with strict Fourth Amendment standards. If the Supreme Court were effectively to outlaw ACOs, moreover, the service would lose what it considers an indispensable tool. Indeed, after the Ninth Circuit enjoined the INS from conducting broad-sweeping factory raids, apprehension rates plummeted in those states affected by the ruling.[136] Whatever the utility of ACOs, however, it is insufficient to offset their attendant harm. This is particularly true since the government can regulate undocumented aliens in more humane and ultimately more effective ways—by penalizing employers who hire unauthorized workers, for instance, or by enforcing wage and safety legislation and thereby reducing the incentive to hire an underground work force.[137]

ARREST WARRANTS

Arrest warrants, even more than administrative search warrants, are dispensed in an haphazard and cavalier fashion. Theoretically, they are required in all but two circumstances—when immigration officers witness an alien attempting to enter the country without inspection, or when they have reason to believe that a given alien is both unlawfully present in the United States and likely to abscond.[138] In practice, however, most deportation cases are initiated without an arrest warrant, either because authorities schedule a hearing without formally arresting the party, or because they conclude that an individual suspected of unlawful presence would escape during the time necessary to secure a warrant.[139] This decision is often based on nothing more than a suspicion that the individual is in the country unlawfully. Under these conditions, a warrant is usually obtained after the fact in order to formalize the custody. When warrants are sought, however, they are often granted automatically, since there are few meaningful standards to guide their dispensation. According to the INA, a warrant of arrest may be issued for any alien whom officers have concluded is illegally present in the United States.[140] The INS has interpreted this statutory grant to mean that warrants may be issued "whenever, in [the named official's] discretion, it appears that the arrest of the respondent is necessary or desirable." What is "necessary or desirable," however, is at no point defined, and according to Leon Rosen, a former immigration official, this apparent qualification is meaningless:

What actually happens is, where they see fit to obtain a warrant, an investigator simply goes to his supervisor and says, "I want a warrant," and the district director signs a warrant, and nobody bothers to prepare an affidavit or read the affidavit to determine whether or not there is probable cause."[141]

According to traditional Fourth Amendment interpretation, warrants are to be issued only by neutral magistrates who are presumably unaffected by the biases and zealotry that can afflict enforcement officers. The INA, however, demands no such impartiality. Even directors of investigation, who are responsible for preparing and executing the agency's case against an alien, are among those officials empowered to issue arrest warrants.[142] This, coupled with the ease with which warrants are issued, prompted the Civil Rights Commission to conclude that "the warrant process (is) an empty gesture that lends a fallacious claim of legitimacy to a subsequent arrest."[143]

CONSTITUTIONAL RIGHTS AND THE DEPORTATION PROCESS

When immigration authorities discover an alien who they believe is in the country unlawfully, they institute deportation proceedings unless the alien "voluntarily departs." Since these proceedings are considered civil in nature,[144] the alien facing deportation is accorded only some, not all, the procedural safeguards provided defendants in criminal proceedings.[145]

Aliens have a right to "fundamental fairness." This evolving concept has no precise definition but, at a minimum, it encompasses the basic guarantees contained in the Constitution's Fifth and Sixth Amendments:[146] individuals are entitled above all to an impartial hearing,[147] which includes notice of the charges against them, the right to cross-examine adverse witnesses and to present evidence on their own behalf, and the right to a judgment by an unbiased magistrate based solely on the evidence.[148]

Congress has also provided the respondent in deportation proceedings with other safeguards not mandated by the Constitution. For instance, the INS bears the burden of proving with "clear, convincing and unequivocal evidence" that the respondent is not only an alien, but a deportable one as well.[149] Congress has also created the Board of Immigration Appeals, distinct from the INS, to which an alien may appeal an adverse decision rendered by an immigration judge. The board's decision is in turn subject to judicial review.

Essential as these constitutional and statutory provisions are, they apply only during the actual deportation proceeding, and consequently benefit only about 6 percent of those ordered to leave the country.[150] Rather than participate in formal deportation hearings, most aliens elect "voluntary departure," and accordingly agree to leave the United States by a specified date. The Immigration Service insists that aliens prefer this procedure since, unlike those who have been formally deported, they are not required to obtain special permission from the INS before returning to the country, nor do they risk the criminal penalties that await those who reenter the United States after leaving under a deportation order.[151]

Voluntary departures, however, are not necessarily as problem-free as the Immigration Service maintains. While aliens who agree to leave facilitate their own reentrance, they also forfeit their right to a hearing, and waive potential forms of discretionary relief. More to the point, are such departures indeed "voluntary?" Do aliens understand the process? Do they appreciate the many forms of relief that are available to those facing deportation? Former INS Commissioner Leon Castillo, for one, doubts that they do, since most aliens have little English-speaking ability and even less understanding of the American legal system or the complexities of immigration law.[152]

The active participation of immigration agents also suggests that at least some aliens who forgo a deportation hearing may not be making a knowing, or intelligent, waiver. These agents naturally prefer that aliens opt for voluntary departure, since this spares their overtaxed agency considerable time and money. They are nevertheless obliged to provide aliens with a full appraisal of their options. This institutionalized conflict of interest must inevitably work to the alien's disadvantage. Given the debilitated state of the INA, voluntary departures are probably indispensable expedients. Congress, however, should at least institute a system in which neutral third parties explain to aliens their range of choices and the consequences attendant upon each.

Even when deportation hearings are conducted, they are sometimes more show than substance. In regions with particularly heavy dockets, such as New York City, the Immigration Service will occasionally hold so-called "mash" hearings—multiple accelerated special hearings—that allow it to process up to sixty aliens on a single morning.[153] The typical hearing lasts about five minutes, including time for translation. Respondents often emerge from these sessions unaware of the fact that they have participated in a hearing, that it is now all over, and that in the process they waived their right to an appeal.

The immigration laws are second only to the Internal Revenue Code in complexity. As a consequence, even if aliens were granted a scrupulously fair deportation hearing, they would still be seriously disadvantaged without a lawyer. Many of those threatened with expulsion nevertheless either lack counsel altogether, or have it only at a stage in the proceeding when such assistance can no longer be optimally effective.

According to the Supreme Court's interpretation of the Sixth Amendment, the government must provide counsel for indigents in any criminal case, whether a misdemeanor or a felony.[154] In a 1975 case a district judge accordingly reasoned that since an alien threatened with deportation faces consequences that are often as serious as those confronting defendants in criminal proceedings, "fundamental fairness" requires the government to provide the former as well as the latter with counsel.[155] His prescription has gone unheeded, however. The INA stipulates that a person in exclusion or deportation hearings may be represented by counsel, but at no expense to the government.[156] In practice, unless attorneys volunteer their services or an alien's circumstances are extraordinary, he or she will probably receive no legal assistance at all.

Beginning with the Wickersham Commission in 1921, every special body impaneled to study American immigration law has recommended that counsel be provided, or at least be made available, during each important step in the deportation process.[157] Charles Gordon, the former General Council of the Immigration Service, observed that aliens represented by counsel were able to avoid an order of deportation more often than those lacking this assistance because lawyers are able to raise points of law, to question the adequacy of the process itself, and to gather relevant evidence.[158] Not surprisingly, the INS assigns a trial attorney to represent its interests at every contested proceeding.

The INA provides that whenever individuals are arrested without a warrant, they shall be advised of their right to the assistance of counsel only after the initial interrogation has occurred, and the decision to institute deportation proceedings has been made.[159] Consequently, even those who are able to retain counsel can benefit from this support only during the actual deportation process itself, and must proceed unassisted during the crucial prehearing stages, when the damaging evidence is often gathered or the inculpating statements declared.[160]

During the pre-trial stages the defendant often feels intimidated by the presence of authority figures and may utter incriminating statements out of ignorance or a desire to please enforcement officers. Since the preliminary processes are conducted in relative secrecy, government officials may even coerce the alien into making damaging statements. Whatever the case, at least those defendants with vested interests in the United

States should have counsel available from the time they are first detained for interrogation.

Since deportations are considered civil proceedings, however, aliens facing deportation are denied not only a right to counsel, but also any right to bail. By virtue of the Eighth Amendment, defendants in criminal cases have a presumptive right to be released on bond.[161] An alien facing deportation, on the contrary, may be detained without bail whenever the attorney general deems this advisable.[162] INS operation instructions further provide that an immigration judge can deny bail whenever there is evidence suggesting that an alien, if released, might either jeopardize the public safety or abscond.[163] These are nebulous guidelines, and whether or not to grant bail ultimately becomes a discretionary and even arbitrary decision. Austin Fragomen, an authority on immigration law, goes further. He contends that in his experience "[the INS] routinely require[s] standard amounts for persons of certain ethnic origins with total disregard of the situation."[164]

According to a recent study commissioned by the INS, the bail system is frequently abused because it operates with neither consistency nor accountability.[165] The study concluded that "there is no discernible pattern—Service wide—to the setting of bond,"[166] and cited two reasons in particular why this is true: (1) the INS has not formulated adequate standards by which to measure bond recommendations, and (2) it fails to gather sufficient information on any given defendant, and as a consequence lacks the basis for determining whether or not he or she would pose a public danger, if released, or would be likely to flee.[167]

With minimum outlay, the Immigration Service could vastly upgrade the system by which it determines bond. As the study advised, it should gather more information on the aliens it processes, particularly the extent to which they have community ties, and devise an objective method by which to determine both appropriate rates and the circumstances under which bail should be set. Both this INS study and the Civil Rights Commission have recommended that once the service detains an alien it should bring him or her immediately before either a special inquiry officer or a magistrate unaffiliated with the INS, who would make an initial bond determination and advise the alien of his or her rights.[168]

Should aliens be allowed to sneak across the Rio Grande, or slip in unnoticed across the Canadian border, and then expect to benefit from the Constitution's many procedural safeguards? Jurists and even lawmakers have grudgingly conceded that they should, and for reasons beyond mere solicitude for the aliens' welfare. Constitutional safeguards must apply because without legal restraints government officials could, through inadvertence as much as intention, mistreat those within their charge. Also, the Constitution should apply for a reason that involves simple political reality: A polity cannot forbear substantial illegality in one area of public life without itself being diminished.

UNDOCUMENTED MIGRATION: PROPOSED SOLUTIONS

Many proposals, ranging in scope from the simple to the monumental, have been suggested for combatting undocumented migration. One demographer recommends that no visitor be allowed into the country without a return ticket in his or her pocket;[169] others argue the futility of policing the borders at all, and submit that restrictive immigration laws be abandoned altogether.[170] Among these wide-ranging proposals three in particular have received serious consideration by one or more of the select commissions that have convened over the last fifteen years to study the "phenomenon" of undocumented migration: (1) a program to legalize the status of specific groups of undocumented residents; (2) a "guest" or temporary worker program; and (3) a system of employer sanctions applicable to those who knowingly hire aliens not authorized to work in this country.

In 1980, the Reagan Administration's Interagency Taskforce on Immigration recommended that many of the country's undocumented residents be allowed to regularize their status. In justifying this proposal, Attorney General William French Smith noted that "[w]e have neither the resources, the capability, nor the motivation to uproot and deport millions of illegal aliens, many of whom have become, in effect, members of the community"[171] Although they frequently disagree on the scope of this legalization program, or the manner of its implementation, most other study groups have also recommended that an amnesty be accorded undocumented residents who have lived in the United States for a prescribed period.[172] Congress is currently considering the Immigration Reform and Control Act, or so-called Simpson-Mazzoli Bill, that provides for the institution of such a program.[173]

While an amnesty is a humane and probably unavoidable expedient, many in Congress are nevertheless reluctant to support its passage. They are worried about attendant costs, especially as newly legalized aliens become eligible for social services.[174] Their main concern, however, is that the American public will regard an "amnesty" as nothing more than a reward for those who "successfully sneak across the border."[175]

Even if Congress passed a legalization program, however, its success is problematic. When Canada and Australia implemented amnesties, they were able to attract only a small percentage of eligible aliens because the intended beneficiaries either regarded the program with suspicion, or found its stipulations confusing and restrictive.[176] In fashioning a legalization program, legislators therefore face a dilemma. The majority of their constituents will support such a program only if it provides recipients with minimal public benefits and is selective in character. On the other hand, participation in the program will probably correspond directly to the generosity of its terms.

In addition to recommending a limited amnesty, the Reagan taskforce advocated the implementation of a temporary worker program in which a prescribed number of aliens would be admitted to work in the country for an indefinite period of time.[177] According to its proponents, such a program would redirect undocumented migration into legal channels, provide employers in agriculture and other enterprises dependent on seasonal labor with a guaranteed work force, and protect participants from the exploitation that an illegal status invites.

Opponents of a temporary worker program—and they are many, including most members of the Select Commission—rejoin that such a solution is counter-productive and inherently exploitative.[178] As evidence they cite this country's experience

with the bracero program, which accelerated, rather than reduced, the pace of illegal migration from Mexico,[179] or the guest
worker programs instituted in Western Europe after World War
II. According to economist David North, the consequences of
the European experiment were "almost universally grim":[180]
several million "temporary" lodgers became instead permanent
inhabitants, and subsequently imported their families as well.
In the process, they displaced indigenous labor and otherwise
debased working conditions. Those counseling against a temporary worker program point out that, since its participants are
welcomed only as long as the country needs their cheap labor,
they are inevitably shunted into an underclass where they remain ineligible for most of the rights and privileges of citizenship.[181]

Every panel commissioned since 1973 has recommended
penalizing employers who knowingly hire undocumented
workers.[182] An employer sanction provision also provides the
keystone of the Simpson-Mazzoli bill.[183] Despite the uncertainty which otherwise colors any discussion of undocumented
migration, one point is universally conceded: Migrants come to
the United States in search of jobs; the availability of employment is by far the largest "pull" factor.[184] The United States,
which is the only industrialized country in the world without
employer sanctions, also perpetuates an injustice. Although
undocumented workers are subject to exploitation and deportation, even fines and jail sentences, the immigration laws in-
sulate from any liability whatsoever those who would profit from
their labor.[185]

Theoretically, then, a system of employer sanctions is both
sensible and just. Yet business people, civil libertarians, and
members of ethnic minorities fervently oppose its imposition.
Foremost among their fears is that employers, anxious to avoid
liability, will discriminate against "foreign looking" applicants.
Daniel E. Leach, former vice president of the Equal Employment Opportunity Commission, is one of many who maintains
that employers, if subject to penalties for hiring illegal aliens,
will either selectively ask for proof of legal residence (from
members of ethnic minorities only), or refuse to hire them altogether "to be on the safe side."[186]

To prevent discrimination on the basis of race or national origin, sanctions must be coupled with some type of identification system by which employers can ascertain the eligibility of prospective employees. Whether the system relies upon existing documentation, or a new "universal identifier," critics maintain that the costs of establishing and/or verifying this documentation will be formidable.[187] They are concerned, moreover, that poor people will have trouble securing the necessary documentation, and that such a verification system will only aggrandize the profits already realized by a flourishing underground industry devoted to the mass production of fraudulent documents.

Civil libertarians predict that Americans will experience an even greater erosion of privacy if so-called "universal identifiers" are instituted. One governmental study concluded that such identifiers "could serve as the skeleton for a national dossier system to maintain information on every citizen (and resident) from cradle to grave."[188] While the card itself poses only a minimal threat, the authors of this study worry that the data it supplies will eventually be automated, integrated with other record-keeping systems, and processed to yield a highly sophisticated profile of every eligible worker in this country.[189]

The proposed guest-worker and employer-sanctions programs represent massive, expensive, and potentially counterproductive measures that perhaps would be unnecessary if existing health and wage laws were vigorously enforced, in particular the Fair Labor Standards Act, the National Labor Relations Act, and the Occupational Safety and Health Act. Their effective implementation would guarantee salutary results. Enforcement machinery already in existence could be utilized, potentially discriminatory remedies avoided, and the employment of undocumented workers discouraged since employers required to provide decent wages and working conditions would lose a prime incentive for hiring underground labor.

Those advocating this vigorous enforcement, however, and even those promoting employer sanctions or other remedial steps, concede that short of erecting a "combat zone" around the country's borders, or imposing surveillance and investigative measures more appropriate to a police state than an open

5

Refugees

The novelist Heinrich Boll has referred to the twentieth century as "[t]he Century of refugees and prisoners,"[1] and others have described it as the "century of the homeless man,"[2] or the "Era of the Dispossessed."[3] Hannah Arendt suggests that refugees in fact symbolize modern society. As the victims of extreme nationalism, minorities and stateless people are "the most symptomatic group in contemporary politics."[4]

Refugee movements constitute a major destabilizing force in the world. According to one conservative estimate, more than one hundred million men, women, and children have become displaced persons since 1900, perhaps twice as many as in the preceding two centuries.[5] Since 1980 tens of thousands of people have sought refugee status in the United States alone—Cubans and Haitians, Jews from the Soviet Union and Afghani exiles, Indochinese "boat people," Poles and Salvadorans.[6] President Reagan recently warned, moreover, that the situation would worsen if other "feet people" start marching north from Central America.[7]

No one knows how many refugees there are in the world.[8] This uncertainty is compounded by the elusive nature of the term itself. At a minimum the term signifies those individuals who have been driven from their homes by political, social, or religious pressure.[9] Hannah Arendt characterizes refugees as those human beings who are considered extraneous or undesirable by a state that tolerates no one unable or unwilling to contribute to its glorification.[10] Others, like Aristide Zolberg, would broaden the term to include those whose suffering stems not only from political or religious persecution, but also from abject hunger, thwarted ambitions, or even from a profound sense of estrangement—Paul Robeson and Richard Wright, for instance, and the other American blacks who sought social acceptance by living abroad.[11]

Refugees create problems that normal-flow immigrants do not because their arrival is often *en masse*, unanticipated, and abrupt. Countries of first asylum consequently have little room for choice and no time for preparation. Unlike ordinary immigrants, refugees usually arrive destitute and desperate, bereft the family ties or special skills that facilitate assimilation. By accepting refugees in substantial numbers, a country thus embarks on a high-risk venture. Although refugees as a class traditionally have enriched their adopted countries in manifold ways, a receiving state is never guaranteed positive returns.

REFUGEES IN AMERICAN HISTORY

From 1975 until 1980 the United States accepted as many refugees as the rest of the world combined.[12] During a campaign speech, President Reagan attempted to account for this generosity:

Can we doubt that only a divine Providence placed this land, this land of freedom, here as a refuge for all those people in the world who yearn to breathe free? Jews and Christians enduring persecution behind the Iron Curtain, the boat people of Southeast Asia, Cuba, and of Haiti.[13]

President Reagan took some license with history because this country's refugee policy has traditionally ranged from indifferent to reactive.[14] Indeed, the United States had no refugee policy at all before World War I, although its absence was not crucial since the country had few barriers to immigration in general. Such absence became crucial before World War II, however, when in deference to the national origin quota system, established in 1921, the United States refused to admit hundreds of thousands of Jewish refugees attempting to escape Nazi persecution. After the war the country also refused to sign a series of international conventions designed to facilitate refugee re-settlement, again primarily because a substantial influx of southern and eastern Europeans would undermine the quota system.[15]

After World War II, the Truman Administration, influenced both by humanitarian impulses and the desire to prevent a war-ravaged Europe from succumbing to communism, succeeded in circumventing the quota system. It passed the Displaced Persons Act in 1948, which with subsequent amendments authorized the admission of more than 400,000 people from Central Europe.[16] Congress expressly stipulated, however, that any visas issued beyond a country's statutory limit would be counted against future quotas.

When Congress passed the McCarran-Walter Act in 1952,[17] it codified a long established administration practice whereby the attorney general, at his discretion, would grant temporary asylum, or parole, to aliens. This power was intended only as an expedient to admit individual aliens under emergency conditions. In 1956 it became the vehicle by which President Eisenhower authorized the admission of more than 38,000 Hungarian refugees,[18] and thereafter the parole power was used so extensively that by 1979 it was the principal means by which more than one million refugees had entered the country.[19]

The McCarran Act initiated a fundamental shift in United States policy by providing that hereafter the country would offer asylum to those individuals who fled either Communist-dominated or Middle-Eastern regimes.[20] Persecuted people from other regions would now be officially excluded. As a consequence, in 1952 the President's Commission on Immigration and Nationality concluded in its final report that "[t]he United States is one of the few major democratic countries of the free world whose present laws impede and frequently prevent asylum."[21]

Congress first distinguished between refugees and other immigrants in 1965, when it created within the framework of the INA a "seventh preference" quota reserved for those fleeing persecution. Under this quota, only 17,000 aliens were entitled to enter the country in any one year, and then only if they came from Communist or Communist-dominated countries in the eastern hemisphere. By 1980, when the seventh preference category was repealed, it was applicable worldwide, but still only 17,400 refugees could enter annually.[22]

In emergency situations this ceiling was unrealistically low, and under any circumstance it was unduly restrictive. Consequently, the attorney general again invoked his parole power to admit hundreds of thousands of refugees whom the immigration laws could not accommodate, including more than 690,000 Cubans who have sought sanctuary in the United States since the collapse of the Batista regime in 1954,[23] and the more than 360,000 Indochinese who fled here between 1975 and 1980.[24] The United States admitted both groups in part for humanitarian reasons, and, in the case of the Indochinese, in part because public officials felt morally obliged to rescue those whose lives were jeopardized by their association with this country before or during the Vietnam War. Both groups of refugees were fleeing Marxist regimes, and this as well partly accounts for the fact that they were admitted readily and in bounteous numbers.

In 1968 the United States became a party to the United Nation's 1951 Convention Relating to the Status of Refugees, as amended by the 1967 Protocol.[25] This document defines a refugee as basically any person unable to live in the country of his or her nationality due to a "well-founded fear of persecution for reasons of race, religion, nationality, membership in a particular social group or political opinion."[26] Individuals who qualify for refugee status may apply for asylum in the country to which they have fled. Signatories are obliged to honor the principle of *nonrefoulement*, which prohibits a host state from returning refugees to a country where they would face persecution. Although the United States became a party to the Protocol, it refused to adopt its definition of a refugee, and even after Congress abolished the quota system in 1965 it continued to admit refugees largely on the basis of their national origin.

By the late 1970s most members of Congress were dissatisfied with the country's refugee policy. In the absence of any adequate mechanism to regulate admissions, the attorney general was admitting refugees virtually at his discretion, and he, rather than Congress, was determining their numbers and characteristics. Many legislators were also troubled by the restrictive aspects of this policy, but its emendation nevertheless remained a low priority until the events of 1979 jolted them into action. In that year more than 200,000 refugees, mainly Indochinese "boat people" and Soviet Jews, entered the country.[27] Although their plight gripped the public's imagination, their sudden arrival also strained the adaptive capacities of American society and signaled the need for a mechanism by which to admit and resettle refugees in a systematic manner.

THE REFUGEE ACT

This "mechanism" became the Refugee Act of 1980.[28] This act, whose substance had been debated intermittently for four decades, and intensively for three years, was finally passed by Congress and signed by President Carter on March 17, 1980. It is a fastidiously crafted document intended to create a system that will be "coherent and comprehensive," rather than "reactive and *ad hoc*."[29] The act eliminated prior geographic and ideological restrictions and adopted a definition of refugee that conforms to the one embodied in the United Nations Protocol. Accordingly, a refugee is now defined as

every person who, owing to a well-founded fear of being persecuted for reasons of race, religion, nationality, membership in a particular social group, or political opinion, is outside the country of his nationality and is unable or, owing to such fear, is unwilling to avail himself of the protection of that country.[30]

This definition suggests that the critical factor distinguishing those eligible for admission is that they flee for reasons that are political and not primarily economic. In deciding among eligible political refugees the act stipulates that the United States should be guided by "special humanitarian concerns."[31] This caveat has been interpreted to mean that preference should be accorded those fleeing countries, such as Vietnam, with which the United States has an unusually close social, economic, political, or cultural association. Preference for individuals associated with this country is reasonable, since their refugee status may result, at least indirectly, from United States policy. Unfortunately, this caveat also infects the Refugee Act with an ideological bias: By according preference to those with whom the United States has "special humanitarian concerns," the Administration is able to favor exiles from Communist-dominated regions with almost the same frequency as it did before the Refugee Act became law.[32]

After defining a "refugee," the 1980 act instituted an admissions process that was intended to be orderly and predictable. For the past thirty years, substantial numbers of refugees had entered the country outside the formal immigration channels, occasionally creating glaring discrepancies between authorized and actual admissions. The 1980 act provides that refugees, previously admitted in limited numbers as "seventh preference" immigrants, would now be admitted under a new and entirely independent quota. Based on the average number of refugee admissions during the last twenty years, 50,000 eligible individuals would be accepted annually through fiscal year 1982, after which the yearly allocation would be determined by the President "after consultation with Congress."[33] This provision for consultation is important, because it represents Congress's first attempt to reserve for itself a role in the formulation of refugee policy, and by so doing, reduce the discretionary power previously exercised by the executive branch.

The act established no statutory quota after 1982, since its drafters believed that a fixed annual allotment would be unrealistic and even unjust. By allowing the President to determine a ceiling for each fiscal year, its drafters sought to meet the demands of order and predictability, on the one hand, and the realities of a turbulent world, on the other.[34] For better or worse, the act's flexibility was evidenced during the first two years of its existence, when the number of refugees vastly exceeded the established quota.[35] Less than 100,000 refugees entered the country in either 1982 or 1983, however, and while the number of official admissions is unlikely to fall beneath the Refugee Act's 50,000 baseline figure, barring extraordinary circumstances the authorized flow will probably continue to be moderate.[36]

The 1980 act also created two new federal agencies. One, the Office of Refugee Resettlement, is authorized to fund and administer all related domestic programs. The second, the Office of United States Director for Refugee Affairs, is empowered to advise the President on relevant policy and to coordinate the myriad activities of the federal agencies involved in the admission and resettlement of refugees. Congress also agreed to reimburse states and voluntary organizations for the cash and medical assistance they provide refugees during the first three years subsequent to their admission.[37]

The act provides for the admission of both "refugees" and "asylees"—the former being those aliens who are applying for admission to the United States from another country, the latter being those who are seeking admission at either a United States land border or port of entry.[38] The act authorizes the attorney general, or, by delegation, an INS district director or immigration judge, to grant asylum to any alien who meets the new definition of refugee. It also establishes a separate procedure for adjudicating asylum claims, independent of a deportation or exclusion proceeding. Applicants at any port of entry may either appear before the district director for a consideration of their claims, or apply for asylum during the course of a deportation or exclusion hearing. When asylum is granted, aliens are entitled to remain in the United States until their "well-founded" fear of persecution ceases to exist or, under some circumstances, to adjust their status to that of permanent resident. They are also eligible for the same federal assistance that refugees receive.[39]

The 1980 act stipulates that the merits of an individual claim, rather than geographic or ideological considerations, are to be determinative in the selection process. This stipulation has been substantially undermined by another provision in the Refugee Act that permits the President—and, by extension, the Department of State—to determine how many refugees from specific geographic areas may enter the country each year. The State Department often accords certain classes of applicants—Polish militants, for instance, or Saigon evacuees—presumptive eligibility based on their country of origin. Individual members are then only required to demonstrate that they are not otherwise excludable.

By granting presumptive eligibility the State Department ex-

pedites the screening process and eases a petitioner's burden
of proof. Geographic preferences frequently preempt other
considerations, however, with the result that applicants from
non-Marxist countries are still disadvantaged. In fiscal year 1984,
for instance, less than 14 percent of the proposed allocations
are reserved for non-Communist areas.[40] Latin America and
Africa, regions with enormous refugee populations, together
receive only 5 percent of the total.[41]

State Department participation in the refugee-selection process makes geographic, and hence ideological, bias almost inevitable, since the Department often subordinates other factors
to foreign policy considerations, in particular the Administration's relationship with the applicant's home country. This tendency is reflected not only in the refugee allocation process, but
also in the content of its advisory letters, upon which the INS
relies in its effort to determine whether or not a claimant's fears
of persecution are substantial. Letters from the State Department also influence immigration judges, who study their findings before deciding whether a decision to grant or withhold
asylum is based on the "totality of the evidence." Yet, as the
Ninth Circuit Court of Appeals observed in *Kasravi v. INS*, "[a]
frank, but official discussion of the political shortcomings of a
friendly nation is not always compatible with the high duty to
maintain advantageous diplomatic relations."[42] Moreover, if the
President certifies that Haiti, for instance, or El Salvador, is
making progress in the area of human rights, the State Department can scarcely concede that an applicant for asylum from
either country risks political persecution without embarrassing
and even countering the Administration.

In order to minimize the bias in refugee selection, in 1980 the
Select Commission on Immigration and Refugee Policy (SCIRP)
recommended that in its distribution of refugee numbers the
Administration base its determination on specific, individual
characteristics as well as geographic preferences.[43] This recommendation does not go far enough, however. Unless decision-
makers are insulated from heavy-handed partisan pressures,
particularly from the State Department, then even when individual merit is a factor it will inevitably be outweighed by other
considerations based on political expediency.

THE MARIEL BOATLIFT

Until recently this country's experience with asylees, as opposed to refugees, consisted of nothing more than an occasional request from individuals or small groups. This pattern was abruptly disrupted in 1980 by events that demonstrated both the difficulty of predicting human behavior and the inadequacy of the Refugee Act when massive numbers of people flee to the United States as a country of first asylum. In 1980, when the Refugee Act first went into effect, the unexpected arrival of hundreds of thousands of aliens effectively sabotaged its operation. Within the space of twelve months the United States received 800,000 immigrants—more than all other countries in the world combined.[44] Among these newcomers were 375,000 people who either entered as refugees or sought asylum once here, including some 10,000 Haitian "boat people" and 125,000 Cubans.[45]

The United States was particularly unprepared for the influx of Cubans, and the circumstances surrounding their arrival constitutes an extraordinary chapter in recent American history. In March 1980 a busload of Cubans rammed into the gates of the Peruvian Embassy in Havana, where they were granted sanctuary. Soon some 10,000 of their fellow citizens joined them—all of whom, as it turned out, sought political asylum in the United States. The United States granted their request immediately, a predictable response, given the country's long tradition of hospitality toward those fleeing Castro's Communist regime.

What began as a public relations "coup" for the United States, however, turned into a political triumph of sorts for Castro, who announced that the United States could have not only every one encamped in the Peruvian Embassy, but also another contingent whose members he personally would select. He urged Cubans living in Florida to retrieve their relatives, and the latter responded with alacrity. Thus began the Mariel boatlift, or so-called Freedom Flotilla, during which more than 3,000 boats, passing one another coming and going, dotted the waters between Miami and Mariel Bay.

At the outset of the boatlift, President Carter pledged that the

United States would provide "an open heart and open arms" to the new arrivals.[46] By the time the Casto government closed Mariel Bay on September 26, this meant extending open arms not only to the aunts, uncles, sisters, and brothers of Cubans in Miami, but also to those whom Castro himself had selected as their traveling companions—some 20,000 reputed criminals, mental patients, sociopaths—those he called the "scums and worms" of society.[47]

Meanwhile the Haitians also came, although not in a Freedom Flotilla but in ragtag dinghies with tree trunk masts. They had been coming ever since 1972 but always in small groups. The Haitians, too, sought political asylum in the United States, but they received treatment that differed markedly from that accorded the Cubans. The United States government uniformly labeled the Haitians "economic" migrants, and made every attempt to expel them from the country.

President Carter's promise to receive the Cubans with "open arms" became increasingly difficult to honor as the initial contingent of 10,000 was multiplied many times over, and supplemented with an infusion of Haitians. The country had absorbed thousands of refugees before, but under terms of its own devisement and according to well developed transition plans. Now, the size and abruptness of the new deluge made orderly resettlement impossible.

The Carter Administration was waist-deep in a political quagmire. By its perceived mismanagement of the influx, it contributed to the disaffection already felt by a citizenry suffering from economic travail. Mindful that a presidential election was only a few months away, it thus attempted to assuage the public at large without simultaneously alienating either of two significant power blocs—the large and politically active Cuban community in South Florida and black Americans who juxtaposed the treatment traditionally granted Cubans with that provided the Haitians.[48]

As reporter Paul Lehman noted, the Carter Administration was "caught between the Cubans, whom it did not wish to refuse, and the Haitians, whom it did not wish to admit."[49] The Administration therefore "waffled." It concocted a scheme designed to antagonize no major constituency and, at the same time, avoid the high costs associated with the Refugee Act. It announced that Cubans and Haitians who had entered the United States between April 21, 1980, and June 19, 1980, would receive a new immigration classification, "Cuban-Haitian Entrant," [50] which would permit them to remain in this country until their status was resolved. (The June 19 cutoff date was later extended to October 10, 1980.[51]) By the terms of this scheme, which Congress subsequently ratified, the government would provide "entrants" with resettlement aid and public assistance, and for a period of three years, it would reimburse states and localities for their attendant expenses.[52]

The benefits of this *ad hoc* remedy were considered twofold: (1) it would provide a politically palatable means for accepting the Cubans, whom the government had intended to admit from the outset and who, at any rate, could not be returned since Castro refused to readmit them; (2) it enabled the government to provide Haitians with temporary asylum without compelling it to concede that as a class they merited refugee status.[53]

The Cuban-Haitian Entrants were, in effect, granted parole, an ironic development since the Refugee Act had been passed to prevent the large-scale use of this mechanism. When used as intended, parole is a means by which individual aliens, outside the country, may be admitted on a conditional basis pending determination of their legal status. As such, it represents a humane response to unanticipated and temporary situations. In this case, however, the government used parole to grant indefinite residence to battalions of aliens already physically present in the country—including many eligible to apply for political asylum. Recipients were admitted, effectively for permanent residence, without proving that as individuals they feared any sort of persecution in their countries of origin.

The Cuban-Haitian Entrant Program proved a poor substitute for the Refugee Act. It saved the government no money[54] and it created what remains an administrative monstrosity. Because the new arrivals were considered "special entrants," rather than refugees, machinery established under the Refugee Act lay unused while *ad hoc* expedients were spliced together. The result was semi-chaos. Inexperienced personnel, unsure of their mission, maneuvered among confused lines of authority and operated more or less at cross-purposes.[55]

As the *National Law Journal* declared in a headline, "Carter Help[ed] Refugee Law Flunk First Test."[56] Indeed, by circumventing the Refugee Act, the Cuban-Haitian Entrant Program threatened its future viability. In the process the government reactivated the public's suspicion that the country lacked any refugee policy at all and that the admission of aliens was "out of control."

The Carter Administration's decision to bypass the Refugee Act, while unfortunate, may nevertheless have been unavoidable given the enormity of the influx. The Cuban-Haitian crisis revealed that the machinery established by the 1980 act was incapable of dealing with present migratory phenomena. Those drafting the act anticipated, based on past averages, that no more than 5,000 aliens would seek asylum in any one year, and accordingly designed an administrative system equipped to handle roughly that number.[57] Under this system, INS personnel must determine whether each individual applicant has suffered, or is in danger of suffering, persecution. This is a cumbersome and time-consuming process, allowing administrators to accommodate at most several thousand—certainly not some tens of thousands—claimants a year.

There probably will be increasing numbers of claimants each year. Two immigration scholars, John Scanlan and G. Leoscher, estimate that as many as 50,000 individuals from Latin America and the Caribbean will flee to the United States annually in order to escape political turbulence in their region.[58] As a consequence, unless the Refugee Act is redrafted to provide for the expeditious processing of large-scale claims, the Immigration Service will either routinely bypass it or be crushed in the backlog.

Under current procedures those applying for asylum bear the burden of proving that they as individuals have a well-founded fear of persecution, a requirement in no other asylum-granting country and one not mandated by the language of either the Refugee Act or the United Nations Protocol.[59] This burden is onerous, considering the difficulty a lone applicant faces in assembling witnesses and corroborative data. It also represents the single most time-consuming component in the asylum process. The INS and State Department could accord due consideration to individual claimants and still grant presumptive eligibility to aliens who come from regions where human rights violations are common, or who are members of identifiable subclasses that frequently suffer abuses in a particular society. By instituting this single reform the government could benefit asylum seekers, and also revivify the Refugee Act by relieving its administrators of the need to process every claimant on an individual basis.

THE HAITIANS

In December 1980, the attorney general declared that "it is imperative that the question of long-term status of Cuban-Haitian Entrants be given early, priority attention."[60] His admonition notwithstanding, some four years later these entrants are still living with their fuzzy immigration ranking, waiting for Congress to pass a law that would allow them permanent residence in the United States. In the meanwhile most of the Cubans are faring considerably better than their Haitian counterparts.[61]

When Castro sealed Mariel Bay on September 26, at least 125,000 Cubans had come to the United States. Two years later most of them were free, and many were settled in the same communities that since 1959 had welcomed almost 700,000 of their fellow nationals.[62] By comparison, the number of Haitians who have arrived since 1972 is trifling.[63] For the majority of them, however, the United States has been less a haven than a battleground, where for the past twelve years they have suffered discrimination more sustained and multiform than any other group of aliens. Whether undocumented Haitians come to the United States in order to escape Jean-Claude Duvalier's brutal regime, or the island's equally brutal poverty, from the time they first disembarked on the Florida shore in 1972 the United States government has labeled them "economic," as opposed to "political," migrants, and denied almost all of their requests for asylum.[64]

Even before the Refugee Act became law in 1980, the INA provided claimants for asylum with a number of procedural rights, including a fair hearing, the right to retain counsel, and the opportunity to confront and cross-examine adverse witnesses.[65] Since the government had predetermined that Haitians could not be legitimate refugees, however, until 1978 these rights were either abridged or suspended altogether whenever a member of their class sought asylum.[66] By 1978 a dedicated alliance of public interest lawyers and religious activists had succeeded in publicizing the Haitians' plight, and under orders from its new commissioner, Leonel Castillo, the INS began treating them with considerably more respect.[67]

Castillo's reforms were short-lived. Soon after he assumed office Haitians started coming to the United States in twice their former numbers,[68] precipitating fear among government officials that a "black tide" was inundating the country's southeast. As a consequence, in 1978 the Immigration Service launched the so-called "Haitian Program," a well-coordinated operation in which INS and State Department officials, with encouragement from the White House, conspired to process and expel Haitians as rapidly as possible.[69]

While the Haitian Program was in operation several public interest groups brought a class action suit on behalf of 5,000 Haitian nationals, all facing expulsion, whose applications for asylum had been processed at a rate up to 150 per day between July of 1978 and May of 1979.[70] Although plaintiffs cited sixteen grounds for action, their case coalesced around two basic complaints: (1) the government had deprived them of meaningful hearings at the administrative level; and (2) it had denied them equal protection by subjecting them to much harsher treatment than other similarly situated aliens.

On July 25, 1979, Federal District Judge James Lawrence King issued an injunction prohibiting the Immigration Service from deporting any more Haitians until a full-scale hearing could be conducted. On July 2, 1980, he issued a final, 180-page opinion in *Haitian Refugee Center v. Civiletti*.[71] His findings were unequivocal: the INS had intentionally and systematically denied due process to the Haitians and subjected them to relentless discrimination in violation of every applicable law, treaty, administrative regulation, and operating procedure. Government memoranda revealed that immigration officials had prejudged every one of the five-thousand-some cases included in the class action.[72] In one INS memorandum, Haitians were explicitly depicted as immigrants seeking to escape poverty and not persecution;[73] in a second, they were described as "threatening the community's well being socially and economically."[74] Still a third memorandum discussed ways in which the government could discourage Haitian migration—by intercepting them at sea, for instance, and towing them to Guantanamo, where they would be deprived of support services.[75] Proof that a Haitian's fate was predetermined was indicated in the Immigration Service's own records, which eliminated altogether the column listing accepted asylum applications.[76]

Judge King therefore concluded that the service had violated its duty to decide each claim on its merit,[77] and accordingly that it had deprived plaintiffs of their right to due process. Additional evidence, submitted in abundance, bolstered this conclusion. For instance, the INS failed to suspend deportation hearings upon the filing of Haitian asylum claims. Indeed, it proceeded directly to a finding of deportation. By so doing, it compelled the Haitians to incriminate themselves—that is, concede deportability—in order to apply for asylum. Although INS operating instructions flatly outlawed this practice, the agency's regional commissioner stated at the time that "[these] instructions should be canceled, or, if not canceled, [they] should at least be suspended as far as the Haitians are concerned."[78]

Immigration judges threatened those who attempted to exercise their Fifth Amendment right to remain silent, and ultimately denied them both further access to counsel and permission to work pending the final disposition of their cases. By administrative fiat, the INS also demanded that Haitians, alone among claimants, submit their official applications for asylum within ten days after requesting them—a Draconian time limit calculated to prevent them from securing the evidence crucial for their defense.[79]

The Immigration Service typically schedules six asylum hearings a day, and allocates approximately ninety minutes for each. It summoned Haitians to hearings at the rate of sixty, eighty, even 150 a day and even including time for translation no session exceeded thirty minutes.[80] No more than seven attorneys were available at any one period to service Haitians on a full-time basis, and once the accelerated hearings began their workloads became overwhelming. The same lawyer was occasionally scheduled for as many as fifteen simultaneous hearings, many at different locations several blocks apart.[81] Accustomed to spending twenty hours preparing for a hearing, they could now devote only thirty minutes to any case, however complicated. Even then, the INS frequently attempted to discourage counsel from volunteering their services.[82]

Judge King reiterated that in processing the Haitians' applications, the Immigration Service had committed a variety of procedural irregularities, thereby violating the due process clause of the Fifth Amendment.[83] This ruling, certainly justified, was predictable since state and federal courts routinely upset governmental action on procedural grounds. Judge King exceeded the limits of conventional jurisprudence, however, by holding that the Fifth Amendment obliges the federal government to accord asylum applicants not only due process, but also equal protection.

As the record abundantly demonstrated, the Haitians alone had been singled out for disparate treatment. Among aliens seeking asylum, they alone had been systematically denied work authorizations and incarcerated indefinitely in "holding" camps. They alone had been subjected to arbitrary deadlines and accelerated and truncated proceedings. Judge King therefore accused the government of subjecting an entire class of people to racial discrimination:

The Haitians allege that the actions of the INS constitute impermissible discrimination on the basis of national origin. They have proved their claim. This Court cannot close its eyes to possible underlying reasons why these plaintiffs have been subjected to intentional "national origin" discrimination. The plaintiffs are part of the first substantial flight of black refugees from a repressive regime to this country. All the plaintiffs are black. Prior to the most recent Cuban exodus all of the Cubans who sought political asylum . . . were granted asylum routinely. None of the over 4000 Haitians processed during the INS program at issue in the lawsuit were granted asylum. No greater disparity can be imagined.[84]

In conclusion, Judge King ordered the INS to submit a detailed plan for the individualized, nondiscriminatory, and fair processing of the plaintiffs' asylum applications. He also enjoined the government from expelling any member of their class until the court approved this plan.[85] His order was vindication for the plaintiffs, of course, and the squadron of volunteers dedicated to their welfare. Unfortunately, however, Judge King's admonitions did little either to benefit Haitians who were not parties to the suit, or to chasten an Immigration Service intent upon their speedy expulsion.

In a series of related cases, "Louis I, II, and III," the Haitian Refugee Center (HRC) again challenged the INS,[86] initially on behalf of undocumented Haitians who had been subjected to accelerated mass hearings. The initial case burgeoned, however, into a nation-wide class action suit, with HRC lawyers eventually representing more than a thousand detained Haitians. These Haitians spent months and sometimes more than a year in holding centers and federal penitentiaries throughout the United States and Puerto Rico awaiting a ruling on the legality of their detention.

The case came before Federal District Court Judge Alcee Hastings in September 1981. In this case, *Louis v. Meissner*,[87] plaintiffs introduced substantial evidence, which the government at no point contested, that since March of 1981 the Department of State and and INS had executed a campaign to process and expel Haitians as expeditiously as possible. The Immigration Service had conducted mass hearings in which thirty Haitians at a time had been locked in a single room, denied access to counsel, and provided Creole translators who were so inept that plaintiffs were unable to comprehend the proceedings or learn of their rights. The service also began transferring those Haitians represented by counsel to remote areas throughout the country, such as Otisville, New York, or La Tuna, Texas, prompting an unusually strong response from Judge Hastings:

Having made a long and perilous journey on the high seas to South Florida, these refugees, seeking the "promised land," have instead been subjected to a human shell game in which the arbitrary INS had sought to scatter them to locations that, with the exception of Brooklyn, are all in desolate, remote, hostile, culturally diverse areas, containing a paucity of available legal support and few if any Creole interpreters. In this regard, INS officials have acted as haphazard [sic] as the rolling seas that brought these boat people to this great country's shores. Indeed, even though INS officials have been rudderless in the enunciation and application of an immigration policy, when they decided to move the Haitians to these remc te areas, they acted with laserlike precision.[88]

At the conclusion of this preliminary hearing, the judge enjoined the INS from either deporting, or proceeding with exclusion hearings against, any of the class members unrepresented by counsel. The government did not appeal this preliminary injunction. In a subsequent case, *Louis v. Meissner* ("Louis II"),[89] the district court dismissed many of the allegations in the original complaint. Thus in March 1982, when the full trial commenced in *Louis v. Nelson* ("Louis III"),[90] the focus shifted to the legality of the government's detention process.

The government's new detention procedure was instituted shortly after President Reagan assumed office. Acting upon the advice of the Administration's Immigration "Task Force," President Reagan and Attorney General William French Smith announced, on July 30, 1981, that hereafter the government would "detain undocumented aliens" pending their exclusion hearings.[91] By so doing they reversed a twenty-seven-year practice of paroling aliens into the community until their admissibility could be determined.

Before new rules and regulations may take effect, the Administrative Procedure Act (APA)[92] ordinarily requires federal agencies to publish them in the Federal Register and allow the public sixty days in which to respond. The INS instituted its new detention policy, however, without providing this "notice-and-comment" period. As a consequence, district Judge Eugene Spellman declared the new policy "null and void,"[93]

and ordered the government to parole—under strict conditions—every person covered by the class action suit.[94]

When the case, now called *Jean v. Nelson*,[95] reached the Elev-
enth Circuit on appeal in 1983, Judge Phyllis Kravitch spoke for
the court. She agreed with the lower tribunal that the government's detention policy constituted a "rule" that must be issued in accordance with APA procedures, and she chastised the
government for flaunting the act's presciptions. Because the new
rule governing detentions had never been subject to formal debate or formal promulgation, regulations for its specific application were never developed. According to testimony at the trial,
not a single person in the entire chain of command from the
attorney general to the immigration officers at the Krome Avenue Processing Center outside Miami, where the Haitians were
incarcerated, acknowledged ever giving or receiving instructions regarding which of the excludable aliens would be detained.[96] Immigration inspectors were therefore left with "un-
guided and unfettered discretion" to enforce the policy however
they chose.[97] Although Haitians were few in number relative to
similarly situated Cubans and Mexicans, the inspectors nevertheless implemented the new policy as though it were intended to apply "solely and uniformly" to them.[98] The Elev-
enth Circuit thus concluded that the Immigration Service had
practiced "a stark pattern of discrimination" based on nationality.[99]

Statistics introduced at the trial showed that among excludable aliens, Haitians were subject to detention in vastly disproportionate numbers. One expert witness, after reviewing the
statistics comparing the extent to which Haitians as opposed to
non-Haitians were detained in New York State, concluded that
in a nonbiased world the chance of so many Haitians being incarcerated was "on the order of less than two in ten billion
times."[100]

Respected members of the immigration bar and high-ranking
INS and Department of Justice officials also testified that Haitians were selectively and persistently targeted for mistreatment.[101] The government attempted to refute these charges, but
none of its witnesses were involved in the parole-granting pro-

cess. Consequently Judge Kravitch concluded that "their self-serving affirmations of good faith fail to constitute a rebuttal," and she enjoined the government from enforcing its detention policy in a discriminatory way.[102]

In both *Louis v. Nelson* and *Jean v. Nelson*, the courts emphasized that the government must not implement any policy without observing strict standards of fairness, although at the same time they suggested that the substance of these policies was beyond their concern. Thus, neither the district nor the circuit court examined the constitutionality of a program that would subject Haitians to indefinite incarceration, or explored the possibility that protracted detention might be a means by which the Immigration Service sought to induce Haitians to abandon their quests for asylum. Rather, they implied that the government could reinstate any detention policy it chose, providing only that it conform to procedural regulations and avoid selective enforcement.

The government accordingly complied with the APA regulations, and then reinstated its detention policy.[103] Aliens unable to post $2,500 in bond are now incarcerated for months and, as administrative backlogs continue to mount, perhaps soon for years. Now, however, Haitians are not the only ones confined to these holding camps. Aliens from many other countries supplement their ranks, in particular a growing number of Salvadorans.[104]

THE INTERDICTION PROGRAM

After he heard that Judge Spellman had ordered the government to parole over 1,000 refugees, Marc Garcia, the radio commentator known as "Marcus" to the several hundred Haitians at the Krome Avenue Processing Center, shouted out, "They are going to free you," "They have to free you." The Haitians responded with cries of jubilation: "Viktova Net!" (Complete victory).[105] Neither Judge Spellman's nor Judge Kravitch's rulings represented a "complete victory," however. Both rulings rested in part on procedural technicalities, and benefited only those aliens covered by the lawsuits. Neither ruling could do anything to protect the men, women, and children who are intercepted by the United States Coast Guard in the waters between Haiti and the Florida coast.

After Ronald Reagan won the presidency, he assured an anxious nation that the country would regain "control of its borders."[106] Accordingly, on September 29, 1981, he negotiated a cooperative agreement with Haiti's Duvalier regime to prevent the unauthorized migration of Haitian nationals.[107] Through an interdiction program, the United States now patrols the Windward Passage between Haiti and Cuba, and turns around any vessel suspected of harboring individuals who intend to violate either United States or Haitian immigration laws. The Coast Guard is empowered to fire upon any craft that fails to halt upon command for inspection.[108]

The United States and Haiti agreed upon procedures to safeguard the rights of those who advance a legitimate claim for asylum. A Haitian naval officer, INS examiner, and two interpreters are stationed on board each Coast Guard vessel. Whenever individuals request asylum, the immigration examiner affords them the opportunity to supply documentation or otherwise establish their refugee status. Though unsuccessful applicants are not afforded a formal hearing process, as required under the INA, the service maintains that since the interdictions are occurring on the high seas they are beyond the act's jurisdiction. Any applicant who presents a legitimate claim for asylum is brought to the United States for a full hearing though this is not required by law.[109]

The service's logic is weak; it argues that since interdictions occur on the high seas they are beyond the reach of domestic law, yet at the same time it asserts jurisdiction over vessels intercepted in those waters. Furthermore, while the INS insists that aliens who posit a legitimate claim for asylum are provided full hearings back in the United States, during the almost three years in which the interdiction program has been operating rare are the claims that have been considered "legitimate."[110]

The New York Times accused the INS of conducting "walrus courts" aboard the Coast Guard vessels.[111] Indeed, it strains credulity to believe that Haitians, usually poor, illiterate, and frightened, would carry with them documentary evidence, or possess the wherewithal on board a crowded vessel to convince an immigration officer that they possess a well-founded fear of persecution. Furthermore, since these interviews are conducted in the presence of Duvalier's security officers, and frequently in Haitian territorial waters, only the most stout-hearted would risk a frank catalogue of their fears.

Regardless of whether its domestic law applies on the open seas, the United States is a signatory to the United National Protocol Relating to the Status of Refugees. The procedures implemented aboard the Coast Guard vessel may violate Article 33 of this document.[112] This article obliges signatories to honor the principle of *nonrefoulement*, which prohibits them from returning any alien to a country where his or her life or freedom would be threatened.

The interdiction program may also contravene both the Universal Declaration of Human Rights,[113] which affirms the right of individuals to leave any country, including their own, and the freedom-to-travel provisions in the Helsinki Accords.[114] Certainly the United States does not require exit visas from its own citizens, and it has been quick to condemn the Soviet Union for restricting the right of its nationals to emigrate. Nevertheless, by its own initiative, the United States has agreed to enforce a law that prohibits Haitians from leaving their homeland without an exit permit. Moreover, since in practice few Haitians receive permits who are not enthusiastic supporters of the Duvalier regime,[115] by contributing to the enforcement of this law the Administration may turn back the very people most likely to be refugees.

From a narrow and short-term perspective the Reagan Administration's interdiction program has been successful. Since its inauguration the number of Haitians who have entered the country without authorization has decreased dramatically.[116] In the larger sense, however, the program can scarcely be considered successful because the United States is enforcing the laws of a regime that has been characterized as "the most repressive on earth."[117]

"POLITICAL" VERSUS "ECONOMIC" REFUGEES

Judges Kenyon, King, and most of their colleagues in the federal judiciary are acting with unprecedented vigilance to safeguard the statutory and constitutional rights of those seeking asylum. Their vigilance has benefited many aggrieved aliens, irrespective of their national origin—in particular the Haitians, but also the Salvadorans, whom government officials have treated with persistent abuse.[118] Federal judges are limited in the remedies they can prescribe, however, which is as it should be since they are nonelected officials neither authorized nor equipped to formulate policy. They can oblige the government to accord aliens procedural fairness, but they cannot require it to grant asylum to any particular individual or class of individuals. Among the tens of thousands of people potentially eligible for refugee status, choices must be made and ultimately those choices are political ones entrusted to the legislative and executive branches. Members of these branches frequently base their decisions on factors that have little to do with the abstract merits of competing claims.

According to government officials, one "factor" is most influential: whether aliens come to escape political persecution, or to seek economic opportunity. They steadfastly maintain that most Haitians, Salvadorans, and other Third World migrants come to the United States in quest of economic gain.[119] S. Scott Burke, head of the State Department's asylum division, recently stated that in his view

most who leave Haiti do so for economic reasons and have never been attacked for political reasons. I would want to escape, too. I'd probably hop on a boat, too. But that doesn't mean I'd have a fear of persecution.[120]

He noted that in his opinion Salvadorans also migrate primarily for monetary reasons.

There may be truth to Mr. Burke's allegations, for in El Salvador the average worker brings home less than $600 a year, and the country's economy is in tatters.[121] Haiti is even poorer, so poor, in fact, that it ranks not among Third but among Fourth World countries and gives rise to statistics that sound hyperbolic: 66 percent of Haitian children suffer from malnutrition, for instance, and while 5 percent of the population accumulates 50 percent of the national income, 60 percent subsists on as little as sixty dollars a year.[122]

Poverty, then, and hope for a better life, must surely encourage Haitians and Salvadorans to migrate. Nationals of both countries live amid violence and political repression, however, and this could also inspire their flight. The office of the United Nations High Commissioner of Refugees has accorded refugee status to Salvadorans, who by most accounts are being killed by armed forces and paramilitary groups sometimes at the rate of several hundred a day.[123] During the first half of 1982 alone, between 2,500 and 3,000 civilians lost their lives in both calculated and random assaults.[124]

Conditions in Haiti are even worse. Judge King concluded in *Haitian Refugee Center v. Civiletti* that the island is governed by an "apparatus of repression,"[125] which creates conditions that are "stark, brutal and bloody."[126] Before reaching this conclusion, Judge King had studied a barrage of evidence attesting to the systematic human rights abuses perpetuated first by Francis Duvalier and then, since 1971, by his son, Jean Claude, or "Baby Doc," who, like his father, has proclaimed himself "President for Life."[127]

Authorities can argue with equal fervor that Haitians or Salvadorans—or indeed aliens from most other underdeveloped countries—are fleeing to the United States for economic or for political reasons, but ultimately the distinction is increasingly artificial and even irrelevant in today's world, where economic and political conditions are often inextricably meshed. As the *Detroit Free Press* observed in an editorial,

in the hard-bitten world of refugees, political and economic hardships often go hand-in-hand. The Cubans resent their government because it has mismanaged the economy—and their lives. The Haitians face political reprisals for objecting to economic conditions."[128]

What about states that refuse to utilize international aid to alleviate starvation or to irrigate parched land? Are their nationals, then, victims of economic or political repression? What about people living in totalitarian countries, where the state as the main employer determines who will work, or who will be dragooned into labor camps?

What about Haiti? Its government collects and disburses all

public funds. According to the Lawyer's Committee for International Human Rights, and even a United States Department of State report issued in 1979, for more than two decades the country's centralized administration of revenue has resulted in massive government corruption and the gross mismanagement of public funds.[129] Extortion and fraud are so ubiquitous, in fact, that one observer has characterized Haiti as a "kleptocracy"— a government by thieves.[130] Judge King concluded in *Haitian Refugee Center v. Civiletti* that the country's economy is a function of its political system:

> Much of the Haitian's poverty is a result of Duvalier's efforts to maintain power. Indeed, it could be said that Duvalier has made his country weak so that he could be strong. To broadly classify all of the class of plaintiffs as "economic refugees," as has been repeatedly done, is therefore, somewhat callous. Their economic situation is a political condition.[131]

Distinctions between economic and political migrants are scarcely tenable from either a logical or moral perspective, and America's persistence in honoring this distinction may even be unwarranted from a legal point of view. In 1980 Congress passed the Refugee Act, and with great hoopla eliminated pre-existing geographical and ideological barriers. In accordance with the United Nations Protocol on the Status of Refugees, Congress agreed to consider every claim for asylum on its merits. Notwithstanding this act, however, the country continues to welcome those fleeing left-wing or Marxist regimes, and to rebuff those seeking to escape so-called right-wing or authoritarian ones. Immediately upon passage of the 1980 act, the Department of State established new guidelines for the processing of asylum claims. People fleeing communist countries were to be considered "politically sensitive," it instructed, and accorded "immediate action."[132]

As a result of such bias, while in fiscal year 1982 more than 5,000 Haitians applied for asylum, it was granted to seven.[133] The same year more than 18,000 Salvadorans applied for asylum, and it was granted to sixty-nine.[134] By contrast, the United States approved 297 asylum requests from claimants in Soviet-dominated Afghanistan, thereby accommodating almost 50 percent of its applicants.[135] In the first three years after the Refugee Act was adopted, moreover, the United States did not admit a single Haitian, Salvadoran, or Guatemalan as part of its annual refugee admission process. During this same period it authorized the admission of more than half a million refugees from communist countries in Indochina and East Europe, while reserving space for only 1,000 refugees from all of Latin America (excluding Cuba).[136] The Administration's proposed refugee allocations for fiscal year 1984 are equally skewed. Less than 14 percent of the total is reserved for non-Communist areas.[137]

The United States not only welcomes, but frequently encourages, migration from Communist-dominated countries. Cubans, Soviet Jews, Armenians, and Afghanis are warmly received. Poles and other Eastern European nationals continue to be admitted in maximum numbers, and they are spared even normal INS processing.[138] The United States grants asylum to nationals from Communist states even when they defect for reasons that are understandable but scarcely compelling. In the spring of 1983, for instance, the Immigration Service granted asylum to Hu Na, a young Chinese tennis star who chafed under the mild restraints that China imposed.[139] About the same time, the service also granted asylum to two Soviet musicians who maintained—as Mikhail Baryshnikov and many other talented Russians had done earlier—that their artistic freedom was curtailed.[140]

A dual standard is similarly evidenced in the western hemisphere. While Salvador Allende was Chile's Marxist president, the United States welcomed anyone fleeing the country; once the authoritarian General Augusto Pinochet seized power in September 1974, however, the doors of this country were closed to Chilean exiles.[141] Particularly striking is the contrast between the traditional reception granted Cubans fleeing Castro, on the one hand, and Haitians fleeing the Duvalier regime, on the other.[142]

Under his prosecutory discretion the attorney general may grant temporary haven, or so-called "extended voluntary departure," to aliens living in or visiting the United States until violence in their home lands subsides. For instance, Poles who

were in the United States in 1981 when martial law was declared in their country have been allowed to remain until conditions improve there. The government has granted the same
privilege over the years to other aliens as well—Chileans, Czechs,
Ethiopians, Afghanis. Despite importunings from Congress and
voluntary agencies, however, the Reagan Administration recently reaffirmed its determination to withhold even temporary
sanctuary from most Salvadorans.[143]
Why this reflexive preference for anyone fleeing a Marxist
state? One reason is that Americans believe life under a Communist dictatorship must be intolerable for everyone, whereas
those living in authoritarian regimes can exist relatively unmolested as long as they eschew active political involvement. According to related logic, individuals possess virtually no rights
in totalitarian states, whereas in authoritarian countries they
enjoy at least limited ones. The Department of State points out,
for example, that in Haiti there is freedom of religion.[144] According to official explanation, furthermore, those fleeing left-
wing regimes are coerced into abandoning their homelands,
while those fleeing right-wing ones do so voluntarily; the former are said to be "pushed," the latter "pulled."[145] Finally, defectors from Marxist states are purportedly subject to inevitable
persecution upon their return, while their counterparts from
authoritarian polities are ignored or only mildly sanctioned.[146]
These reasons may be politically palatable, but they do not
adequately account for the preference system that governs
America's refugee policy. Rather, this policy rests foremost on
the conviction that between free enterprise democracy and state
socialism there can be no compromise and only limited coexis-
tence. As a consequence, the United States should bypass no
opportunity to achieve a substantial or even symbolic victory
over "communism." In this zero-sum calculation, any defeat for
communism becomes perforce a victory for democracy, and any
authoritarian regime merits support as long as it is aligned ideologically with the United States.
The United States could scarcely welcome defectors from right-
wing polities without acknowledging that an ally is found
wanting, that perhaps morally it is indistinguishable from the
enemy. By contrast, every time a disaffected Russian or Cuban

or Pole seeks asylum in the United States this reaffirms the superiority of democratic capitalism. Thus in a recent case an immigration judge confirmed the obvious when he observed that in an effort to avoid embarrassing friendly governments, the Department of State advises the INS to deny asylum to their nationals whenever possible.[147] Recently an official from the Department of State noted the same phenomenon, explaining that many in the Reagan Administration were opposed to granting asylum to any of the Salvadorans because "this would leave the impression that there are refugees from El Salvador and that El Salvador does not protect its people."[148]

There is a second major reason for the country's preference system: Its not unreasonable fear that abandonment of the distinction between economic and political refugees will mean inundation by hordes of poor people from the Third World, and especially the western hemisphere. As President Reagan phrased it, the country will be overwhelmed once the "feet people" start marching north from Central America.[149] Indeed, government officials are candid in voicing this fear. One Department of State spokesman explained that "if we let in the Haitians, we will have to let in half of South America and Africa."[150] S. Scott Burke, Deputy Assistant Secretary of State, made the same observation:

We don't think it is wise to set a precedent that when a country has random violence, a war, insurgency, or it is poor, any refugee would be accepted. . . . We do not have the legal or moral obligation to accept all the people who want to come here from around the world.[151]

The government's attitude toward Salvadoran and Haitian migrants is therefore understandable. They are poor people, desperate to improve their lot in life, and if they are granted sanctuary in the United States then peasants from the Dominican Republic and Honduras and every other "banana republic" will expect similar hospitality. Both Haiti and El Salvador, moreover, are governed by regimes that are solidly pro-American, and as such they represent valuable allies in this country's perfervid campaign to rid its neighborhood of Communists.

RECOMMENDATIONS

Social scientists predict that in coming decades the number of human exiles will range in the tens of millions. From economic or political or religious compulsion, they will drift inexorably toward the few countries in the world that are prosperous and free.[152] Whether animated by moral imperatives or sheer necessity, the United States should consequently amend its own system for processing refugees, and encourage the development of international institutions that can better anticipate, minimize, and accommodate large-scale human displacement.

Since international institutions alone are capable of handling massive refugee movements, the United States should cooperate fully with the Office of the United Nations High Commissioner of Refugees (UNHCR). This office, in operation since 1951, attempts to resettle refugees and to safeguard their welfare. Neither the UNHCR nor any other international body, however, is equipped to intercede with countries that either forcibly banish their own citizens or that generate the insufferable conditions that compel their defection. There is not even an international convention that would impose sanctions on regimes such as those in Uganda or Cambodia or Cuba that expel their own nationals.

The United States should encourage the adoption of a convention that would outlaw forcible mass expulsions. It should endeavor as well to establish regional institutions that would facilitate joint efforts by neighboring countries to process and resettle refugees. By evidencing such cooperation in the late 1970s, the United States and other countries of Northern and Central America succeeded in resettling tens of thousands of Indochinese with relative smoothness.[153] Regional mechanisms must be institutionalized, however; America's experience in 1980 with the Cuban "boat people" demonstrates that once refugees have landed in the United States, it is thereafter difficult to relocate them in other countries.

The United States should also revise the Refugee Act in order to establish a more judicious and efficient asylum process. Foremost, immigration agents must be encouraged to treat their subjects with greater sensitivity—to regard them without the preconviction that most are impostures.[154] They should also be well schooled in immigration law, and provided with thorough and up-to-date information on the status of identifiable religious, ethnic, and social classes in various countries. While the Department of State should continue providing immigration officials with this information, it should no longer submit advisory opinions or otherwise assume an active role in determining who receives asylum, since in so doing it unduly politicizes the process.[155] In lieu of advisory opinions the Immigration Service should follow the practice of European countries and rely on recommendations submitted by the UNHCR.

Procedures for reviewing asylum applications are so unwieldy that less than four years after passage of the Refugee Act there was already a 200,000-claim backlog.[156] Legitimate refugees are penalized, as a result, because they must wait indefinitely for a resolution of their status. More seriously, because of this backlog lawmakers are convinced, not without cause, that many aliens seek asylum without any bona fide claim in order to "gain time" in the United States while their applications wind their way through the bureaucratic backways. As a consequence, Congress is seriously considering a bill that would sharply curtail the availability of administrative and judicial review for asylee applicants.[157] The Reagan Administration has also proposed an "Immigration Emergency Bill" that would not only restrict judicial review,[158] but also vest the attorney general with absolute discretion to decide whether or not to detain aliens during an "immigration emergency" pending a determination of their eligibility.[159]

Congress could streamline the asylum process, and thus obviate the need for restrictive amendments, by establishing a special immigration court exclusively devoted to the processing of asylum applications. Its judges should be well trained in the applicable law, and insulated from the compromising pressures that emanate from both the INS and the Department of State. A second reform would further simplify the asylum process. The United States should identify discrete classes that are particularly subject to persecution in a given society, and relieve their individual members of the need to document their fears with extensive written or oral testimony. As observed earlier, this evidentiary requirement imposes an excessive burden on the claimants and unnecessarily prolongs the adjudicatory process.[160]

Even the finest scheme for upgrading the asylum process will be of limited benefit, however, as long as the Immigration Service continues summarily to exclude many aliens. When individuals at a port of entry seek admission to the United States, government officials are required by both the Refugee Act and the United Nations Protocol to inform them of their right to apply for asylum and to instruct them in the requisite procedure. Since immigration officials are frequently reluctant to honor this right, either a UNHCR representative or some other independent official with equivalent expertise should be stationed at ports of entry to provide aliens with this information.

The United States could accommodate many more refugees than it now admits without significantly jeopardizing the public's standard of living.[161] It could certainly do more to relieve hardship if it granted temporary sanctuary—or extended voluntary departure—on a more generous basis to aliens from beleaguered countries. Even at its most generous, however, the United States can accept only a fraction of those who seek and merit asylum, but it can adopt a selection system that is less ideologically biased and more equitable than the present method.

The United States should first distinguish between "degrees of desperation." While this is an unpleasant undertaking, no alternative is more just as long as choices must be made. The government, then, must admit the individual who faces starvation, but not the young man thwarted in his artistic ambition; the religious apostate who risks incarceration and perhaps death, but not the political activist prohibited from desecrating a flag.

As long as choices must be made, the United States should implement a second policy. In determining who shall receive refuge it should accord preference to those whose distress it is unable or unwilling to ameliorate in other ways.[162] In a revealing article in *The New York Times*, political analysts suggested that the ruling coalition in El Salvador believes it can violate human rights with impunity because the United States will never suspend the country's large-scale economic and military assistance.[163] If this government were willing to discharge every weapon in its diplomatic arsenal, however, perhaps it could induce or even compel regimes, especially authoritarian ones with whom it wields particular influence, to respect human rights.

Similarly, if the United States were willing to provide substantial amounts of economic and other developmental assistance, and deploy it strategically, it might reduce the unemployment, hunger, and desperation that also induce people to flee.[164] It might be that no amount of diplomatic and material intervention can appreciably mitigate the conditions that foster refugee movements. Unless the United States risks this intervention, however, it is obliged to admit those whose suffering it has either abetted or left unallayed.

Conclusion

Noncitizens generally fare pretty well in this country. Refugees and permanent resident aliens possess many of the "rights and privileges" of native-born residents, and members of either class can attain citizenship with relative ease. Temporary visitors— so-called "nonimmigrants"—and even undocumented aliens are entitled to due process and most of the Constitution's substantive rights.

The fabled "Golden Door," however, through which tens of millions have entered the United States, is not untarnished. Aliens continue to be admitted and excluded from the country in a capricious and discriminatory manner. Once here, they can secure their status only by conducting themselves with utmost circumspection; noncitizens can be deported or excluded on hundreds of grounds, and certainly for speech or deportment that offends the administration in power.

In an imperfect world the Golden Door can never regain its legendary splendor. This book is dedicated to the proposition, however, that it can be reconditioned and polished. Accordingly, scores of reforms are suggested throughout the text that would benefit America's immigrant population. These reforms are important, apart from their intrinsic value, because they represent realizable objectives. Ultimately, however, they point beyond themselves.

Aliens will never receive the treatment that befits their human status until the country experiences a fundamental institutional and philosophic reorientation. This reorientation depends upon two related phenomena. One the Supreme Court must assume greater responsibility for the rights of noncitizens, and thus abandon the notion that its role is minimal whenever it examines federal policy that affects their well-being. Two the United States and eventually every other country must cease to revere, and indeed genuflect before, the twin altars of "citizenship" and "sovereignty."

JUDICIAL ABDICATION AND THE RIGHTS OF ALIENS

Although the Supreme Court is willing to upset particularly untenable state schemes that discriminate against this country's alien population, it has effectively abdicated any responsibility toward them when it reviews congressional or executive action that is similarly discriminatory. As a result, not once in its history has the Court invalidated on substantive grounds federal policy that affects the rights of noncitizens.

Why this deference to federal legislation? The Court has provided a number of explanations. It has frequently stated that the political branches possess "plenary power" over noncitizens as an adjunct of sovereignty:

It is an accepted maxim of international law, that every sovereign nation has the power, as inherent in sovereignty, and essential to self-preservation, to forbid the entrance of foreigners within its dominion, or to admit them only in such cases and upon such conditions as it may see fit to prescribe.[1]

Since sovereign powers arise from extra-constitutional sources, the Court suggests that in the exercise of such powers the government is largely insulated from judicial review.

The authority to conduct foreign affairs, moreover, is constitutionally committed to the political branches, a fact further contributing to the judiciary's caution. As the Court noted in *Harisiades v. Shaughnessy*, "[a]ll policy tied to the conduct of foreign affairs . . . is entrusted so exclusively to the political branches of government as to be largely immune from judicial inquiry or interference."[2]

The Court's reluctance to upset federal policy may ultimately stem from simple fear—fear that if it interfered with one aspect of the immigration scheme it might thereby unravel a vastly complicated and interconnected system; or fear, alternatively, that its interjection into areas assertedly beyond its competence might precipitate a chain of calamitous events.[3]

Despite these justifications, the Court's submissiveness is unnecessary. Decisions relating either to the admission or, under some circumstances, the expulsion of aliens, may implicate foreign affairs and be therefore the particular province of the political branches. Most cases affecting noncitizens, however, involve neither so-called "sovereign prerogatives" nor foreign policy considerations, but rather issues that the Court is not only competent, but also obliged to resolve, issues in which the rights of individuals are pitted against the asserted needs of the government. What possible foreign policy objectives, for instance, are served by denying elderly aliens the right to participate in a contributory scheme for medical insurance?[4]

Neither is judicial abdication justified by the language of the Constitution. Where does this document support the notion that the judiciary can intervene in only the most limited way whenever the political branches adversely affect the rights of noncitizens? The Constitution empowers Congress to establish a "uniform rule of Naturalization," and perhaps incidentally to regulate commerce. Nowhere in the Constitution is there express authority for Congress to control immigration, or deportation, or to prescribe conditions under which aliens might remain in this country. Even if there were express authority however, this would not be dispositive. In other areas where the political branches are supposedly vested with plenary power—areas relating to the regulation of commerce, or internal security, or even foreign affairs—the Court has not hesitated to assert itself.[5]

The judiciary's reflexive deference is thus neither necessary nor constitutionally mandated. To the extent it is also premised upon respect for the government's so-called "sovereign prerogatives," it is dangerous as well. The "sovereign," or "inherent" power doctrine is at odds with this country's entire constitutional system, which is constructed on the fundamental premise that unchecked and unreviewable power is by definition dangerous—appropriate for a despotism but not a republic.[6]

Over the years the Court's submissiveness has prompted several of its members to express disagreement and even dismay. Justice Felix Frankfurter, for instance, revealed his misgivings in a 1953 case:

> In light of the expansion of the concept of substantive due process as a limitation upon all powers of Congress, even the war power . . . much could be said for the view, were we writing on a clean slate, that the Due Process Clause qualifies the scope of political discretion heretofore recognized as belonging to Congress in regulating the entry and deportation of aliens. . . .
> But the slate is not clean. As to the extent of the power of Congress under review, there is not merely "a page of history" . . . but a whole volume. We are not prepared to deem ourselves wiser or more sensitive to human rights than our predecessors, especially those who have been most zealous in protecting civil liberties under the Constitution.[7]

As Gerald Rosberg points out, Frankfurter's words are ironic because in recent decades the Court has repeatedly shown itself willing to "deem [itself] wiser or more sensitive to human rights than [its] predecessors."[8] The entire equal protection revolution that began in full force in the 1950s is largely a repudiation of past doctrine. Just one week before Justice Frankfurter made the above statement, in fact, he was a member of a unanimous Court that in *Brown v. Board of Education*[9] upset a major constitutional principle that had reigned for half a century.

While individual members may regret the Court's deferential posture, the majority is apparently unwilling to abandon it. As a result, the Court will presumably continue to support federal officials, as it has in the past, even when they sanction flagrant discrimination on the basis of race or national origin,[10] or affront fundamental notions of fairness by banishing long-term resident aliens for past activity that was perfectly legal when undertaken.[11]

By renouncing at the outset any attempt to balance the individual rights of noncitizens against the real or purported needs of the government, the Court compounds their vulnerable status and even encourages the political branches to enact legislation adverse to their interests. Resident aliens become "easy targets." They are unable to retaliate against abusive legislators at the election polls, and the Court suggests that they are unable to rely upon the judiciary for more than perfunctory assistance. Policy-makers are thus free to enact legislation that penalizes noncitizens, perhaps in order to enhance the economic well being of their constituents, perhaps only to vent a "bare desire to discriminate against a politically unpopular group."[12]

CITIZENSHIP AND SOVEREIGNTY: TWO DANGEROUS ABSTRACTIONS

This country's alien population would benefit significantly if the Supreme Court intervened more actively in its behalf. Such intervention is unlikely but not inconceivable. What *does* seem inconceivable, at least in the near future, is that the United States will forsake obsolescent and dangerous attachments, without which even a vigilant judiciary cannot ultimately protect the rights of noncitizens. The United States—and ultimately every other country—must loosen its attachment to the related concepts of "citizenship" and "sovereignty."

At least when examining state legislation, the United States judiciary has recently demonstrated a new appreciation for the rights of noncitizens. Underlying virtually every one of its opinions, however, is the implicit and hence irrebuttable assumption that the distinction between citizen and alien is fundamental. Until the 1970s, courts routinely sustained thousands of state and federal laws that restricted the activities aliens could pursue. By so doing, they implied that only a citizen is fit to own a gun or a fishing license, to serve as a cemetery sexton, shave someone's beard, or in fact, to participate in any activity affecting the public weal.

During the last several decades, the Supreme Court has limited the occasions in which Congress could denaturalize individuals, but in defending this laudable objective it further aggrandized the concept of citizenship. In a 1957 case, for instance, Chief Justice Earl Warren proclaimed that citizenship [is] man's basic right, for it is nothing less than the right to have rights. Remove this priceless possession and there remains a stateless person, disgraced and degraded in the eyes of his countrymen.[13]

In 1971, the Supreme Court held in *Graham v. Richardson*[14] that resident aliens merit particular judicial solicitude, and it proceeded to nullify a number of discriminatory state statutes. At the same time, it has repeatedly invoked the so-called "political community" doctrine to validate other state policies that disadvantage noncitizens. According to this doctrine, a state retains the sovereign right to protect the "character and needs" of its political community, and thus might consider only citizens for those positions that involve the formation or execution of high-level policy. Recently, however, the Court has sustained legislation that disqualifies aliens from participating in many activities related only peripherally to the "character and needs" of this community. It has thereby contributed anew to the exaltation of the citizen and the correlative denigration of the noncitizen, and in the process it has encouraged parochialism and divisiveness at a time when both are particularly indefensible.

Even less appropriate to a nuclear age than an emphasis on citizenship is a veneration for "sovereignty"—another tyrannizing abstraction that breeds in nations an arrogant willfulness and concomitant disdain for the imperatives of the international order. The United States guards its "sovereign" prerogatives with jealous fervor, and given its pre-eminent status thereby encourages other nations to respond in kind.

The American judiciary has emphasized time and again that by virtue of their sovereign prerogatives, the political branches possess virtually unfettered power over noncitizens. In *Knauff v. Shaughnessy*, for instance, the Court stressed that Congress may exclude any alien from the country, in accordance with whatever procedures it sees fit to prescribe, because "the exclusion of aliens is a fundamental act of sovereignty."[15]

While the United States condemns other nations for violating United Nations Charter obligations, it steadfastly maintains that these same obligations have no force within its own borders in the absence of domestic legislation. Moreover, most international human rights agreements are not in force in the United States, nor are the bulk of covenants and agreements concerning labor conditions sponsored by the International Labor Organization. The United States has ratified only human rights agreements, such as the United Nations Charter or the Universal Declaration of Human Rights, that lack the status of law and hence impose no international obligations. Since the United States Constitution does not prohibit either the President or Congress from violating international law, the judiciary is rarely troubled when federal policy contravenes its prescriptions.

There is one commanding reason why the United States has failed to ratify many international conventions: By so doing it would thereby forfeit a modicum of its sovereign authority. That other nations should participate even marginally in the country's internal affairs is as unacceptable to Congress as is the specter of the country's compulsory submission to the judgments of an international tribunal.

In the second half of the twentieth century, scarcity of resources and unemployment, overpopulation and political turbulence have already given rise to human migration staggering in scope, subjecting both sending and receiving countries to devastating dislocations. Multinational institutions alone are capable of forestalling or at least palliating this phenomenon, but only if they are endowed with sufficient resources and authority. Yet the United States, like most other countries, is not only reluctant to strengthen these institutions, but in fact contributes to their debilitation. In homage to its sovereign interests it will suffer no restraint on its power to admit or exclude aliens virtually at will, or to conduct its affairs without unsolicited interference from any supranational authority.[16]

So-called "sovereign" interests are usually short-term self interests, which as such must be vindicated by a legitimizing ideology. These ideologies, in turn, further imperil international institutions because they suggest that the fissures between developed and developing nations are so deep that ultimately munitions and not mediation are inevitable. Third World countries believe that since developed nations have contributed to the welter of ills that afflict their societies, the developed nations are obliged to assist in the birth of a "new world order" and, more important, to honor what Third World nations maintain is a universal right to migrate.[17] Residents of the United States and other developed countries often resent these assumptions; they contend that the overpopulation and underdevelopment characteristic of Third World nations are largely attributable to their "irresponsible" failure to promote birth control, economic development, and democratic institutions.

Self-righteousness is an indulgence developed nations can no longer afford, however, any more than they can afford a policy of indifference to the plight of their neighbors. If not from altruism, then from sheer self-interest, they are obliged to help those neighbors ameliorate the conditions that compel mass migration.[18] This obligation, in turn, raises hard questions. Do nations continue to bear responsibilities toward others even if meaningful assistance would necessitate a modest or even significant reduction in their standard of living? If it would require them to sacrifice any of their sovereign prerogatives?

According to a central tenet of sovereignty, every nation has the right to exclude from its territory any and all whom it chooses, and indeed for any reason it chooses. This assumption raises a fundamental question, however: Given the demographic realities of the twentieth century, is it ethically justifiable for any country to close its borders for reasons that are less than compelling? These are telling questions, because in answering them both individuals and nations reveal whether or not they are willing to become responsible members not only of the family of nations, but also of the family of man.

Notes

INTRODUCTION

1. An alien is "any person not a citizen or national of the United States." Immigration & Nationality Act, § 101, 8 U.S.C. § 1101(a) (1980).
2. Maurice Davie, *World Immigration*, pp. 11–12.
3. For discussion see Reverend Theodore M. Hesburgh, "Opening Remarks at Wingspread Conference on Immigration and Refugee Policy," Racine, Wisconsin, March 28–9, 1981, p. 8 (citing Roper Polls, Sept. 1979 and June 1980).

Father Hesburgh was chairman of the Select Commission on Immigration and Refugee Policy (hereinafter referred to as SCIRP)—a panel of high-level public and private officials created by Congress in 1978 to study, and make recommendations for reforming, the country's immigration laws. In a speech delivered after the SCIRP issued its final report, Father Hesburgh pointed out that in 1938 and 1939, as the American public became generally more aware of Hitler's persecutions, it nevertheless remained opposed to any proposal that would increase the number of refugee admissions. According to a Gallup poll he cited, 67.4 percent of the American people favored a total ban on refugee admissions, and only 4 percent of the population approved of a proposal to raise immigration quotas. Another 18.2 percent favored letting refugees in only under the strict quota restrictions then in effect, which meant—as Father Hesburgh observed—"condemning tens of thousands to their deaths." Ibid., p. 8.

The public's support for refugee admissions remains low. In a Gallup poll conducted in August 1979, 57 percent of the respondents opposed allowing the Indochinese "boat people" to enter the country, and only 32 percent favored their admission. In a second poll, conducted in May 1980, George Gallup asked if refugees suffering from oppression should be admitted or excluded until unemployment fell below 5 percent. Sixty-five percent of the sample favored excluding political refugees until unemployment had declined. Edwin Harwood, "Alienation: American Attitudes Toward Immigration," *Public Opinion*, June-July 1983, p. 50.

4. Kevin McCarthy and David Ronfeldt, *United States Immigration Policy and Global Interdependence*, p. 1.

5. For official figures through fiscal year 1980, see "Immigration by Country, For Decades 1820–1980," Table Two, *1980 Statistical Yearbook of the United States* (Washington, D.C.: G.P.O., 1980), pp. 1–4; John M. Crewdson, "New Administration and Congress Face Major Immigration Decisions," *The New York Times*, Dec. 28, 1980, pp. 1, 120; Michael Teitelbaum, "Right Versus Right: Immigration and Refugee Policy in the United States," *Foreign Affairs*, 59, p. 23.

For estimates of both legal and illegal immigration since 1980, see McCarthy and Ronfeldt, *United States Immigration Policy*, p. 1; Jacob Siegel, Jeffrey Passel, and J. Gregory Robinson, "Preliminary Review of Existing Studies of the Number of Illegal Residents in the United States," p. 18.

6. Hesburgh, "Opening Remarks at Wingspread Conference," p. 10.

After examining nationwide poll data, compiled by Gallup since 1945, Wayne Cornelius concluded that since 1945 Americans have consistently favored levels of immigration even lower than that allowed by United States law. "America in the Era of Limits," pp. 9–16.

7. For discussion see Ch. 4, infra.

8. One new, well-financed organization, Federation for American Immigration Reform (FAIR), merits particular note because it is the first "national organization formed solely to abolish illegal immigration," and, according to its descriptive brochure, "to set a limit for total legal immigration consistent with the realities of the 1980's." "The FAIR Way," published by FAIR, Washington, D.C.

FAIR is notable, as well, because of the influence it has already amassed in official circles during its brief existence. Fran Westner, assistant to Illinois Congressman Henry Hyde, told this author that FAIR is at least occasionally privy to information that "we can't get from the INS (Immigration and Naturalization Service)," and consequently that "we can call FAIR for this data." Interview with author, Washington, D.C., May 22, 1981.

9. Quoted in Leon F. Bouvier, Testimony Before Joint Hearing of the Senate and House Subcommittees on Immigration and Refugee Policy, Washington, D.C., May 7, 1981, p. 13.

10. Editorial, "Immigration and Purity," *The New York Times*, Dec. 16, 1982, p. 26.

11. Over the past decade at least 50 percent of the legal and illegal immigrants to the United States were Spanish-speaking. Teitelbaum, "Right Versus Right," p. 26.

12. "Immigration and Refugee Policy: The Most Pressing Social Issues of the 80's?" Feb. 1982, no. 205 (Sen. Mark O. Hatfield, Backgrounder).

13. Carl T. Rowan and David M. Mazie suggested this figure, after undertaking a review of estimates offered by various official bodies. "Melting Pot is Brimming," *Newark Star-Ledger*, Jan. 2, 1983, p. 13.

14. Quoted in Hatfield, "Backgrounder."

15. Ibid. See also Dr. William Overholt, "A Global Survey of Political-Economic Tensions Which Could Stimulate Refugee or Rapid Migrations, 1980–2000." Paper prepared for SCIRP, Sept. 17, 1979.

16. Act of June 27, 1952, ch. 477, 66 Stat. 163 (hereinafter cited as the INA). This statute is set forth in 8 U.S.C. § 1101 et seq. (1980). Regulations of the Immigration and Naturalization Service (INS) are found in 8 C.F.R. (1978).

CHAPTER 1

1. Quoted in FAIR, "Immigration Report," 4 (March 1983).

The material in this section was gathered largely from the following sources: "United States Immigration Policy and the Public Interest," Staff Report of SCIRP, pp. 161–216 (hereinafter cited as Staff Report); Oscar Handlin, *The Uprooted*; Marcus Lee Hansen, *The Immigrant in American History*; Arthur Mann, *The One and the Many*, pp. 71–96.

2. John Jay expressed this longing in *The Federalist* Number 3: "Providence has been pleased to give this one connected country to one united people—a people descended from the same ancestors, speaking the same language, professing the same religion, attached to the same principles of voting, very similar in their manner and custom." Alexander Hamilton, James Madison, and John Jay, *The Federalist*, ed., James Fletcher Wright (New Haven, Connecticut.: Yale University Press, 1961), p. 94.

3. *Notes on the State of Virginia*, ed. William Peden (Chapel Hill, North Carolina: University of North Carolina Press, 1955), pp. 83–85. Elsewhere Jefferson explained why he disagreed with the popular de-

sire to encourage immigration: "Every species of government has its specific principles. Ours perhaps are more peculiar than those of any other in the universe." Most immigrants would come from "absolute monarchies," and thus be unable to accept the free principles of American government. Even worse, immigrants would teach tyrannical ideas to their children. Jefferson thus recommended, as the most prudent course, to allow the population to grow through natural increase.

Most colonial leaders agreed with Jefferson that the United States would be well advised to adopt a neutralist stance in preference to one that encouraged migration. George Washington, for instance, gave the following advice to John Adams:

> My opinion, with respect to immigration, is that except of useful mechanics and some particular descriptions of men or professions, there is no need of encouragement, while the policy or advantage of its taking place in a body (I mean the settling of them in a body) may be much questioned; for, by so doing, they retain their language, habits and principles (good and bad) which they bring with them.

Quoted by Milton Gordon, *Assimilation in American Life*, p. 90.

4. The Alien and Sedition Acts of 1798 were imposed by the Federalist Administration of John Adams; they were abrogated two years later when Thomas Jefferson became President and his Democratic Republican supporters gained a majority in Congress.

5. Naturalization Act, 2 Stat. 153 (1802); I.N.A. § 312, 8 U.S.C. § 1423 (1980).

6. Mann, *The One and The Many*, p. 81.

7. Under the English common law, which was based on the *jus soli*, or "law of the place of one's birth," the principle of "indelible allegiance" was assumed. As a consequence, for decades Great Britain claimed the right to impress naturalized American seamen who were born in Britain—an action that constituted one of the causes for the War of 1812. For discussion see Edward S. Corwin, *The Constitution and What It Means Today*, p. 67.

Although the right of expatriation had been assumed by American leaders since the time of the Declaration of Independence, Congress explicitly sanctioned it in 1868: "The right of expatriation is a natural inherent right of all people, indispensable to the enjoyment of the rights of life, liberty, and the pursuit of happiness." Act of July 27, 1868, ch. 249, 15 Stat. 223 (1868).

Britain never formally acknowledged this principle, but in 1870 Parliament recognized that an individual ceased to be a British subject once he voluntarily became a citizen of another sovereign. During the same period the United States secured similar concessions from other states. Mann, *The One and The Many*, pp. 82–83.

8. The persistent notion of American "exceptionalism" has been commented upon by myriad historians and social scientists. See, e.g., Louis Hartz, *The Liberal Tradition in America*; Daniel Bell, "The End of American Exceptionalism," p. 199; Henry Steele Commager, *The Empire of Reason*.

9. Quoted in *The Founders of the Republic on Immigration, Naturalization and Aliens*, ed. Madison Grant and Charles Stewart Davison (New York: Charles Scriber's Sons, 1928), p. 90.

10. Quoted in Gordon, *Assimilation in American Life*, p. 89.

11. John Higham, *Strangers in the Land: Patterns of American Nativism 1860–1925*.

12. For discussion see Bruce Campbell, *The Golden Door: The Irony of Our Immigration Policy*.

13. The typical members of nativist alliances were those whom Seymour Martin Lipset and Earl Raab refer to as the "once hads"—embittered individuals who blame their own and the country's perceived shortcomings on foreign people and ideas. *The Politics of Unreason*, pp. 23–24.

14. For discussion see Higham, *Strangers in the Land*, pp. 30–105.

15. Act of March 3, 1875, ch. 141, 18 Stat. 477. Criminals and prostitutes were excluded under this act.

16. For discussion see Staff Report, pp. 727–735.

17. Act of Aug. 3, 1882, 22 Stat. 214.

18. Act of Feb. 26, 1885, 23 Stat. 332, and Act of Feb. 23, 1887, 24 Stat. 414. This exclusion presented the aspiring immigrants with a dilemma. While they could gain admission to the United States only by demonstrating that they would not become a "public charge," they were also forbidden to reveal any employment offer that could be considered prearranged.

19. Ch. 126, 22 Stat. 58 (1882). This act suspended the immigration of Chinese laborers for ten years, excepting only those who had been present in the United States as of November 17, 1880. Congress also rendered the Chinese ineligible for United States citizenship once the act became operative.

In 1884 the act was broadened to encompass all subjects of China, and any one of Chinese descent who lived in any other country. Four years later Congress passed a third law extending the suspension of immigration to all but a select class of Chinese. After several interim extensions, the Chinese Exclusion Act was extended indefinitely in 1904, and it remained in effect until 1943. Act of April 27, 1904, 33 Stat. 428.

Although these exclusionary provisions were frequently challenged by American residents of Chinese descent, their constitutionality was upheld by state and federal courts. In one case, *Fong Yue Ting v. United States*, 149 U.S. 698 (1893), the Supreme Court sanctioned a particularly invidious provision, adopted in 1892, that required Chinese laborers to obtain certificates of residence within a specified time or face deportation. In order to obtain the certification, Congress stipulated that the alien must produce a credible white witness who would testify that he was an American resident prior to the passage of the act.

20. For discussion see Milton Konvitz, *The Alien and the Asiatic in American Law*; R. D. McKenzie, *Oriental Exclusion*.

21. Hawaii experienced a similar phenomenon. Japanese nationals imported to work in the pineapple fields remained even after their services were no longer needed. Eventually they became solid components of the Hawaiian middle class. See Kevin McCarthy and David Ronfeldt, *United States Immigration Policy and Global Interdependence*, p. 3.

22. For discussion see Stanford Lyman, *The Chinese Americans*, pp. 69–70.

23. California, for example, passed legislation requiring that every foreign miner and fisherman acquire a license in order to work, although the laws were enforced almost exclusively against the Chinese. In another instance, San Francisco adopted an ordinance regulating the operation of laundries, which was similarly applied only to the Chinese until the Supreme Court declared this selective enforcement violative of the equal protection clause of the Constitution's Fourteenth Amendment. *Yick Wo v. Hopkins* 118 U.S. 356 (1886). For an excellent discussion of official discrimination against Asians, particularly on the East Coast, see McKenzie, *Oriental Exclusion*, pp. 24–33.

24. California State Senate, Special Commission on Chinese Immigration, "Chinese Immigration: Its Social, Moral and Political Effects," 1876, quoted in Staff Report, p. 180.

25. Gentlemen's Agreement of 1907, U.S. Dept. of State, *Papers Relating to the Foreign Relations of the United States 1924*, 2 vols. (Washington, D.C.: G.P.O., 1939), p. 339.

During this time members of Congress also attempted to prevent blacks from immigrating to the United States. In 1915 an amendment was introduced in the Senate to exclude "all members of the African or black race." The amendment was approved, but subsequently defeated in the House of Representatives after an intense campaign by the NAACP. See *Crisis* 9 (February 1915), p. 190.

26. The only territory excluded from the barred zone included parts of Afghanistan and Russia, and what was then Persia. For discussion see U.S. Commission on Civil Rights, *The Tarnished Golden Door*, p. 9 (hereinafter cited as the Civil Rights Comm'n Report.).

27. U.S. Const., Amend. XIV, § 1.

28. Congress is empowered "[t]o establish a uniform rule of naturalization." U.S. Const., Art. I, § 4.

29. Act of July 14, 1870, 16 Stat. 256.

30. Mann, *The One and The Many*, p. 89.

31. Ibid. Background material for this section on citizenship is drawn largely from Mann, pp. 89–94, and Sidney Kansas, *Citizenship of the United States of America*, pp. 28–61.

32. *Elk v. Wilkins*, 112 US 94 (1884).

33. The Fourteenth Amendment defines a native-born citizen as one "born or naturalized in the United States, and subject to the jurisdiction thereof." U.S. Const., Amend. XIV, § 1.

34. 6 F. Rptr. 256, 258 (U.S.C.C. 1880).

35. Ibid., at 259. One district court concluded that the meaning of "free white person" was to be determined by reference to the meaning the term naturally would have been given when it was used in the first naturalization act of 1790. Thus, the term would refer to all persons belonging to the European races and their descendants. *Ex Parte Shahid*. 205 F. Rep. 812 (1913).

36. Ibid., at 256.

37. *In re Rodriguez*, 81 F. Supp. 337 (W.D. Tex. 1897).

38. Jones Act, ch. 145, § 5, 39 Stat. 951 (1917).

39. Act of June 2, 1924, ch. 233, 43 Stat. 254.

40. *Wong Kim Ark*, 169 U.S. 649, 704 (1898). See also *Fong Yue Ting v. U.S.*, 149 U.S. 698, 716 (1893) ("Chinese persons not born in this country have never been recognized as citizens of the United States, nor authorized to become such under the naturalization laws").

41. When Congress passed the Nationality Act of June 29, 1906, ch. 3592, 34 Stat. 596, persons of Japanese ancestry applied for naturalization in accordance with the procedures prescribed in that act. The Supreme Court foiled their efforts, however, by holding that the 1906 Act was restricted by earlier congressional statutes that rendered the Japanese ineligible for citizenship. *Ozawa v. U.S.*, 260 U.S. 178 (1922).

The 1924 National Origin Act prohibited from entering the country aliens who were ineligible for citizenship (Act of May 26, 1924, ch. 190, § 14, 43 Stat. 153). Thus, by virtue of the Supreme Court's 1922 ruling,

Japanese were effectively barred altogether from entering the United States.

Since natives of Korea owed allegiance to the Mikado of Japan, and are of the Mongol race, they were similarly ineligible for naturalization. *Petition of Easurk Emsen Charr*, 273 F. Rep. 207 (1921). See also *U.S. v. Javier*, 57 App. D.C. 303, 22 F. 2d 879 (1927) (Filipino, being neither "a free white person" nor of "African descent," not eligible for citizenship).

42. *In re Young*, 715 F. Rep. 715, 717 (1912).

43. *U.S. v. Thind*, 261 U.S. 204 (1923) (Hindus); *U.S. v. Cartozian*, 6 F. 2d 919 (1925) (Armenians). See also *In re Najour*, 174 F. Rep. 735 (1909) (Syrians, coming under the same racial classification as Armenians, are also ineligible for citizenship).

44. U.S. Bureau of the Census, *Historical Statistics of the United States, Colonial Times to 1970* (Washington, D.C.: G.P.O., 1975), I, reprinted in Staff Report, pp. 172–73.

45. *The American Scene*, ed. Leon Edel (Bloomington, Indiana: The University of Indiana Press, 1968), p. 64.

46. Charles Keely, "United States Immigration: A Policy Analysis," p. 14.

47. Quoted in Jenna Weissman Joselit, "Perceptions and Reality of Immigrant Health Care, 1840–1920," paper prepared for SCIRP (New York: Historical Consultants, 1980), in Staff Report, p. 178.

48. Ibid.

49. Ibid.

50. Ibid.

51. "United States Immigration Commission, 1907–1910," Report of the Immigration Commission (Dillingham Commission).

52. Act of March 3, 1903, ch. 1012, § 2, 32 Stat. 1213. "Anarchists" are currently excludable under I.N.A. § 212, 8 U.S.C. § 1182(a)(18)(A) (1980).

53. Susan S. Forbes and Peter Lemos, "A History of American Language Policy," paper prepared for SCIRP (New York: Historical Consultants, 1980), p. 148.

54. Their sentiments were endorsed by many influential publications of the day, including the *Nation* magazine. While the *Nation* conceded that a language requirement would drastically curtail immigration from everywhere but the British Isles, it concluded that "we are under no obligation to see that all races and nations enjoy an equal chance of getting here." "The Language Test for Immigrants" (April 16, 1891), p. 312.

55. Act of Feb. 5, 1917, ch. 29, § 3, 39 Stat. 875. The act exempted

from the literacy requirements close relatives of citizens and resident aliens.

56. Congressional Record, 54th Cong., 1st Sess., 28 Cong. Rec. 2816–20, (1896), quoted in *The New Immigration*, ed. John J. Appel, p. 126.

57. Act of Feb. 5, 1917, ch. 29, § 3, 39 Stat. 874. The 1917 act also excluded persons of "constitutional psychopathic inferiority," men attempting to enter the country for immoral purposes, chronic alcoholics, stowaways, vagrants, those with one or more attacks of insanity.

58. Act of Oct. 16, 1918, ch. 186, § 1, 40 Stat. 1012.

59. *Immigration Law and Defense*, Student ed., § 2.4.

60. For discussion see Mann, *The One and The Many*, pp. 136–48.

61. Ibid., p. 137.

62. Table, "The Origins of U.S. Population by Region, 1821–1979," in Staff Report, pp. 172–73.

63. (Boston: 1926), p. 261, quoted in Mann, *The One and The Many*, p. 126.

Apostles of restrictionism found an incongruous ally in organized labor. Although labor did not endorse a racialist philosophy, it urged a limitation on immigration, which it perceived as undermining its efforts to unionize and secure adequate wages and working conditions. Labor thus found itself aligned with the so-called "100 Percenters"—eugenicists and other white supremacists who urged restrictionism in order to preserve the purity of United States institutions and culture. For discussion see Staff Report, p. 193.

64. Act of May 19, 1921, ch. 8, 42 Stat. 5.

65. Act of May 26, 1924, ch. 190, 43 Stat. 153.

66. For discussion see Civil Rights Comm'n Report, pp. 9–10.

67. Staff Report, p. 300.

68. The United States made a feeble effort to accommodate some refugees. In 1940, for instance, the State Department permitted consuls outside of Germany to issue visas to German refugees whenever the German quota remained unfilled. As writers of the Staff Report observed, however, the measures were altogether too few and too late to help most victims of Nazi persecution. Staff Report, p. 199.

69. Ibid.

70. Those refugees who were able to enter the United States under existing quotas were still required to satisfy all of the other preconditions for entry, and a substantial number were denied visas because they might become "public charges." Staff Report, pp. 199–200.

71. Earlier, when it became independent in 1934, the Philippines had received a small quota. The quota system had also been eased for the Chinese, who were wartime allies, and again in 1946 when Con-

gress, eager to rally support against Japan, lifted its barriers against the nationals of India. See Staff Report, p. 307.

72. For discussion see Ch. 5 infra.

73. Act of June 28, 1940, ch. 439, 54 Stat. 670 (codified as amended at 50 U.S.C. §§ 781–835 (1976 & Supp. V 1981).

74. The Alien Registration Act required the registration and finger-printing of all aliens who were either present in the United States or who were seeking permission to enter.

75. Act of June 20, 1941, ch. 209, 55 Stat. 252.

76. Act of June 21, 1941, ch. 210, 55 Stat. 252, amending Passport Act of May 22, 1918, ch. 81, 40 Stat. 559.

77. Internal Security Act of 1950, ch. 1024, Title I, § 7, 64 Stat. 993 (codified as amended at 50 U.S.C. §§ 781–835 (1976 & Supp. V 1981).

78. For discussion see Ch. 2 infra.

79. Quoted by David Margolick, "Reprise on McCarran Act," The New York Times, June 4, 1982, pp. B1 & 6.

80. Act of June 27, 1952, ch. 477, 66 Stat. 163.

81. Harry Rosenfield, who wrote extensively on immigration law, aptly described the act:

It is probably accurate to say of the Immigration and Naturalization Act that few laws enacted by Congress are longer and more complex, or have been sub-ject to greater and more widespread criticism by successive Presidents of the United States, by both national political parties, and by individual citizens and representative American organizations.

"Necessary Administrative Reforms in the I.N.A. of 1952," Fordham Law Review, p. 145.

82. Quoted in Staff Report, p. 203.

83. If an alien was more than one-half Asian but of mixed back-ground—for example, a combination of Cambodian, Vietnamese, and French—he or she would be "charged" to a special "Asia-Pacific Tri-angle" quota of one hundred established specifically to accommodate people of mixed Asian background.

84. U.S. Dept. of Commerce, Statistical Abstract of the United States (Washington, D.C.: G.P.O., 1957), p. 91.

85. "Reprise on McCarran Act," pp. B1 & 6.

86. I.N.A., § 212, 8 U.S.C. § 1182(a)(15) (1980). In the 1952 act Congress reenacted the bulk of the exclusionary provisions in the 1950 Subversive Activities Control Act, but it waived exclusion for aliens who had belonged to a proscribed organization at least five years in the past, and who thereafter actively opposed its tenets and practices. I.N.A., § 212, 8 U.S.C. § 1182(a)(28)(I) (1980).

87. President's Commission on Immigration and Naturalization, *Whom We Shall Welcome.*

88. Staff Report, p. 205.

89. Act of Oct. 3, 1965, Pub. L. No. 89–236, 79 Stat. 911.

90. Weekly Compendium of Presidential Documents, 1, No. 11 (Monday, 11 Oct. 1965), p. 365.

91. U.S. Dept. of Justice, Labor, and State, Interagency Taskforce on Immigration Policy, Staff Report, pp. 192–193.

92. The 1976 Amendments to the INA increased the allotment from two hundred to six hundred. Pub. L. No. 94–571, 90 Stat. 2703 (1976).

93. For discussion see Civil Rights Commission Report, pp. 16–18.

94. For discussion see U.S. Congress, House, *House Report No. 94–1553*, 94th Cong., 2d Sess. Sept. 15, 1976, p. 4.

95. Act of Oct. 20, 1976, Pub. L. No. 94–571, 90 Stat. 2703.

96. Act of Oct. 5, 1976, Pub. L. No. 95–412, 92 Stat. 907 (1978 revisions). Congress, concerned about the number of Indochinese refugees arriving in the United States, created a single, worldwide ceiling so that visas could go wherever the refugee need was greatest, unimpeded by hemispheric limits. Staff Report, p. 212.

97. Refugee Act of 1980, Pub. L. No. 96–212, 94 Stat. 102 (1980) (codified in scattered sections of 8 U.S.C.). For discussion see Ch. 5 infra.

98. U.S., Congress, House, Committee on the Judiciary, Hearings before the Subcommittee on Immigration, Citizenship, and International Law, 94th Congress, 2d. Sess. (Washington, D.C.: G.P.O., 1976), pp. 362–363.

99. In 1980, for instance, no European country came near depleting its 20,000-person allotment for quota immigration. The United Kingdom came closest, with 9,150 visa applications. Austrians applied for 171 visas, and residents of Luxembourg sought only 28. By contrast, applicants from both Korea and Mexico easily reached the 20,000 ceiling. 1980 Statistical Yearbook of the INS, Table 7.

100. For discussion see Civil Rights Comm'n Report, pp. 13–18.

101. "The Characteristics and Role of Illegal Aliens in the U.S. Labor Market," U.S. Dept. of Labor Research & Development Contract No. 20–11–74–21 (1976), p. 8.

102. 1980 Statistical Yearbook of the INS, "Immigrants Admitted, By Type of Admissions: FY 1966–1980," Table 3.

The high priority that United States immigration law assigns to family reunification furthers the humane goal of reuniting relatives, and by so doing it also promotes family and societal stability. The system's heavy commitment to family reunification has nevertheless been criticized, both because it penalizes aspiring immigrants from countries that were subject to quotas until 1965, and because it discourages an optimal level of "seed migration," that is, immigration by those with skills and training that are valuable to United States society. Economists David North and Allen Le Bel, for instance, believe that the nation's welfare would be better served if visa preferences were linked less to family relationships and more to the country's manpower needs. Their views are discussed in Inter-Agency Task Force on Immigration Policy, Staff Report, Depts. of Justice, Labor, and State, March 1979, reprinted in *Selected Readings on Untied States Immigration Policy and Laws*, p. 410.

By according preference to the relatives of United States citizens and resident aliens, moreover, the present system creates a "chain reaction" that is potentially unlimited. A son, for instance, may immigrate to the United States and, in time, become a citizen. He is then entitled to have his immediate family enter without restrictions, and under the current preference system he can petition to bring in his siblings and their immediate families. Among those considered to be within the immediate family are spouses, who can in time become citizens, and in turn sponsor their parents who are still living abroad.

103. For discussion see Kenneth Brill, "Refugee Law and Policy," p. 126.

104. For discussion see, e.g., A. Salem, "The United Nations and the International World of Physics," *Bulletin of Atomic Scientists* 24 (Feb. 1968), pp. 14–16; Harry Johnson, "Some Economic Aspects of the Brain-Drain," *Pakistan Development Review* 7 (Autumn 1967), pp. 379–411.

105. I.N.A., § 212, 8 U.S.C. § 1182(a) (1980).

106. I.N.A., § 212, 8 U.S.C. § 1182(a)(15) (1980).

107. For discussion see Ch. 3 infra.

CHAPTER 2

1. Up to 270,000 "quota" migrants are allowed to enter the United States each year for permanent residence. I.N.A., § 101, 8 U.S.C. § 1101(a)(20) (1980). An indeterminate number of nonquota immigrants, who are close relatives of United States citizens, are also permitted to enter each year. In 1981, for example, 480,000 aliens were admitted to the United States for permanent residence. "U.S. Gross Immigration, 1976–1981," Table 5 in SCIRP, Final Report, U.S. Immigration Policy and the National Interest (1981), p. 93 (hereinafter cited as Final Report).

2. To acquire permanent residence status, an alien must obtain an

immigrant visa by which he or she is "lawfully accorded the privilege of residing permanently in the United States as an immigrant in accordance with the immigration laws." I.N.A. § 101, 8 U.S.C. § 1101(a)(20) (1980). Upon entry a resident alien may live anywhere in the United States and engage in any activity permitted by law. Ibid., § 1101(a)(15). After five years of residence in this country, most permanent aliens become eligible for citizenship. Ibid., § 1427(a). Only three years of residency are required, however, for the naturalization of an alien whose spouse is a United States citizen. Ibid., § 1430.

3. Aliens are ordinarily required to pay the same taxes as citizens, although Congress grants limited exemptions to specified subclasses. Tax Guide, Ch. 1 & 2, 1–4; 26 C.F.R. § 1.871.2(b) (1980).

4. 40 U.S.C. app. § 456(a)(1) (1980).

5. For instance, although resident aliens ordinarily enjoy the rights guaranteed by the First Amendment, they may nevertheless be deported for certain speech or political activity that the government finds objectionable. See Ch. 2 infra.

With few notable exceptions, however, resident aliens enjoy most constitutional protections. See, e.g., *Yick Wo v. Hopkins*, 118 U.S. 356 (1886) (equal protection of the laws); *Russian Volunteer Fleet v. U.S.*, 282 U.S. 481 (1931) (just compensation); *Nishimura Ekiu v. U.S.*, 142 U.S. 651 (1892) (habeas corpus); *Wong Wing v. U.S.*, 163 U.S. 228 (1896) (Fifth and Sixth Amendment guarantees in criminal trials).

6. See n. 2 supra.

7. *Fong Yue Ting v. U.S.*, 149 U.S. 698, 736 (1893) (dissenting opinion).

8. Congress was authorized to enact a "uniform rule of Naturalization" (U.S. Con., Art. 1, § 7); citizenship was made a precondition for high elected national office. U.S. Con., Art. 1, § 2 (Congressman), ibid., § 3 (Senator), ibid., Art. 11, § 11 (President).

State citizenship provided a means of access to the federal courts, but as Alexander Bickel pointed out, only one of several means. (Bickel noted that the Judiciary Act of 1789 established, under the diversity jurisdiction, a number of avenues to the federal courts). "The Passive Virtues," *Harvard Law Review*, p. 369.

Finally, while the privileges and immunities clause of Article IV generally requires states to treat the citizens of other states on a parity with their own, a state was not allowed to discriminate against parties solely because they held no citizenship in a particular state. U.S. Const., Art. IV § 2.

9. For a discussion of the thesis that the Constitution's framers intended that the distinctions between citizens and aliens be minimal,

see Elizabeth Hull, "Resident Aliens, Public Employment, and the Political Community Doctrine," *The Western Political Quarterly*, pp. 231–236.

10. For discussion see Gerald Rosberg, "Aliens and Equal Protection: Why Not the Right to Vote?" *Michigan Law Review* 75, pp. 1092–1136.

11. I.N.A., § 221, 8 U.S.C. § 1201(g) (1980).

12. The negative decisions of consular officers are theoretically subject to review by a supervisory consul. These supervisors, however, frequently serve more than one consulate, or are themselves overburdened with casework. In either case, they lack the time necessary to subject these decisions to more than perfunctory review. For discussion see Civil Rights Comm'n Report, p. 50.

The State Department may also review consular decisions, but only with regard to questions of law. Factual determinations remain within the absolute discretion of the consular officer. 22 C.F.R. § 42.130(c) (1979). Moreover, parties adversely affected by a consul's action cannot seek redress in the federal courts, since the judiciary has repeatedly held that administrative determinations in this area are final unless judicial review is authorized by explicit statutory language. See, e.g., *Ulrich v. Kellogg*, 30 F. 2d 984 (D.C. Cir. 1929); *Estrada v. Ahrens*, 296 F. 2d 690 (5th Cir. 1961).

13. The Commission's findings are compiled in a final report, *The Tarnished Golden Door*. This report, together with personal interviews conducted by the author, have provided the primary source material for the section on "visas."

14. Testimony of Sister Adela Arroyo, Director of Catholic Services for Immigrants in San Antonio, Texas, Texas Open Meeting, Transcript, vol. 5, p. 7, in Civil Rights Comm'n Report, p. 49.

15. Civil Rights Comm'n Report, pp. 47–48.

16. See n. 12 supra.

17. McDonald Testimony, Texas Open Meeting Transcript, vol. 3, p. 92, in Civil Rights Comm'n Report, p. 51.

18. The I.N.A. lists thirty-three specific classes of excludable aliens. I.N.A., § 212, 8 U.S.C. § 1182(a)-(j) (1980).

19. I.N.A., § 234, 8 U.S.C. § 1224 (1980).

20. I.N.A., § 212, 8 U.S.C. § 1182(a)(14) (1980).

21. In *Ludecke v. Watkins*, 335 U.S. 160 (1948), the Supreme Court upheld a governmental policy, in effect during World War II, that provided for the summary internment and deportation of "enemy aliens" without a hearing. The Supreme Court reasoned that the government's action was a war power not subject to judicial review.

America's treatment of its Japanese-Americans remains a sad illustration of the extent to which resident aliens of foreign ancestry can be persecuted during periods of international tension. During World War II not only Japanese aliens, but even those who were United States citizens, whose sons were in some cases defending this country as members of the armed forces, were subject to curfews, the confiscation of their property, and eventually to compulsory internment until the cessation of hostilities. See *Hirabayashi v. U.S.* 320 U.S. 81 (1943); *Korematsu v. U.S.*, 323 U.S. 214 (1944).

22. I.N.A., § 241, 8 U.S.C. § 1251(a)-(f) (1980).

23. Recently, for instance, Congress has provided that the attorney general, "at his discretion," might suspend deportation proceedings when the alien has resided in the United States at least seven years, exhibited good moral character, and demonstrated that deportation would result in extreme hardship, I.N.A., § 244, 8 U.S.C. § 1254(a)(I) (1980).

For discussion see Sam Bernsen, "Needed Revision of Grounds of Exclusion," *In Defense of the Alien*, pp. 47–50.

24. *Nishimura Ekiu v. U.S.*, 141 U.S. 651, 659 (1892).

25. *Ng Fung Ho v. White*, 259 U.S. 276, 284 (1922).

26. See, e.g., *Bugajewitz v. Adams*, 228 U.S. 585, 591 (1913). (Deportation is "simply a refusal by the government to harbor persons whom it doesn't want.")

Although the federal courts continue to categorize deportation proceedings as "civil" in nature, they are no longer as willing to assume that deportation results in no hardship. See, e.g., *Lennon v. I.N.S.*, 527 F. 2nd 187, 193 (2d. Cit. 1975). ("[d]eportation is not, of course, a penal sanction. But in severity it passes all but the most Draconian penalties.")

27. See, e.g., *MacKay v. Alexander*, 268 F. 2nd 35 (9th Cir. 1950) (the Constitutional prohibition against bills of attainder not applicable in civil proceedings); *Fong Yue Ting v. U.S.*, 149 U.S. 698, 730 (1893) (Eighth Amendment's prohibition against cruel and unusual punishment also inapplicable in civil proceedings).

28. I.N.A., § 241, 8 U.S.C. § 1251(a)(11) (1980).

29. *Marcello v. Bonds*, 349 U.S. 302 (1955). Marcello never left the United States, despite the goverment's sustained efforts to deport him, because no other country was willing to accept him. See *Marcello v. Kennedy*, 194 F. Supp. 748 (D.C. 1961); *aff'd* 312 F. 2nd 874 (1970); *Marcello v. Attorney General*, 347 F. Supp. 898 (D.C. 1972); *Marcello v. INS*, 694 F. 2d 1033 (1982); cert. denied, 103 S. Ct. 3112 (1983).

30. Alien Registration Act of 1940, ch. 439, 54 Stat. 670 (8 U.S.C. 137).

31. Internal Security Act of 1950, ch. 1024, § 22, 64 Stat. 1006 (8 U.S.C. Supp. IV 37).

32. *Galvan v. Press*, 347 U.S. 522 (1954).

33. Ibid., at 530–532.

34. Ibid. Frankfurter's assertion—that there is a "whole volume" of support for the Court's position that Congress exercises virtually unfettered discretion in areas relating to the entry and deportation of aliens—has been vigorously disputed by a number of legal scholars. See, e.g., Louis B. Boudin, "The Settler Within Our Gates" (points 1–3), *New York University Law Review*, pp. 266, 451, 634; Siegfried Hesse, "The Constitutional Status of the Lawfully Admitted Permanent Resident Alien," *Yale Law Journal*, pp. 262–297.

35. I.N.A., § 241, 8 U.S.C. § 1251(a)(6)-(7) (1980).

36. 355 U.S. 115 (1977). "Meaningful association" was defined as conscious knowledge of membership in a "distinct and active political organization." Ibid., at 120. Individuals did not have a "meaningful" association if they only joined the Communist party in order "to fight for something to eat," ibid., at 117, or operated a party bookstore only in order to secure "the necessities of life," ibid. at 121.

37. 374 U.S. 469 (1963).

38. See, e.g., *Rehman v. I.N.S.*, 544 F. 2d 71 (2d. Cir. 1976). *Rehman* involved § 241(a)(11) of the INA, which explicitly provides for the deportation of any alien convicted for the possession or use of drugs or narcotics, including marijuana. The petitioner, however, was a small-time first-offender, and thus the Second Circuit devised a way to avoid this harsh penalty: it reasoned that while petitioner had, indeed, been convicted for possessing hashish, in an analogous case involving federal law, the simple possession of this drug could be expunged from the record, in which case there would be no "conviction." Since the petitioner's conviction could be similarly expunged, the Court concluded that it provided inadequate grounds for his expulsion.

See also *Wong Yang Sung v. McGrath*, 339 U.S. 33 (1950); *Lok v. I.N.S.*, 548 F. 2d. 37 (2d. Cir. 1977).

The judiciary does not invariably construe statutes in a way calculated to benefit the alien, however. A 1984 case is illustrative: In *I.N.S. v. Phinpathya* (No. 82–91), the Supreme Court held that § 244(a)(I) of the INA (8 U.S.C. § 1254[a][I]), setting seven years of "continuous physical presence" in the United States as a precondition for a suspension of deportation, is to be interpreted narrowly. Thus a unanimous Court concluded that even a brief or casual trip out of the country at any point during the seven years constitutes a violation of the standard.

39. I.N.A., § 241, 8 U.S.C. § 1251(a)(E) (1980).

40. I.N.A., § 241, 8 U.S.C. § 1251(b)(I) (1980). The Supreme Court sustained the INA provisions that eliminated the statutes of limitation and rendered the deportation statutes retroactive. By so doing, the Court permitted the INS to proceed with the expulsion of aliens who had attained a status of nondeportability under the prior law. See Lehman v. Carson, 353 U.S. 685 (1957).

41. Harisiades v. Shaughnessy, 342 U.S. 580, 601 (1952) (dissenting opinion).

42. U.S. Const., Art. 1, § 8.

43. For discussion see Ch. 1 supra. In 1915 the Supreme Court upheld a federal provision stipulating that whenever a woman married a foreigner she would automatically assume his nationality. The Court reasoned that the provision reflected "the ancient principle of the identity of the husband and wife." Mackenzie v. Hare, 239 U.S. 299 (1915).

44. U.S. v. McIntosh, 283 U.S. 605, 615 (1931).

45. See, e.g., Repouille v. U.S., 165 F. 2d 152, 154 (2d. Cir. 1947):

The phrase "good moral character" set[s] as a test, not those standards which we might ourselves approve, but whether "the moral feelings, now prevalent generally in this country" would "be outraged" by the conduct in question: that is, whether it conformed to "the generally accepted moral conventions current at the time."

46. Most federal courts, however, no longer believe an applicant's sexual preference bears any relevance to his or her eligibility for naturalization. In a 1971 decision, for instance, a New York tribunal disregarded the recommendation of the INS and granted citizenship to a homosexual on the ground that aliens' private consensual behavior has no bearing on their moral character. In re Labady, 326 F. Supp. 924 (S.D.N.Y. 1971). See also Nemetz v. I.N.S., 647 F. 2d 432 (4th Cir. 1981).

47. Thus the INA prohibits anyone associated with "subversive" doctrines from becoming a citizen. § 313, 8 U.S.C. § 1424(a)(d) (1980). "Attached to the principles of the Constitution" also implies a willingness to serve in the armed forces during war. Consequently, the following classes are also ineligible for citizenship: persons who deserted the United States during wartime in order to avoid military service, or who were unwilling to bear arms for the United States. I.N.A., § 314, 8 U.S.C. § 1425; aliens who claimed exemption from military service solely because of alienage. I.N.A., § 315, 8 U.S.C. § 1426.

Those individuals who went to Europe, Canada, or otherwise evaded the draft between August 4, 1961, and March 28, 1973, have apparently been granted an unconditional pardon by the President. See Pres. Proc. 4483, 42 F.R. 4391 (1977).

48. 320 U.S. 118 (1943).

49. The I.N.A. provides that anyone who has been a member of a Communist organization during the preceding ten years may be denied naturalization, and the government is not required to prove that the individual personally advocated Communist tenets. § 313, 8 U.S.C. § 1424(c). An exception is made for those whose membership occurred when they were under sixteen years of age, if it was involuntary, or if such membership was necessary to secure the necessities of life. I.N.A., § 313, 8 U.S.C. § 1424(d).

50. I.N.A., § 312, 8 U.S.C. § 1423 (1980); 8 C.F.R. 312.

51. The nature of the questions depends upon the applicant's age, background, the length of time he or she has resided in the United States, and the "opportunities available and efforts made to acquire the requisite knowledge, and any other elements or factors relevant" to the government test. I.N.A., § 312, 8 U.S.C. § 1428 (1980). An applicant who fails the test is offered at least one opportunity to retake it.

52. I.N.A., § 337, 8 U.S.C. § 1448(a)(4) (1980).

53. 8 C.F.R. § 337.1(b).

54. Denaturalization occurs only when the government can prove that citizenship was improperly obtained in the first place. See *Federenko v. U.S.*, 449 U.S. 490 (1981). "Denaturalization" should not be confused with "expatriation"; the former is a civil proceeding to abrogate a status wrongfully obtained, whereas the latter is a voluntary renunciation of citizenship.

55. In *Schneider v. Rusk*, 377 U.S. 163 (1964), for instance, the Supreme Court held that naturalized citizens could not be stripped of their status simply because they lived in another country for several years. The Court reasoned that in mandating this penalty Congress deprived naturalized citizens of a right to which native-born ones were entitled, thereby offending section one of the Fourteenth Amendment.

Three years later the Court declared in *Afroyim v. Rusk*, 387 U.S. 253 (1967), that persons born or naturalized in the United States are citizens under the Fourteenth Amendment, and therefore cannot be deprived of their citizenship by an act of Congress. In the same opinion, the Court held that a citizen has "a constitutional right to remain a citizen in a free country unless he voluntarily relinquishes that citizenship." Ibid., p. 268.

The Court's broad holding in *Afroyim* may have been narrowed by subsequent cases. In *Rogers v. Bellei*, 401 U.S. 815 (1971), in particular, the Court held that the *Afroyim* rule applied only to "constitutional" citizens, as defined by the Fourteenth Amendment, and not to foreign-born ones naturalized according to standards prescribed by Congress. (Persons outside the United States acquire citizenship under an Act of Congress, rather than from any language in the Constitution.)

In *Bellei* the Court reasoned that since Congress can legitimately impose special conditions for obtaining citizenship, it could also impose special requirements for its retention as long as these requirements were not "irrational, arbitrary, or unfair." Ibid. By virtue of its holding in *Bellei*, however, for the first time the Court established separate standards for constitutional and nonconstitutional citizens, and called into question whether citizenship, once conferred, represents a fundamental right that cannot be revoked absent the voluntary action on the part of the bearer, or a privilege that can be conditioned by Congress.

56. *Trop v. Dulles*, 356 U.S. 86, 101 (1958). In an earlier case the Court had expressed the same sentiment: "Denaturalization, like deportation, may result in the loss of all that makes life worth living." *Knauer v. U.S.*, 328 U.S. 654, 659 (1946).

57. See, e.g., *Federenko v. U.S.*, 449 U.S. 490, 505–506 (1981), in denaturalization proceedings

the burden of proof is upon the government to prove its case by clear, unequivocal, and convincing evidence. . . . [M]ere preponderance of the evidence which leaves the issue in doubt will not suffice.

58. United States district attorneys are authorized to institute denaturalization proceedings when they have reason to believe citizenship "[was] illegally procured or [was] procured by concealment of a material fact or by willful misrepresentation." I.N.A., § 340, 8 U.S.C. § 1451(a) (1980). In *Federenko v. U.S.*, ibid., for instance, the Court upheld the revocation of defendant's citizenship on the ground that he had lied on his visa application by denying that he had served as a concentration camp guard in Poland during World War II.

59. *Eichenlaub v. Shaughnessy*, 338 U.S. 521 (1950) is illustrative. This case involved two natives of Germany who became naturalized citizens in the 1930s. In 1944 Eichenlaub pled guilty to serving as an agent for a foreign government without having registered with the State Department, and his citizenship was subsequently annulled on the ground that it was fraudulently obtained. The second party to the case was convicted of violating the Espionage Act of 1917; he, too, was stripped of his citizenship on the same ground and ordered deported.

60. See *Knauer v. U.S.*, 328 U.S. 601 (1949) (German sympathizers); *Harisiades v. Shaughnessy*, 342 U.S. 580 (1952) (Communist sympathizers). For discussion see C. Herman Pritchett, *Civil Liberties and the Vinson Court*, pp. 102–104.

61. I.N.A., § 340, 8 U.S.C. § 1451(c) (1980).

62. Citizenship can also be revoked if an individual, within ten years after naturalization, is convicted of contempt for refusing to testify before a congressional committee regarding his or her alleged subversive activities. I.N.A., § 340(d), 8 U.S.C. § 1451 (d) (1980).

63. This fact prompted a sharp dissent in a 1946 case, *Knauer v. U.S.*, 328 U.S. 654 (1946). In this case petitioner had unsuccessfully argued that the government had unconstitutionally stripped him of his citizenship. Justices Frank Murphy and Wiley Rutledge agreed; they maintained that as long as the government can strip foreign-born individuals of their citizenship, then all naturalized citizens would be

timorous and insecure because blanketed with the threat that some act or conduct, not amounting to forfeiture for others, will be taken retroactively to show that some prescribed condition had not been fulfilled and be so adjudged.

Ibid., p. 678.

64. *Lem Moon Sing v. U.S.*, 158 U.S. 538, 547 (1895).

65. U.S. Const., Amend. XIV, cl. 1.

66. 118 U.S. 356 (1886).

67. For discussion see Hull, "Resident Aliens and the Equal Protection Clause," *Brooklyn Law Review*, pp. 4–11; Rosberg, "Protection of Aliens from Discriminatory Treatment by the National Government," *Supreme Court Review*, pp. 293–98.

68. Chief Justice Earl Warren explained the rationale underlying minimal scrutiny analysis:

State legislatures are presumed to have acted within their constitutional power despite the fact that, in practice, their laws result in some inequality. A statutory discrimination will not be set aside if any state of facts reasonably may be conceived to justify it.

McGowan v. Maryland, 366 U.S. 420, 425–426 (1961).

The rational relationship test is an easy one to satisfy, and when courts apply it they generally validate the statute. According to Professor Gerald Gunther, in fact, the test provides "minimal scrutiny in theory and virtually none in fact." "Forward: In Search of Evolving Doctrine on a Changing Court," *Harvard Law Review*, p. 8.

69. U.S. Const. Art. I, § 8, cl. 4.

70. See *Hines v. Davidowitz*, 312 U.S. 52, 66–67 (1941):

where the federal government, in the exercise of its superior authority in this field (immigration and naturalization), has enacted a complete scheme of regulation and has therein provided a standard for the registration of aliens, states cannot, inconsistently with the purpose of Congress, conflict or interfere with, curtail or complement, the federal law, or enforce additional or auxiliary regulations.

The preemption doctrine, as usually understood, is used to overturn state laws in areas where the state normally has concurrent powers with the federal government. This legislation is ordinarily not considered "preempted," however, unless federal law has "occupied" the field, or state policy conflicts with federal law or treaties. See Edward S. Corwin, *The Constitution and What it Means Today*. pp. 223–225. The Supreme Court in *De Canas v. Bica*, 424 U.S. 351 (1976), may have signaled its intention to relax the preemption doctrine under certain circumstances. *De Canas* is the only case in which the Supreme Court assessed the constitutionality of a state statute penalizing undocumented aliens. At issue was a California law that made it illegal for an employer to "knowingly employ an alien who is not entitled to lawful residence in the United States." Cal. Lab. Code § 2805(a) (West 1971).

The California law was challenged on the ground that it represented an unconstitutional incursion into the federal power over immigration, and hence was preempted by federal law. Justice William Brennan, speaking for a unanimous Court, rejected the challenge and noted that any attempts to preempt the field must be indicated by Congress in clear and manifest terms, and such intent will not be presumed. 424 U.S. at 357.

The Court held, in addition, that in enacting the INA Congress did not intend to preempt all state laws affecting undocumented aliens; rather, the central concern of the INA was the terms and conditions of entry into this country, and the subsequent treatment of aliens lawfully residing here. Ibid., at 359.

In recent cases in other areas the Supreme Court has also refused to presume or infer a congressional intent to preempt state legislation. See, e.g., *N.Y. State Dept. of Social Services v. Dublino*, 413 U.S. 405 (1973); *Goldstein v. California*, 412 U.S. 546 (1973).

71. 239 U.S. 33 (1915).

72. Ibid., at 42.

73. Judge Benjamin Cardozo's opinion in *People v. Crane*, 214 N.Y. 154, 108 N.E. 427, aff'd 239 U.S. 195 (1915), upholding a statute limiting employment in public works projects to citizens, reflects the rationale underlying the public interest doctrine. He found that a state "may

legitimately consult the welfare of its own citizens, rather than that of aliens, in the allocation of the state's resources," and that "[w]hatever is a privilege, rather than a right, may be made dependent on citizenship." Ibid., at 164, 108 N.E. at 430.

74. *Gizzarelli v. Presbrey*, 44 R.I. 333, 335, 117 A. 359, 360 (1922). A California court used the same reasoning to explain why a state might limit many occupations to citizens. Its explanation also underscored the fact that statutory discriminations against aliens would be upheld if the judiciary was able to adduce any conceivably reasonable motive for their enactment:

> It cannot be assumed that the Legislature did not have evidence before it, or that it did not have reasonable grounds to justify the legislation, as, for instance, that unnaturalized foreign-born persons and persons who were convicted of a felony were more likely than citizens to . . . engage in dangerous practices against the government in times of peace or war, or to resort to force in defiance of the law. To provide against such contingencies would plainly constitute a reasonable exercise of the police power.

Ex Parte Ramirez, 193 Cal. 633, 650, 226 P. 914, 927 (1924).

75. "Resident Aliens and the Right to Work," *Hastings Constitutional Law Quarterly*, p. 1037. See also *Miller v. City of Niagara Falls*, 207 App. Div. 798, 202 N.Y.S. 549 (4th Dept. 1924) (ordinance prohibiting aliens from selling soft drinks held constitutional because it served the welfare of the community); *Commonwealth v. Hana*, 195 Mass. 262, 81 N.E. 149 (1907) (peddlers licenses denied to aliens because of the opportunities to swindle purchasers).

76. States continue to restrict the ownership of land by aliens. See, e.g., Ill. Ann. Stat. ch. 6, § 2 (Smith-Hurd. Supp. 1980) (aliens may hold land for only six years); N.J. Stat. Ann. § 46: 3–18 (West Supp. 1980) (only "alien friends" may hold land). The Supreme Court has yet to invalidate these laws, partly because of a long tradition that considers the regulation of land and land ownership the domain of the states. See note, "Foreign Direct Investment in U.S. Real Estate: Xenophobic or Principled Reaction?" *University of Florida Law Review*, pp. 491–520.

77. 334 U.S. 410 (1948).

78. Ibid., at 417.

79. See Ch. 1 supra.

80. 334 U.S. 410, 420 (1948).

81. 403 U.S. 365 (1971).

82. The petitioners in *Graham* challenged an Arizona statute that required recipients of disability payments to be United States citizens

or residents for at least fifteen years, and a Pennsylvania statute that denied general assistance benefits to noncitizens.

83. Justice Harry Blackmun, speaking for the Court, explained that while a state may validly seek to limit its expenditures, it may not do so by means of an invidious classification, the use of which violated "a general policy" embodied in

[t]he Fourteenth Amendment and the laws adopted under its authority . . . that all persons lawfully in this country shall abide "in any state" on an equality of legal privileges with all citizens under nondiscriminatory laws.

403 U.S. at 374 (quoting *Takahashi v. Fish & Game Comm'n.*, 334 U.S. 410, 420 (1948).

84. 403 U.S. at 376.

85. Ibid., at 372, quoting *U.S. v. Carolene Products Co.*, 304 U.S. 144, 152–153, n. 4 (1938).

86. For a discussion of "suspect" classes, see Ch. 2 infra.

87. For discussion of the rationale underlying the "strict scrutiny" standard, see *McLaughlin v. Florida*, 379 U.S. 184, 191–192 (1964).

88. 347 U.S. 483 (1954).

89. See, e.g., *Missouri ex rel. Gaines v. Canada*, 305 U.S. 337 (1938) (states must either provide black students with graduate and professional schools equal to those provided whites, or integrate the facilities); *Sweatt v. Painter*, 339 U.S. 629, 637 (1950) (a segregated Negro law school cannot provide its students with "those qualities which are incapable of objective measurement but which make for greatness in a law school."); *McLaurin v. Okla St. Regents*, 339 U.S. 637 (1950) (segregating a black student from his peers, even within the same institution, deprives the minority student of his Fourteenth Amendment right to an equal education).

90. Prior to *Graham* the Supreme Court had not once invalidated a statute that discriminated against aliens solely on the basis of the equal protection clause; rather, it had relied on the preemption doctrine, either alone or in conjunction with the equal protection clause. See Hull, "Resident Aliens and the Equal Protection Clause," *Brooklyn Law Review*, p. 11. Moreover, the Court had not adjudicated a single case involving resident aliens since *Takahashi v. Fish & Game Commission*, 334 U.S. 410 (1948), twenty-three years earlier.

91. Ironically, however, only a few months after *Graham* the Court refused to apply the same rigorous standards to classifications based on gender, despite considerable pressure from feminists and their supporters. In *Reed v. Reed*, 404 U.S. 71 (1971), the Court avoided the question whether classifications based on gender were suspect by ap-

plying the rational relationship test to invalidate a gender-based provision of a state statute. Ibid., at 76. Two years later, in *Frontiero v. Richardson*, 411 U.S. 677 (1973), only four members of the Court agreed that gender-based classifications were suspect. Ibid., at 691 (plurality opinion).

92. *In re Griffiths*, 413 U.S. 717 (1973).
93. *Examining Board v. Flores de Otero*, 426 U.S. 572 (1976).
94. *Nyquist v. Mauclet*, 432 U.S. 1 (1977).
95. For discussion see Ch. 2 infra.
96. 413 U.S. 634 (1973).
97. N.Y. Civ. Serv. Law § 531(I) (McKinney 1973).
98. 413 U.S. at 641 (quoting Brief for Appellants at 22). The state argued that aliens' divided loyalty and obligations might impair their objectivity and good judgment in the performance of civil service employment. Ibid.
99. Ibid., at 643.
100. Ibid., at 647.
101. 435 U.S. 291 (1978).
102. N.Y. Educ. Law § 215(3) (McKinney 1972).
103. 435 U.S. at 297.
104. Ibid., at 299–300.
105. Ibid., at 300 n.9.
106. Ibid., at 304 (quoting *Nyquist v. Mauclet*, 432 U.S. 1, 11 (1977).
107. Ibid., at 308. Justice Stevens also suggested that New York's desire to confine its police to the citizenry had less to do with notions of a political community than with considerations of political patronage and nepotism. Ibid., at 308, 309 n.2.
108. 441 U.S. 68 (1979).
109. N.Y. Educ. Law § 3001(3) (McKinney 1970).
110. 441 U.S. at 82 (1979).
111. Ibid., at 78.
112. 454 U.S. 432 (1982).
113. Calif. Govt. Code § 1031(a) requires "public officers or employees declared by law to be peace officers" to be citizens; § 830.5 of the Penal Code declares probation officers and deputy probation officers to be "peace officers."
114. 427 F. Supp. 158, 170 (C.D. Calif. 1977).
115. 454 U.S. at 442.
116. Ibid. The Supreme Court agreed in December 1983, to rule on the constitutionality of a Texas law, similar to ones in eighteen other states, that prohibits aliens from serving as notary publics. *Bernal v. Fainter*, 52 L.W. 2105. The United States Court of Appeals for the Fifth

Circuit had upheld the Texas restriction on the ground that notary publics perform functions that affect the "character and needs" of the political community. *Vargas v. Strake,* 710 F. 2d 190, 195 (5th Cir. 1983). 117. Earlier Chief Justice Burger drew the same distinction:

although we extend to aliens the right to education and public welfare, along with the ability to earn a livelihood and engage in licensed professions, the right to govern is reserved to citizens.

Foley v. Connelie, 435 U.S. 291, 297 (1978).
118. See n. 8 supra. For discussion of the framers' concept of the role of citizenship see Hull, "Resident Aliens, Public Employment, and the Political Community Doctrine", *The Western Political Quarterly,* pp. 233–39.
119. For discussion see Alexander Bickel, "Citizenship in the American Constitution," *Arizona Law Review.* pp. 369–387.
120. Ibid., at 380, 387.
121. Pub. L. 88–352, § 701(b), 78 Stat. 254, reenacted, Pub. L. 89–554, 80 Stat. 523, 5 U.S.C. § 7151.
122. 29 C.F.R. § 1606.1(d) (1972).
123. 414 U.S. 86 (1973).
124. Ibid., at 93. In compliance with the Supreme Court's holding in *Espinoza,* the Equal Employment Opportunity Commission revised its guidelines. Now in order to establish discrimination under the 1964 Civil Rights Act, plaintiffs must establish that a citizenship requirement intentionally or in effect discriminates on the basis of national origin. 29 C.F.R. 1606.1.
125. While the Supreme Court held on almost purely semantic grounds that Title VII of the Civil Rights Act does not prevent private employers from discriminating on the basis of alienage, this may not be the last word on the subject. In 1974, in *Guerra v. Manchester Terminal Corp.,* 498 F. 2d 641 (5th Cir. 1974), the Fifth Circuit Court of Appeals held that such discrimination is prohibited by § 1981 of the 1866 Civil Rights Act, which provides, essentially, that "[a]ll persons within the jurisdiction of the United States shall have the same right in every State and Territory . . . that is enjoyed by white citizens." Ch. 114, 16 Stat. 144 (1870), 42 U.S.C. § 1981 et. seq. (1970). Legal scholars have contested this interpretation, however, and until the Supreme Court rules otherwise private employers presumably retain the right to discriminate on the basis of alienage.
126. 426 U.S. 67 (1976).
127. 426 U.S. 88 (1976).
128. The equal protection clause of the Fourteenth Amendment ap-

plies only to state action. However, the Supreme Court has interpreted the Fifth Amendment—which prohibits the government from depriving any person of "life, liberty or property, without due process of law"—as imposing on the federal government many of the same strictures that the equal protection clause imposes on states. For discussion see *Bolling v. Sharpe*, 347 U.S. 497, 499–500 (1954).

129. In *Mathews v. Diaz*, 426 U.S. 67 (1976), the Court pointed out that it accorded federal provisions only minimal scrutiny because

[t]he equal protection analysis . . . involves significantly different considerations because it concerns the relationship between aliens and the States rather than between aliens and the Federal Government.

Ibid., at 84–85. As the Court explained, the standard of review is relaxed when a federal statute dealing with immigration is challenged because

the decision in those matters may implicate our relations with foreign powers, and since a wide variety of classes must be defined in light of changing political and economic circumstances, such decisions are frequently of a character more appropriate to either the Legislature or the Executive than the Judiciary.

Ibid., at 81–82. Elsewhere the Court has noted that Congress and the executive branch possess the power, "as inherent in sovereignty, and essential to self preservation, to control the entrance of foreigners and the conditions upon which they might remain in the country." *Ekiu v. U.S.*, 142 U.S. 651, 654 (1892).

130. 426 U.S. 88 (1976).
131. 5 C.F.R. § 338.101 (1979).
132. 426 U.S. at 103.
133. Ibid., at 102–103.
134. Ibid., at 114.
135. Ibid., at 105. The Commission claimed that it had adopted the policy for reasons of "efficiency." This justification was plainly an afterthought, however, since according to the record it had never considered whether, or to what extent, the policy would promote this objective. 426 U.S. at 115.
136. 41 Fed. Reg. 37, 303 (1976).
137. Ibid. The constitutionality of President Ford's order was affirmed in *Vergara v. Hampton*, 581 F. 2d 1281 (7th Cir. 1978).
138. 426 U.S. 67 (1976).
139. 42 U.S.C. § 1395(2) (1976).
140. 426 U.S. at 83.
141. Ibid.

142. 239 U.S. 33, 41 (1915).

143. 430 U.S. 787 (1977).

144. I.N.A., § 101, 8 U.S.C. § 1101(b)(I)(D), § 1101 (b)(2) (1980).

145. 430 U.S. at 792.

146. Ibid., at 800.

147. These groups may in time receive protection under the so-called "intermediate standard of review," which the Supreme Court began to fashion in the early 1970s. When courts examine legislation under this standard, they insist that its classificatory scheme be "substantially related" to an "important governmental objective." See *Craig v. Boren*, 429 U.S. 190, 198 (1976).

The judiciary employs the intermediate standard when it reviews legislation that involves sensitive, but not suspect, classifications. See, e.g., *Trimble v. Gordon*, 430 U.S. 762, 767 (1977) (illegitimacy); *Craig v. Boren*, ibid., (gender).

148. To date the Court has declared only two legislative classifications unequivocally "suspect": race, *Loving v. Virginia*, 388 U.S. I, 9 (1967); and national origin, *Oyama v. California*, 332 U.S. 633, 644–646 (1948).

149. *San Antonio Independent School District v. Rodriguez*, 411 U.S. 1, 28 (1973).

150. See *Brown v. Board of Education*, 347 U.S. 483, 494 (1954) (segregating black school children because of their race stamps them with a "badge of inferiority").

151. *U.S. v. Carolene Products*, 304 U.S. 144, 152, 153 n.4 (1938).

152. 304 U.S. 144 (1938).

153. Ibid., at 152, 153 n.4.

154. See note 148 supra.

155. *Graham v. Richardson*, 403 U.S. 365 (1971).

156. Indeed, Chief Justice Burger explained in *Graham v. Richardson* that aliens are "suspect" precisely because they are "a prime example of a discrete and insular minority that lacked a political voice to protect itself against the majority." 403 U.S. 365, 372 (1971).

157. Every state restricts the right to vote to citizens, leaving resident aliens virtually no opportunity to assert their rights in the political forum. See Rosberg, "Aliens and Equal Protection: Why Not the Right to Vote?" p. 1092.

CHAPTER 3

1. See I.N.A., § 101, 8 U.S.C. § 1101(a)(15)(A)-(L) (1980).

2. *Fiallo v. Bell*, 430 U.S. 787, 796 (1977).

3. See *Bridges v. Wixon*, 326 U.S. 135, 161 (1945) (Murphy, J., concurring).

4. See, e.g., *Chew v. Colding*, 344 U.S. 590, 596 n.5 (1953):

The Bill of Rights is a futile authority for the alien seeking admission for the first time to these shores. But once an alien lawfully enters and resides in this country he becomes invested with the rights guaranteed to all people within our borders. Such rights include those protected by the First and Fifth Amendments and by the due process clause of the Fourteenth Amendment. None of these provisions acknowledge any distinctions between citizens and resident aliens. They extend their inalienable privileges to all "persons" and guard against any encroachment on those rights by federal or state authority.

5. The Supreme Court stressed this point in *Shaughnessy v. U.S. ex rel Mezei*, 345 U.S. 206, 212 (1953):

It is true that aliens who have passed through our gates even illegally, may be expelled only after proceedings conforming to traditional standards of fairness encompassed in due process of law. . . . But an alien on the threshold of initial entry stands on a different footing. Whatever the procedure authorized by Congress is, it is due process as far as the alien denied entry is concerned.

An alien "still on the threshold" is considered an "excludable alien"—a classification that includes not only the alien seeking entry for the first time, but also a number of other more problematic categories. For instance, permanent resident aliens returning to the United States after any significant sojourn abroad are excludable. For discussion see Ch. 3 infra; *Landon v. Plasencia*, 454 U.S. 1140 (1982); *Rosenberg v. Fleuti*, 374 U.S. 449 (1963).

Also excludable are aliens who have been "paroled" into the United States after preliminary processing. See I.N.A., § 212, 8 U.S.C. § 1182(d)(5) (1980). Parole is intended to be a humanitarian expedient by which aliens are allowed to remain in the country while their immigration status is being determined. In order to prevent parolees from acquiring the rights of duly-admitted aliens, however, government officials maintain the fiction that they remain constructively at the border. See *Leng May Ma v. Barber*, 357 U.S. 185, 187 (1958).

Finally, duly-admitted refugees are technically excludable aliens until they have been in the United States for one year, at which time their status is ordinarily adjusted retroactively to that of permanent resident alien. I.N.A., § 207, 209, 8 U.S.C. §§ 1157, 1159(a) (1980).

6. See n.5 supra.

7. See, e.g., *Cheng v. I.N.S.*, 534 F. 2d 1018 (2d Cir. 1976).

8. I.N.A., § 212, 8 U.S.C. § 1182(a)(I)-(31) (1980).

9. *U.S. ex rel. Shaughnessy v. Mezei*, 345 U.S. 306 (1953).

10. 101 F. Supp. 66 (S.D. N.Y. 1951).

11. 345 U.S. at 221.

12. See n.5 supra.

13. Justice Jackson maintained that the case actually involved "a lawful and law-abiding inhabitant of our country for a quarter of a century, long ago admitted for permanent residence, who seeks to return here." 345 U.S. at 219.

14. Ibid., at 220.

15. Ibid.

16. Mezei was finally released after being detained for three years on Ellis Island. His release followed an inquiry by a special panel consisting of renowned attorneys that concluded that there was insufficient grounds for his detention. See Walter Gellhorn, *Individual Freedom and Governmental Restraint* (Baton Rouge, Louisiana: Louisiana State University Press, 1956), pp. 36–38.

17. 59 Stat. 659 ch. 591 (1945); 8 U.S.C. 232.

18. *U.S. ex rel. Knauff v. Shaughnessy*, 338 U.S. 537 (1950).

19. Ibid., at 544.

20. Justice Frankfurter dissented. He found it difficult to believe that Congress would pass the War Brides Act, which was intended to benefit the citizen-husband, rather than the alien-wife, and at the same time penalize the husband by subjecting his wife to the "hazards of an informer's tale without any opportunity for its refutation." Ibid., at 549.

21. Background material for the *Knauff* case has been gathered from two sources: John P. Frank, "The United States Supreme Court: 1949–50," *University of Chicago Law Review* 18 (Autumn 1950), pp. 21–23; Recent Cases, *Catholic University Law Review* (January 1952), p. 42.

22. According to the Appeals Board, there was insufficient evidence to support Mrs. Knauff's exclusion because each of the three witnesses who had testified against her had based his testimony entirely on hearsay evidence. The Board also noted that "there is not the faintest thread of traditional [Communist] Party thinking or Marxist philosophy in her background." Recent Cases, *Catholic University Law Review*, p. 42.

23. Mrs. Knauff made use of her many months on Ellis Island by writing a book detailing her ordeal. See *The Ellen Knauff Story* (New York: W.W. Norton & Co., 1952).

24. During the early and mid-1950s the Supreme Court issued several other opinions that sanctioned the severe treatment of aliens. See, e.g., *Carlson v. Landon*, 342 U.S. 524 (1952) (the government may deny bail to an allegedly deportable alien, on the basis of undisclosed

security information, pending a final adjudication of his case); *Galvan v. Press*, 347 U.S. 522 (1954) (even long-term resident aliens may be deported because of past activities, including ones legal at the time, that Congress subsequently stipulated were grounds for deportation).

25. For an excellent discussion of this phenomenon, see David A. Martin, "Due Process and Membership in the National Community," *University of Pittsburgh Law Review*, pp. 167–173.

26. See, e.g., *Goldberg v. Kelly*, 397 U.S. 254 (1970) (government cannot terminate welfare benefits without requiring a full hearing, including rights of confrontation and cross-examination); *Bell v. Burson*, 402 U.S. 535 (1971) (government cannot suspend the driver's license of an uninsured motorist involved in an accident without a hearing to determine fault).

27. See, e.g. *Louis v. Meissner*, 530 F. Supp. 924 (S.D. Fla. 1981) (aliens applying for asylum entitled to the assistance of counsel); *Haitian Refugee Center v. Civiletti*, 503 F. Supp. 442, 523–526 (S.D. Fla. 1980) (attorneys for asylum applicants entitled to sufficient time in which to prepare a sound case); *Fernandez v. Wilkinson*, 654 F. 2d 1382 (10th Cir. 1981) (prolonged detention of aliens, prior to the completion of an expulsion or deportation proceeding, invalid); *Orantes-Hernandez v. Smith*, 541 F. Supp. 351 (C.D. Cal. 1982) and *Nunez v. Boldin*, 537 F. Supp. 578 (S.D. Tex. 1982) (aliens must be advised of their right to seek asylum before being expelled from the country).

28. In *Landon v. Plasencia*, 454 U.S. 1140 (1982), the Supreme Court noted that "[o]nce an alien gains admission to our country and begins to develop the ties that go with permanent residence, [her] constitutional status changes accordingly." Ibid., at 1148. The Court emphasized, however, that aliens would still be regarded as excludable if their lengthy absence indicates an intent to abandon residence status.

29. I.N.A., § 235, 8 U.S.C. § 1225(c) (1980).

30. See, e.g., *Fiallo v. Bell*, 430 U.S. 787, 792 (1977); *Kleindienst v. Mandel*, 408 U.S. 753, 762 (1972).

31. These measures are contained in the Immigration Reform and Control Act, popularly referred to as the Simpson-Mazzoli bill, which Congress has been considering for the past three years. The bill is named after its principal sponsors, Senator Alan Simpson and Representative Romano Mazzoli. See S.2222, 97th Congress, 2nd Sess., 128 Cong. Rec. S2218 (daily ed. March 17, 1982) (summary of major provisions); H.R. 5827, 97th Cong., 2d Sess. (1982).

On August 17, 1982, the Senate passed S.2222 by a vote of 80 to 19. The bill fared poorly in the House, however, where members of many different groups saddled it with some 300 amendments in an attempt to weaken or eliminate what they perceived as the bill's objectionable features. See 1982 Cong. Quarterly Weekly Reporter 3097.

On February 17, 1983, Senator Simpson reintroduced the bill that had been passed by the Senate the preceding August. S.529, 98th Cong., 1st Sess. (1983). Representative Mazzoli also introduced H.R. 1510, which is identical to the bill that the House Judiciary Committee approved on September 22, 1982. 98th Cong., 1st Sess. (1983). Both bills passed their respective chambers, but a Conference Committee, convened to reconcile the differences between the House and Senate versions, was unable to fashion a satisfactory compromise before the 98th Congress adjourned in late September 1984. The bill will probably be re-introduced in the 99th Congress.

32. The Simpson-Mazzoli bill establishes a new, six-member United States Immigration Board, which is empowered to review all asylum decisions made by immigration law judges. The Senate version of the bill, as reintroduced in 1983, expressly eliminates judicial review with regard to final orders on asylum applications, with the exception of habeas corpus petitions. This effectively prevents the circuit court from reviewing a denial of asylum when it is reviewing a deportation order.

The House bill, as reintroduced in February 1983, is more generous. It would allow the circuit court to review asylum decisions during the course of reviewing exclusion or deportation orders.

33. An increasing number of wealthy foreigners are attempting to invest in United States property. States, fearing a consequent loss of control over their own resources, are responding with new or stiffer restrictions. In deference to a state's historic right to control the land within its borders, federal courts often tolerate reasonable state laws restricting either the amount or type of real property aliens can own. State legislation conditioning the sale or use of real property, however, would never sustain constitutional challenge if it conflicted with federal policy. In *Zschernig v. Miller*, 389 U.S. 429 (1968), for example, the Supreme Court nullified an Oregon statute that permitted a non-immigrant heir to inherit property only upon proof that his bequeathment would not be confiscated by his home state. The Court reasoned that such a stipulation represented an unconstitutional intrusion into the domain of foreign affairs.

34. *Takahashi v. Fish & Game Comm'n*, 334 U.S. 410, 420 (1948).

35. See *Hines v. Davidowitz*, 312 U.S. 52, 66–67 (1941) (Pennsylvania's alien registration law is unconstitutional because Congress, in enacting a federal alien registration law, had occupied the field).

36. See also *Toll v. Moreno*, 458 U.S. I (1981) (state cannot deny college tuition benefits to otherwise eligible nonimmigrant aliens).

37. A nonimmigrant alien can claim a right to work in this country only if the United States government specifically grants this right. See *Pilapil v. I.N.S.*, 424 F. 2d 6 (10th Cir. 1970), *cert. denied*, 400 U.S. 908 (1970). See also *Fiallo v. Bell*, 430 U.S. 787, 794 (1977) ("the conditions and terms of entry into the United States are solely within the discretion of Congress.")

38. I.N.A., § 263, 8 U.S.C. § 1303(a), empowers the attorney general "to prescribe special regulations and forms for the registration and fingerprinting of . . . aliens . . . not lawfully admitted to the United States for permanent residence."

39. The Trading With the Enemy Act provides the Secretary of the Treasury with authority to seize without compensation any property within the territorial jurisdiction of the United States that belongs to enemy aliens. Ch. 106, §§ 1–31, 40 Stat. 411 (codified with amendments at 50 U.S.C. App. §§ 1–6, 7–39 (1976)). The act further authorizes the secretary to freeze the assets of any noncitizens. Theoretically these powers can only be exercised in war time, but in fact they are also exercised whenever the President of the United States proclaims a "national emergency." See *Silesian-American Corp. v. Clark*, 332 U.S. 469 (1947); *Uebersee Finanz-Korp. v. McGrath.* 343 U.S. 205 (1952).

40. See Myres McDougal, Harold Lasswell, and Lung-Chu Chen, "The Protection of Aliens from Discrimination," *American Journal of International Law*, pp. 432–69.

41. See Restatement, Second, Foreign Relations Law of the United States § 166(a), Comments and Reporters' Notes (1965), quoted in Burns H. Weston, Peter Falk, and Anthony D'Amato, *International Law and World Order*, p. 687.

42. Ibid.

43. See McDougal et al., "The Protection of Aliens from Discrimination," pp. 445–450.

44. Speaking in 1910, then United States Secretary of State Elihu Root provided what has become an oft-quoted defense of the international minimum standard:

There is a standard of justice, very simple, very fundamental, and of such general acceptance by all civilized countries as to form a part of the international law of the world. The conditions upon which any country is entitled to measure the justice due from it to an alien by the justice which it accords to its own citizens is that its system of law and administration shall conform to this general standard. If the country's system of law and administration does not conform to that standard, although the people of the country may be content or compelled to live under it, no other country can be compelled to accept it as furnishing a satisfactory measure of treatment to its citizens.

"The Basis of Protection for Citizens Abroad," *American Journal of International Law*, pp. 521–522.

45. This acceptance has not diminished the ardor of those who subscribe to the "equality of treatment" standard, however. Early in the twentieth century those spokesmen were mainly from Latin America, but recently they also include representatives from the Communist countries and the post-colonial states of Africa and Asia. They often consider the international minimum standard an imperialistic tool, utilized in the past by stronger states to exploit the weaker, remaining today as an irritant calculated to exacerbate tensions between citizens and aliens.

Latin Americans, in particular, have long sought recognition as equal participants in the international arena, and have resented any suggestion that their domestic law is inferior to that of "civilized nations," or that its system of justice does not comport with minimum international standards. They have accordingly endorsed the Calvo Doctrine, which in addition to providing the "equality of treatment" standard with theoretical underpinnings, also posits that any remedy to which an injured alien is entitled is determined solely by municipal law.

For discussion see David John Harris, *Cases and Material on International Law*, 2d ed. (London: Sweet & Maxwell, 1979), p. 425; N.S. Guha-Roy, "Is the Law of Responsibility of States for Injuries to Aliens a Part of Universal Law?" *American Journal of International Law*, pp. 863–91.

46. See Restatement, Second, Foreign Relations Law of the United States § 165–166, Comments and Reporters' Notes (1965), quoted in Weston et al., *International Law and World Order*, p. 687.

47. See Richard B. Lillich, "The Current Status of Law of State Responsibility for Injuries to Aliens," *American Journal of International Law*, p. 244.

48. Emeric de Vattel, writing in the nineteenth century, formulated this doctrine, and at least by the beginning of the twentieth century it had become a central tenet of international law. According to this doctrine, the state is an entity comprised of both the sovereign and its citizens, and possesses the right to protect its citizens whenever they are present in foreign territory. It follows that an injury to an alien is perforce an injury to the state of which he is a national:

Whoever ill treats a citizen indirectly injures the state which must protect that citizen. The sovereign of the injured citizen must avenge the deed and, if possible, force the aggressor to give full satisfaction or punish him, since otherwise the citizen will not obtain the chief end of civil society, which is protection.

Quoted in Ram Prakash Anand, *New States and International Law* (Delhi, India: Vikas Publishing House, 1972), p. 39.

49. See Ch. 1 supra.

50. For a list of proposals see Library of Congress, Congressional Research Service, *United States Immigration Law & Policy* (Washington, D.C.: G.P.O., 1979), p. 65. The Reagan administration has also proposed doubling to 40,000-a-year the number of legal immigrants to the United States from both Canada and Mexico. Pub. Papers (Aug. 3, 1981) 17, pp. 829–831.

51. 8 C.F.R. § 2145 (Nov. 13, 1979). The constitutionality of the regulation was upheld in *Narenjii v. Civiletti*, 617 F. 2d 745 (D.C. Cir. 1979).

52. I.N.A., § 241, 8 U.S.C. § 1251(a)(11) (1980).

53. An exception was created by the Federal Youth Corrections Act, which waives deportation for youthful offenders under certain circumstances. 18 U.S.C. § 5021 (1976).

54. Act of July 14, 1960, Pub. L. No. 86–648, § 8, 74 Stat. 505. See I.N.A., § 212, 8 U.S.C. § 1182(a)(23) (1980).

55. For discussion see Sam Bernsen "Needed Revision of Grounds for Exclusion," pp. 45–46.

56. Ibid.

57. 527 F. 2d 187 (2d Cir. 1975).

58. The Second Circuit explained its action:

Deportation is not, of course, a penal sanction. But in severity it passes all but the most Draconian criminal penalties. We therefore cannot deem wholly irrelevant the long unbroken tradition of the criminal law that harsh sanctions should not be imposed where moral culpability is lacking.

Ibid., at 193.

59. I.N.A., § 212, 8 U.S.C. §§ 1182(a)(4) (1980). The material for this section has been gathered largely from *Boutilier v. I.N.S.*, 397 U.S. 118 (1967), and Marc Bogatin, "The I.N.A. and the Exclusion of Homosexuals," *Cardozo Law Review*, pp. 359–96; Sam Bernsen, "Needed Revisions of Grounds for Exclusion," pp. 50–52.

60. Immigration Act of 1917, ch. 29, § 3, 39 Stat. 875.

61. 66 Stat. 163 (1952); I.N.A., § 212, 8 U.S.C. § 1182(a)(4) (1980).

62. See *Boutilier v. I.N.S.*, 387 U.S. 118, 122 (1967).

63. See H. Rptr. 745, 89th Cong., 1st Sess., p. 16.

64. 387 U.S. at 122.

65. Ibid., at 124.

66. Ibid., at 122.

67. I.N.A., § 236, 8 U.S.C. § 1226(d) (1980).

68. Memo of United States Public Health Service, dated August 2, 1979.

69. *The New York Times*, Dec. 16, 1973, p. 1, cited in Bernsen, "Needed Grounds for Exclusion," p. 51.

70. Memorandum from John Harmon, assistant attorney general, to David Crosland, acting commissioner, INS (Dec. 10, 1979), p.9.

71. Dept. of Justice Press Release (Sept. 9, 1980).

72. Ibid. A recent decision by the United States Court of Appeals for the Ninth Circuit enjoined the INS from relying upon even this improvised system. According to the Ninth Circuit, the INS cannot exclude homosexual aliens without a medical certification attesting to their "deviation" or "defect." *Hill v. I.N.S.*, 714 F. 2d 1470, 52 U.S.L.W. 2165 (1983). For a contrary ruling, however, see *In re Petitioner for Naturalization of Longstaff*, 104 S. Ct. 2668 (1984) (cert. denied).

73. See Ch. 3 n.5 supra.

74. David Carliner, *The Rights of Aliens*. p. 113.

75. 8 C.F.R. § 214.2(f)(6) (as amended May 19, 1977). The general prohibition against off-campus work does not forbid an alien studying in the United States from obtaining on-campus employment provided a United States resident is not thereby displaced. Ibid.

76. Carliner, *The Rights of Aliens*. pp. 113–114.

77. Pres. Proc. No. 4702, 44 Fed. Reg. 65,581 (1979) (oil embargo); Exec. Order No. 12,170 44 Fed. Reg. 65,729 (1979) (assets frozen).

78. 8 C.F.R. § 2145 (Nov. 13, 1979).

79. Ibid.

80. *Narenjii v. Civiletti*, 481 F. Supp. 1132 (D.D.C. 1979); 617 F. 2d 745 (D.C. Cir. 1979), *cert. denied*, 446 U.S. 957 (1980).

81. For discussion of the relationship between the Fourteenth Amendment's equal protection clause and the Fifth Amendment's due process clause, see Ch. 2, n.12 supra.

82. 481 F. Supp. at 1139.

83. Ibid., at 1147.

84. 617 F. 2d at 748.

85. Ibid.

86. Ibid.

87. In his concurring opinion Judge George MacKinnon agreed that the government's action was reasonable: The status of the Iranian students could not be dissociated from their connection with their mother country, since an alien "leaves outstanding a foreign call on his loyalties which international law not only permits [the United States government] to recognize, but commands it to respect." Ibid., at 749.

88. Ibid., at 754–755.

89. Ibid., at 755.
90. John M. Crewsdon, "New Administration and Congress Face Major Immigration Decision," *The New York Times*, Dec. 28, 1980, pp. 1, 120. In *Yassini v. Crosland*, 618 F. 2d 1356 (9th Cir. 1980), a case closely related to *Narenjii v. Civiletti*, the Ninth Circuit again deferred to the judgment of the executive branch by sustaining an INS directive that revoked deferred departure dates for deportable Iranians.
91. 617 F. 2d at 747.
92. *Hirabayashi v. U.S.*, 320 U.S. 81, 100 (1943).
93. Judge Wright noted in dissent that

even the cases upholding the right of the Executive, acting pursuant to congressional authorization, to exercise virtually unfettered discretion in expelling "undesirable" aliens from the United States have approved expulsion only upon a scientific claim that the alien has acted in a manner contrary to the interests of the United States.

Narenjii v. Civiletti, 617 F. 2d at 754 n.4.
94. 481 F. Supp. at 1147.
95. In a separate opinion four judges set forth their reasons for wanting to rehear the case, and among those cited was "the fact that the President has taken this action without express authorization from Congress, [creating] a significant factor in the Constitutional balance." 617 F. 2d at 754 n.4.
96. For instance, in *Kent v. Dulles*, 357 U.S. 116 (1958), involving the validity of the Secretary of State's action in denying passports to communists, the Supreme Court emphasized that subordinate governmental officers may restrict individual liberty only if Congress expressly authorizes them to do so:

the right of exit is a personal right included within the word "liberty," as used in the Fifth Amendment. If that "liberty" is to be regulated, it must be pursuant to the law-making functions of Congress. And if that power is delegated, the standards must be adequate to pass scrutiny by the accepted tests. Where activities or enjoyment, natural and often necessary to the well-being of an American citizen, such as travel, are involved, we will construe narrowly all delegated powers that curtail or dilute them.

Ibid., at 129.
97. 581 F. 2d 870 (D.C. Cir. 1978), *cert. denied*, 439 U.S. 828 (1978).
98. I.N.A., § 101, 8 U.S.C. § 1101(a)(15)(H) (1980).
99. 581 F. 2d at 872.
100. Ibid., at 874.
101. Ibid., at 877–878.

102. For discussion see Ch. 1, especially pp. 16–17, 23–26, and 28 supra.

103. Act of March 3, 1903, ch. 1012, § 2, 32 Stat. 1213, 1214 (repealed 1952).

104. Alien Registration Act of June 28, 1940, ch. 439, 54 Stat. 670 (repealed 1952).

105. Internal Security Act of 1950, ch. 1024, title 1, § 22, 64 Stat. 1006 (codified as amended at 50 U.S.C. §§ 781–835 (1976 & Supp. V 1981).

106. Act of June 27, 1952, ch. 477, 66 Stat. 163 (codified as amended at 8 U.S.C. § 1101 et seq. (1976 & Supp. V 1981).

107. I.N.A. § 212, 8 U.S.C. § 1182(a)(27) (1980).

108. Ibid., § 1182(a)(28).

109. Ibid., § 1182(a)(29).

110. "Needed Revisions of Grounds of Exclusion," p. 47.

111. Conference on Security and Cooperation in Europe: Final Act, Aug. 1, 1975, reprinted in 73 Dept. State Bull. 323 (1975), 14 Int'l Legal Mat. 1292 (1975) (hereinafter cited as Accords).

112. Accords, 14 Int'l Legal Mat. at 1313.

113. Pub. L. No. 95–105, § 112, 91 Stat. 848 (1977).

114. Ibid., at § 212(d)(3)(A).

115. Testimony of B. Watson, Hearings Before the Comm'n on Security and Cooperation in Europe, 96th Cong., 1st Sess., on Implementation of the Helsinki Accords, vol. 9, U.S. Visa Policies (April 5, 1974), pp. 49–50.

116. Pub. L. No. 96–60, § 109(d), 93 Stat. 397 (1979).

117. June 9, 1983, p. A–23.

118. Quoted in Tom A. Bernstein, "Political Grounds for Exclusion," *Immigration Law Bulletin* 2, National Center for Immigration Rights, Jan. 1981, pp. 11–12.

119. Dwight James Simpson, "Of Mrs. Kirkpatrick and the Spirit of Free Inquiry," Letter to the Editor, *The New York Times*, March 21, 1983, p. 14.

120. Ibid.

121. United States Representative Barney Frank, who has introduced a bill to repeal many of the most restrictive provisions in the McCarran-Walter Act, was particularly incensed when the State Department denied a visa to Mrs. Allende: "Here we are yelling at the Russians, as we should because they do not have an open society. . .and then we say that Salvador Allende's widow can't come and make a speech." Quoted in E.J. Dionne, Jr., "Barring Aliens for Political Reasons," *The New York Times*, Dec. 8, 1983, p. A–20.

122. See Dionne, Jr., ibid.

123. Bernstein, "Political Grounds for Exclusion," p. 11.
124. Ibid.
125. 408 U.S. 753 (1972).
126. Ibid., at 778 (Marshall, J., dissenting).
127. *Mandel v. Mitchell*, 325 F. Supp. 620, 631 (E.D.N.Y. 1971).
128. 408 U.S. at 766.
129. 130 U.S. 581 (1889).
130. 408 U.S. at 770.
131. Ibid.
132. Editorial, "Alien Ideas Need No Quarantine," *The New York Times*, June 11, 1982, p. 30; Peter Kihss, "50 in Peace Group to Get Visas for Session at UN," *The New York Times*, June 4, 1982, p. B–1.
133. Ibid.
134. David Margolick, "Reprise on McCarran Act," *The New York Times*, June 4, 1982, p. B–1.
135. Kihss, "50 in Peace Group to Get Visas," p. B–1.

CHAPTER 4

1. There is no way of ascertaining with any certainty the number of undocumented aliens who settle in the United States each year, but 500,000 is the estimate most frequently cited. See "Problems and Options in Estimating the Size of the Illegal Alien Population," Report to the Chairman of the Subcommittee on Immigration and Refugee Policy of the Committee on the Judiciary, U.S. Senate (Washington, D.C., G.P.O.) Sept 24, 1982. See also James A. R. Nafziger, "A Policy Framework for Regulating the Flow of Undocumented Mexican Aliens into the United States," *Oregon Law Review*, pp. 67–68.

2. An alien's unauthorized presence in the United States is not a crime under the INA, and individuals who are apprehended are usually subject to deportation rather than criminal sanctions. Thus many people find the term "undocumented alien" preferable to "illegal alien," since the former avoids the implication that one's unauthorized presence in the United States is a crime. The term "undocumented alien" will be used in this book.

Although an alien's unauthorized presence in the United States is not itself a crime, such an individual is often collaterally in violation of one or more specific provisions of the INA. See, e.g., I.N.A., § 264, 8 U.S.C. § 1304(d)(e) (1980) (failure to carry an alien registration receipt card is a misdemeanor).

3. For discussion see Hull, "Los Indocumentados," *Policy Studies Journal*, pp. 638–645.

4. Charles B. Keely and S. M. Tomasi, "The Disposable Worker," p. 10.

5. Quoted in Otis L. Graham, "Illegal Immigration and the New Reform Movement," in FAIR Immigration Paper 11 (Feb. 1980), p. 7.

6. Ibid. Recently former Attorney General William French Smith added to the chorus, claiming that "we have lost control of our borders." Robert Pear, "White House Asks a Law to Bar Jobs for Illegal Aliens," *The New York Times*, July 31, 1981, p. 1.

7. For various estimates of the number of undocumented aliens currently residing in the United States, see, for instance, *Time* (Oct. 16, 1978), p. 58 (eight to ten million); "Unnamed Authorities in the State Department," *The New York Times*, Jan. 16, 1980, p. 8. (As of 1980 "the number of illegal aliens in the United States is at least ten million, and these ranks are swelling at a rate of about two million a year.")

SCIRP employed three demographers to study the existing data, and therefrom estimate the number of undocumented aliens. These demographers, while conceding inadequacies in their source material, nevertheless estimated that "the total number of illegal residents in the United States for some recent year, such as 1978, is almost certainly below 6.0 million, and may be substantially less, possibly only 3.5 to 5.0 million." Jacob Siegel, Jeffrey Passel, and J. Gregory Robinson, "Preliminary Review of Existing Studies of the Number of Illegal Residents in the United States," p. 18.

While their figure has been accepted as reasonable by a number of other officials (see, e.g., Michael Teitelbaum, "Right Versus Right: Immigration and Refugee Policy in the United States," *Foreign Affairs*, p. 23), just as many officials agree with William Fliegelman, former Chief Justice of the INS, who stated that regarding the number of undocumented migrants currently in the country, "only a fool would guess." Interview with author, New York City, May 7, 1981.

8. John M. Crewsdon, "New Administration and Congress Face Major Immigration Decisions," *The New York Times*, Dec. 28, 1980, pp. 1, 120.

9. SCIRP, Final Report, p. 35.

10. *In re Alien Children Education Litigation*, 501 F. Supp. 544, 549 (S.D. Tex. 1980).

11. *Plyler v. Doe*, 628 F. 2d 432, 451 (5th Cir. 1981).

12. Ibid., at 451.

13. Quoted in Sasha Lewis, *Slave Trade Today: American Exploitation of Illegal Aliens*, pp. 154–55.

14. John M. Crewsdon, "Critics Attack Reagan on Immigration Reform," *The New York Times*, Aug. 1, 1981, p. 6.

15. Gregory Jaynes, "More Visitors Entering the U.S. to Stay," *The New York Times*, March 22, 1981, p. 1.

16. "Immigration by Country, For Decades 1820–1980," Table Two, 1980 Statistical Yearbook of the INS, p. 4.

17. Teitelbaum, "Right Versus Right," p. 12.

18. Roper Poll, June 18, 1980, cited in Teitelbaum, ibid., p. 21. See Edwin Harwood, "Alienation: American Attitudes Toward Immigration," *Public Opinion* (June/July 1983), p. 49. Harwood cites the findings of a poll conducted in May 1982, by Audits and Surveys for the Merit Report, according to which 84 percent of the public was either "very" or "fairly" concerned about the number of undocumented aliens in the country. Ibid. In August 1981, moreover, 87 percent of those responding to an NBC News / Associated Press poll said undocumented migration was "very" or "somewhat" serious. Ibid.

19. Early in 1983, for instance, Governor Richard D. Lamm of Colorado suggested that undocumented aliens be denied public health care at a Denver city hospital. William E. Schmidt, "Colorado Governor Seeks to Halt Illegal Aliens," *The New York Times*. Aug. 1, 1983, p. 9. See also U.S.C. § 2015(5) (1976) (undocumented aliens excluded from food stamp programs); 42 U.S.C. § 1382 (a)(I)(B) (1976) (undocumented aliens excluded from supplemental security income program); 45 C.F.R. § 233.50 (1979) (undocumented aliens excluded from Aid to Families with Dependent Children Program); 45 C.F.R. § 248.50 (1976) (undocumented aliens excluded from Medicaid program).

See Robert Lindsey, "Asian-Americans See Growing Bias," *The New York Times*, Sept. 10, 1983, pp. 1, 9; Wayne Cornelius, *America in the Era of Limits: Nativists Reactions to the "New Immigration."*

20. "Approval of Anti-Bilingual Measure Causes Confusion and Worry in Miami Area," *The New York Times*, Nov. 9, 1980, p. A–1. The reporter cited a survey conducted by *The Miami Herald* which found that 71 percent of non-Latin whites who voted supported the ordinance, including 71 percent of those who voted for John B. Anderson in the 1980 presidential election. Supporters of this independent candidate are presumably middle class and liberal Miamians. The author noted that "[s]ignificantly, the ordinance was not opposed by civic groups or a number of liberal politicians." Ibid.

21. In 1981, for instance, a law was passed that designated "English as the official language of the State of Virginia." FAIR, Immigration Report, vol. 2, no. 7, April 1981. In 1983, Mayor Thomas G.Dunn of Elizabeth, N. J., issued a memorandum stipulating that English must be the only language spoken by city employees during working hours.

Suzanne Daley, "Elizabeth Mayor Orders City Hall Employees to Speak English," *The New York Times*, July 18, 1983, p. B–1.

Secretary of Education Terrell Bell is one among many governmental leaders who are outspoken in opposition to federally-funded bilingual programs. In February, 1981, he revoked proposed federal rules that would have required public schools to teach foreign-language-speaking students in their native language. FAIR, Immigration Report, vol. 2, (February 1981).

22. In a recent case, for instance, plaintiffs maintained that by not providing forms written in Spanish the Social Security Administration was denying Hispanics equal access to federal benefits. Federal District Judge Edward Neaher disagreed, concluding that "the valid historical basis and modern rationale for conducting governmental affairs in English is clear: the national language of the United States is English." *Soberal-Perez v. Schweiker*, 549 F. Supp. 1164 (1982). See also *Frontera v. Sindell*, 522 F. 2d 1215 (1975) (the Fourteenth Amendment and civil rights laws do not require that information concerning the civil service examination itself be administered in Spanish to Spanish-speaking applicants).

23. Lewis, *Slave Trade Today*, p. ix. For discussion see Mexican American Legal Defense and Education Fund (MALDEF), "Statement of Position: United States Immigration Policy," p. 2.

24. For discussion see Robert Pear, "Bills in Congress Seek Sharp Reduction in Immigration," *The New York Times*, March 25, 1981, p. A–13. Pear noted that in 1981 there were 2,269 officers in the border patrol, nearly 2,000 of whom were stationed at the United States/Mexico border.

25. Senator Walter Huddleston, 97th Cong., 2d Sess., 126 Congressional Record (daily ed. Dec. 12, 1980), pp. 16462, 16468.

26. Leonard Chapman, "A Look at Illegal Immigration," *San Diego Law Review*, p. 68. This estimate has been disputed by congressional researchers, however, who estimate that visa abusers comprise as much as 25 percent of the undocumented population. Staff Report, p. 30.

27. 458 F. Supp. 569, 583 (E.D. Tex. 1978).

28. Brief for Appellees at 16, *Doe v. Plyler*, 628 F. 2d 448 (5th Cir. 1980).

29. Guadalupe Salinas and Isaias Torres, "The Undocumented Mexican Alien," *Houston Law Review*, pp. 869–70; See also Corwin, *Immigrants—and Immigrants*, pp. 44–45.

30. Staff Report, p. 467.

31. For discussion see Staff Report, pp. 468–469; Civil Rights Comm'n Report, p. 10.

32. Library of Congress, Congressional Research Service, "Temporary Worker Programs: Background and Issues," report prepared for the United States Senate, Committee on the Judiciary (Washington, D.C.: G.P.O., 1980), p. 31.

33. For a discussion on the bracero program see Nafziger, "A Policy Framework for Regulating the Flow of Undocumented Mexican Aliens," pp. 75, 76 n.81; Greene, "Public Agency Distortion of Congressional Will," *George Washington Law Review*, pp. 452–453; Staff Report, pp. 669–673.

34. Civil Rights Comm'n Report, p. 11. This number included not only undocumented aliens but also citizens and legally resident aliens.

35. Library of Congress, Congressional Research Service, *History of the Immigration and Naturalization Service* (Washington, D.C.: G.P.O., 1980), p. 66.

36. Civil Rights Comm'n Report, pp. 84–88.

37. For discussion see Ch. 2 supra.

38. Ibid.

39. U.S. Commission on Civil Rights, "Ethnic Isolation of Mexican Americans in Public Schools of the Southwest," Report I (1970).

40. Brief for Appellees at 15, *Doe v. Plyler*, 628 F. 2d 448 (5th Cir. 1980).

41. 628 F. 2d at 451.

42. For a full discussion of the outlaw theory and related cases, see Comment, "The Legal Status of Undocumented Aliens," *Houston Law Review*, pp. 667–677.

43. Brief at 25, *Doe v. Plyler*, 628 F. 2d 448.

44. *N.L.R.B. v. Sure-Tan, Inc.*, 583 F. 2d 355 (7th Cir. 1978).

45. See, e.g., *Alouso v. State*, 50 Cal. App. 3d 242, 123 Cal. Rptr. 536 (1975), *cert. denied*, 425 U.S. 903 (1976) (undocumented aliens have no right to equal opportunity due to their status and may be denied unemployment benefits); *Pinella v. Board of Review*, 155 N.J. Super. 307, 382 A. 2d 921 (1978) (aliens who had worked in the United States for several years not entitled to unemployment compensation until they can prove their legal immigration status); *Arteaga v. Literski*, 83 Wis. 2d 128, 265 N.W. 2d 148 (1978) (undocumented aliens not entitled to recovery in tort action); *Coules v. Pharris*, 212 Wis. 558, 250 N.W. 404 (1933) (undocumented aliens not entitled to judicial assistance in collecting upaid wages).

46. *Gates v. Rivers Construction Co.*, 515 P. 2d 1020, 1022 (Alaska 1973).

47. 458 F. Supp. at 583.

48. *Janusis v. Long*, 284 Mass. 403, 188 N.E. 228, 230 (1933).

49. See *Williams v. Williams*, 328 F. Supp. 1380 (D.V.I. 1971) (undocumented aliens have access to courts in civil proceedings).

50. *Catalanotto v. Palazzolo*, 46 Misc. 2d 381, 259 N.Y.S. 2d 473, 476 (Sup. Ct. 1965) (undocumented aliens permitted to maintain personal injury action under the Motor Vehicle Indemnification Laws); *Gates v. Rivers Constr. Co.*, 515 P. 2d 1020 (Alaska 1973) (undocumented aliens may sue on an employment contract to recover unpaid wages); See also *Roberts v. Hartford Fire Ins. Co.*, 177 F. 2d 811 (7th Cir. 1949) (undocumented aliens may recover on fire insurance policy).

51. *N.L.R.B. v. Sure-Tan, Inc.*, 583 F. 2d 355 (7th Cir. 1978).

52. *Janusius v. Long*, 284 Mass. 403, 188 N.E. 228 (1933).

53. *Nat'l Bank & Loan Co. v. Petrie*, 189 U.S. 423, 425 (1902).

54. 163 U.S. 228 (1896).

55. 426 U.S. 67 (1976).

56. Ibid., at 80.

57. For discussion see Ch. 2 supra.

58. *Wong Wing v. U.S.*, 163 U.S. 228, 238 (1896), quoting *Yick Wo v. Hopkins*, 118 U.S. 356, 369 (1886).

59. 403 U.S. 365 (1971).

60. 426 U.S. 67 (1976).

61. Ibid., at 80.

62. 457 U.S. 202 (1982). The initial challenge to the Texas education policy was made by the parents and guardians of undocumented alien children living in the Tyler Independent School District. The district court for the Eastern District of Texas found the education policy to be unconstitutional, but refused to issue state-wide relief because the evidence at trial was limited to the impact of excluding children in the Tyler Independent School District. *Doe v. Plyler*, 458 F. Supp. 579 (E.D. Tex. 1978). Sixteen new district court actions were then filed, and ultimately consolidated for trial in the Southern District of Texas. Judicial Panel of Multidistrict Litigation, Rule 10(b); *In re Alien Children Litigation*. 501 F. Supp. 544, n. 6 (S.D. Tex. 1980). After a six-week trial, the court issued a state-wide injunction holding § 21.031 to be unconstitutional. *In re Alien Children Education Litigation*. 501 F. Supp. 544 (S.D. Tex. 1980).

The Court of Appeals for the Fifth Circuit granted a stay of the state-wide injunction issued in the Southern District of Texas. On application of the plaintiff in this case, the stay was vacated by Supreme Court Justice Lewis Powell, and undocumented children in Texas began enrolling in the public schools. *Certain Named and Unnamed Noncitizen Children and their Parents v. Texas*, 448 U.S. 1327 (Powell, Cir. J., 1980).

On the merits, the Court of Appeals later affirmed both trial court decisions, and the cases were consolidated in Texas's appeal of right to the United States Supreme Court. 457 U.S. 202 (1982). Throughout this article the Supreme Court case under discussion will be referred to as *Plyler v. Doe*, and the lower court cases will be referred to as *Doe v. Plyler*.

    63. Tex. Educ. Code Ann. § 21.031 (Vernon Cum. Sup. 1981).

    64. John M. Crewdson, "Access to Free Education for Illegal Alien Children," *The New York Times*, Aug. 26, 1980, p. B–10.

    65. Ibid.

    66. Ibid.

    67. Letter to the Editor, *The New York Times*, Nov. 25, 1981, p. A–22.

    68. Stuart Taylor, Jr., "Conflict Over Rights of Aliens Lies, at the Supreme Court's Door," *The New York Times*, Sept. 28, 1981, p. 17.

    69. Brief for Amicus Curiae, Federation of American Immigration Reform (FAIR), Appeal from the U.S. D. Ct. for the S.D. of Texas, Houston Division, p. 25.

John Tanton, Chairman of FAIR, noted that if the Supreme Court overturned § 21.031 of the Texas Education Code, its action "will probably be used as a wedge to drive open more public programs and benefits—food stamps, public housing, health care, and direct aid—to illegal migrants." "Illegal Aliens Should Not Have the Rights of Citizens," *Christian Science Monitor*, Jan. 29, 1982.

The controversy surrounding *Plyler* provoked different reactions from the Carter and Reagan administrations. During Carter's presidency the Justice Department argued before the Fifth Circuit that § 21.031 of the Texas Education Code was tainted by racism and designed "to harm a vulnerable and unpopular group in an irrational, invidious manner." Stuart Taylor, Jr., "Conflict Over Rights of Aliens Lies at the Supreme Court's Door," *The New York Times*, Sept. 28, 1981, p. 17.

During the Reagan Administration the Justice Department abandoned that position. While the Reagan Administration was reluctant to offend the increasingly powerful Mexican-American constituency, neither could it ignore entreaties from political allies in the Southwest, such as Texas Governor William Clements, Jr., who urged the Justice Department to support the disputed educational policy. Stuart Taylor, Jr., "U.S. Retreats from its Challenge to Texas Law on Alien Schooling," *The New York Times*, Sept. 9, 1981, p. A–26.

Ultimately the Justice Department under the Reagan Administration took no position on the constitutionality of § 21.031. The department explained in its brief that the federal government had no legal "interest" in the case; rather, the constitutionality of the Texas provision should be decided according to state law. The Justice Department did affirmatively argue, however, that the equal protection clause of the Fourteenth Amendment applied to undocumented aliens. Taylor, "Conflict Over Rights of Aliens," p. A–17.

The Justice Department's position was curious. It disavowed any legal "interest" in one of the most significant civil rights cases of the decade. Moreover, while education has traditionally been regarded as the province of the state, for at least half a century the executive branch has assumed that federal issues were raised whenever public officials denied important rights to a discrete class of people. The administration, however, is committed to minimizing federal interference with state operations, and the position adopted by the Justice Department honored that policy.

70. 457 U.S. at 215.

71. Ibid.

72. Ibid., at 219. The status of undocumented alien children is analogous to that of illegitimate children, Justice Brennan continued, and by punishing members of either class a state violates "the basic concept of our system that legal burdens should bear some relationship to individual responsibility or wrongdoing." Ibid., at 456, quoting *Weber v. Aetna Cas. & Sur. Co.*, 406 U.S. 164, 175 (1972).

73. Ibid., at 226. Justice Brennan noted that Dr. Gilbert Cardenas had testified that "fifty to sixty percent . . . of current legal alien workers were formerly illegal aliens." Ibid., at 207, citing 458 F. Supp. at 577.

74. 457 U.S. at 218 n.17, citing Hearing before the Subcommittee on Immigration, Refugees, and International Law of the House Committee on the Judiciary and the Subcommittee on Immigration and Refugee Policy of the Senate Committee on the Judiciary, 97th Cong., 1st Sess. (July 30, 1981).

75. 457 at 230.

76. Ibid.

77. Ibid., at 224.

78. Ibid., at 228.

79. Ibid., at 224.

80. Brief for Appellants at 26, 457 U.S. at 227.

81. According to the copious district court records, moreover, undocumented aliens do not impose a significant burden on the state; on the contrary, they actually underutilize public services "while contributing their labor to the local economy and tax money to the state fisc." 457 U.S. at 228. Certainly the state has ample resources, Justice

Brennan observed, to avoid some form of "educational triage." Ibid., at 229, n.25, quoting *In re Alien School Children Education Litigation*, 501 F. Supp. 544, 579–581 (S.D. Tex. 1980).
82. 457 U.S. at 228.
83. Ibid.
84. By virtue of the so-called Texas Proviso, the United States remains one of the few industrialized countries in the world that refuses to penalize employers who knowingly hire undocumented workers. This proviso stipulates the following:

Any person who willfully or knowingly conceals, harbors, or shields from detection, in any place . . . any alien . . . not duly admitted . . . shall be guilty of a felony, and upon conviction thereof shall be punished by a fine not exceeding $2000.00, or by imprisonment for a term not exceeding five years, or both, for each alien in respect to whom any violation of this subsection occurs: *Provided, however,* that for the purpose of this section, *employment (including the usual and normal practices incident to employment) shall not be deemed to constitute harboring.*

I.N.A., § 274, 8 U.S.C. § 1324(a) (1980) (emphasis supplied).
85. Justices Marshall, Blackmun, and Powell submitted concurring opinions, in which each emphasized the "unique character of the case," and elaborated upon one or more points that Justice Brennan had discussed. Chief Justice Burger wrote the dissenting opinion. He maintained that the majority, in its zeal to become an "omnipotent and omniscient problem solver," usurped the legislative function by formulating policy, instead of interpreting the law. Ibid., at 242.
86. For discussion see Conclusion infra.
87. Testimony of Leon Rosen, New York Open Meeting Transcript, vol 1, pp. 222–223, quoted in Civil Rights Comm'n Report, p. 85.
88. Unauthored, "U.S. Job Squads Arrest Aliens by the Hundreds," *The New York Times*, May 2, 1982, p. E–4; Jo Thomas, "Alien Raids Opened Up Jobs, Aide Says," *The New York Times*, May 7, 1982, p. B–11.
89. Anthony Spinale, quoted in Ronald Sullivan, "Nearly 1000 Are Seized in a Job Sweep of Aliens," *The New York Times*, April 27, 1982, p. 14.
90. U.S. Const., Amend. IV.
91. I.N.A., § 287, 8 U.S.C. § 1357(a)(I) (1980).
92. § 1357(a)(3) grants INS agents authority:

[W]ithin a reasonable distance from any external boundary of the United States, to board and search for aliens any vessel within the territorial waters of the

United States and any railway car, aircraft, conveyance, or vehicle, and within a distance of twenty-five miles from any such external boundary to have access to private lands, but not dwellings, for the purpose of patrolling the border to prevent the illegal entry of aliens into the United States.

The INS defines "reasonable distance" as one-hundred air miles from the border, but it also permits an INS Regional Commissioner to designate any distance from the border as "reasonable" if it is justified by "unusual circumstances." 8 C.F.R. § 287.1.

93. *Almeida-Sanchez v. U.S.*, 413 U.S. 266, 272–273 (1973).

94. 428 U.S. 543 (1976).

95. Ibid., at 559, 563.

96. Ibid., at 562.

97. Ibid., at 572.

98. I.N.A., § 287, 8 U.S.C. § 1357(a)(I) (1980).

99. In *U.S. v. Brignoni-Ponce*, 422 U.S. 873 (1975), the Supreme Court described a "roving patrol":

two officers were observing northbound traffic from a patrol car parked at the side of the highway. The road was dark and they were using the patrol car's headlights to illuminate passing cars. They pursued respondent's car and stopped it saying later that their only reason for doing so was that its occupants appeared to be of Mexican descent. The officers questioned respondent and his two passengers about their citizenship and learned that the passengers were aliens who had entered the country illegally.

Ibid., at 874–75.

100. 422 U.S. 873 (1975).

101. Testimony before the U.S. Comm'n on Civil Rights, Hearing, Wash., D.C., Nov. 14–15, 1978, p. 241, quoted in Civil Rights Comm'n Report, p. 85.

102. 468 F. 2d 1123 (D.C. Cir. 1972).

103. *U.S. v. Salter*, 521 F. 2d 1326 (2d Cir. 1975).

104. *U.S. v. Montez-Hernandez*, 391 F. Supp. 712 (E.D. Calif. 1968).

105. *Illinois Migrant Council v. Pilliod*, 398 F. Supp. 882, 899 (N.D. Ill. 1975), aff'd 540 F. 2d 1062 (7th Cir. 1976).

106. *Cheung Tin Wong v. I.N.S.*, 468 F. 2d 1123 (D.C. Cir. 1972).

107. 540 F. 2d 1062 (7th Cir. 1976).

108. See, e.g., *Marquez v. Kiley*, 436 F. Supp. 100, 112 (S.D. N.Y. 1977); *Au Yi Lau v. I.N.S.*, 445 F. 2d 217, 222 (D.C. Cir. 1971); *Yam Song Kwai v. I.N.S.*, 411 F. 2d 683, 686–688 (D.C. Cir. 1968).

109. 422 U.S. 873, 874 (1975).

110. Ibid. In his testimony before the Civil Rights Commission, David Carliner cited an Immigration Service memorandum that provides:

The dress of an individual plays an important part in choosing to approach an individual and interrogate him. Experience has shown that persons from Latin and South American countries generally will retain their habit of wearing clothing in a style that they were accustomed to in their native countries. Some may be wearing serapes. Others will be dressed in foreign-cut clothing, which is immediately distinguishable. Generally, their garb will be the type that is not associated with persons who have been residents in the New York area for sufficiently long periods of time. Another sign will be the fact that these persons, in addition to their dress, will also be carrying their lunch in brown paper bags.

Quoted in Civil Rights Comm'n Report, p. 85, citing Ben Lambert, INS Assistant Director for Investigation, N.Y. District, memorandum N.Y.C. 50/11, Jan. 16, 1973, printed in U.S., Congress, House, Committee on the Judiciary, Subcommittee on Immigration, Citizenship, and Int'l Law, Review of the Administration of the Immigration and Naturalization Act, 93d Cong., 1st Sess. (1973), p. 32.

111. 548 F. 2d 715 (7th Cir. 1977).
112. 392 U.S. 1 (1968).
113. Ibid., at 20–22.
114. See, e.g., *Dunaway v. N.Y.*, 442 U.S. 200 (1979). In this case the Supreme Court overturned the plaintiff's conviction on the ground that police officers, who brought the plaintiff to headquarters for custodial interrogation, lacked sufficient information to support a warrant for his arrest.
115. 436 F. Supp. 100 (S.D. N.Y. 1977).
116. Ibid., at 113–114.
117. Ibid., at 114.
118. 468 F. 2d 1123 (D.C. Cir. 1972).
119. Ibid., at 1129.
120. A former immigration officer detailed the havoc that can arise when the INS encourages this practice:

[P]erhaps we haven't witnessed in this country before a situation where family members, neighbors, can take vengeance and wreak vengeance upon one another simply because they can turn in some one who is undocumented. It has broken up families. It has caused terrible human suffering, and all of this because of the state of present legislation.

Rev. Bryan Karvelis, Testimony before the N.Y. State Advisory Committee to the U.S. Comm'n on Civil Rights, open meeting, New York City, Feb. 16–17, 1978, vol. I, p. 121.

121. I.N.A., § 287, 8 U.S.C. § 1357(a)(I) (1980).
122. 467 F. Supp. 170 (D.D.C. 1978).
123. See National Lawyer's Guild, *Immigration Law & Defense*, § 7.1.

124. *U.S. v. Harris*, 403 U.S. 578 (1970); See also *Aguilar v. U.S.*, 378 U.S. 108 (1964).

125. Testimony before the U.S. Comm'n on Civil Rights, Washington, D.C. hearing, in Civil Rights Comm'n Report, pp. 269–270.

126. 480 F. Supp. 1078 (D.D.C. 1979).

127. 659 F. 2d 1981 (D.C. Cir. 1981).

128. Ibid., at 1225.

129. Ibid.

130. Ibid.

131. Ibid., at 1226.

132. 681 F. 2d 624 (1982).

133. No. 82–1271 (April 17, 1984). Justice William H. Rehnquist wrote the majority opinion.

134. No. 82–1271. Justice William Brennan wrote a dissenting opinion, which Justice Thurgood Marshall joined. They agreed that the entire work force had not been seized, but pointed out that "only through a considerable feat of legerdemain" could the individual questioning not be regarded as a seizure. Ibid. Justice Brennan described the raid as a "frightening picture of people subjected to wholesale interrogation" under conditions calculated to intimidate. Ibid.

135. Quoted in Linda Greenhouse, "Justices Will Decide on Limitations for Raids for Illegal Aliens," *The New York Times*, April 26, 1983, p. A–20.

136. Ibid.

137. For discussion see Ch. 4 infra.

138. I.N.A., § 287, 8 U.S.C. § 1357 (a)(2) (1980).

139. Carliner, *The Rights of Aliens*, p. 91.

140. I.N.A., § 287, 8 U.S.C. § 1357(a)(2) (1980).

141. Testimony before the New York State Advisory Committee to the U.S. Comm'n on Civil Rights, open meeting, New York City, Feb. 16–17, 1978, vol. 1, p. 120, in Civil Rights Comm'n Report, p. 85.

142. For discussion see Civil Rights Comm'n Report, p. 111.

143. Ibid., p. 112.

144. See Ch. 2 supra.

145. See I.N.A., § 242, 8 U.S.C. § 1252(a)-(h) (1980).

146. Ibid., § 1252(b).

147. See *Wong Yang Sung v. McGrath*, 339 U.S. 33 (1950).

148. I.N.A., § 242, 8 U.S.C. § 1252(b)(I) (1980).

149. 8 C.F.R. § 242.14(a); See *Woodby v. I.N.S.*, 385 U.S. 276 (1966).

150. I.N.S., 1978 Annual Report, Table 28, p. 126.

151. I.N.A., § 212, 8 U.S.C. § 1182(a) (1980).

152. Letter to Louis Nunez, Staff Director, U.S. Comm'n on Civil Rights, Sept. 28, 1979, quoted in Civil Rights Comm'n Report, p. 101.

153. For discussion see Susan Sussman, "The Disgrace Known as the I.N.S.," *Rights* 28 (June-Aug. 1982), p. 9.

154. See *Gideon v. Wainwright,* 372 U.S. 335 (1963); *Powell v. Alabama,* 287 U.S. 45 (1932).

155. *Aguilera-Enriquez v. I.N.S.,* 516 F. 2d 565, 571 (6th Cir. 1975) (dissenting opinion).

156. A 1959 regulation also requires INS officials to inform aliens threatened with deportation of the possibility of obtaining free legal services. 8 C.F.R. § 242.1; § 242.16.

157. Nat'l Comm'n on Law Observance and Enforcement (Wickersham Comm'n), *Report on the Enforcement of the Deportation Laws in the United States* (Washington, D.C.: G.P.O., 1931).

158. "Right to Counsel in Administrative Proceedings," *Minn. Law Review,* pp. 878–79.

159. I.N.A., § 292, 8 U.S.C. § 1362 (1980). A few lower courts have suggested that appointed counsel may even be necessary if the case against the alien is complicated. See, e.g., *Aguilera-Enriquez v. I.N.S.,* 516 F. 2d 565, 568 (6th Cir. 1975). These tribunals have adopted a position that is far from widespread, however.

160. The Supreme Court pointed out in *Escobedo v. Illinois,* 378 U.S. 478 (1964), in fact, that in criminal cases the "right to use counsel at the formal trial [would be] a very hollow thing [if] for all practical purposes, the conviction is already assured by pretrial examination." Ibid., at 487.

161. U.S. Const., Amend. VIII: "Excessive bail shall not be required, nor excessive fines imposed, nor cruel and unusual punishment inflicted." See also the Bail Reform Act of 1966, 18 U.S.C. §§ 3141–51 (1976), which creates an explicit right to bail.

162. I.N.A., § 242, 8 U.S.C. § 1252(a) (1980). Habeas corpus proceedings are still available for detained aliens, however, under a "reasonable dispatch" standard. I.N.A., § 106, 8 U.S.C. § 1105(a)(9) (1980).

163. Operations Instructions 242.6c.

164. Testimony before the N.Y. State Advisory Committee, pp. 245–246, in Civil Rights Comm'n Report, p. 106.

165. INS, "A Comparison of the Bond-Setting Practices of the I.N.S., with that of the Criminal Courts" (Bruce D. Beaudin, consultant) (July 26, 1978), pp. 20–31.

166. Ibid., at 32.

167. Ibid.

168. See Civil Rights Comm'n Report, p. 114.

169. According to David S. North, Director of the Center for Labor and Migration Studies,

[r]equiring a nonrefundable airline ticket . . . would not discourage legitimate tourists, but it would save INS millions in funds now spent for airline tickets for expelled aliens. Further, it might discourage some potential visa abusers [by increasing the cost of a trip to the United States].

Statement to the Subcommittees on Immigration of the Judiciary Committees, U.S. Senate and House of Reps., May 7, 1981, p. 8.

170. For discussion see Staff Report, p. 5.

171. Testimony Before Subcommittee on Immigration and Refugee Policy and House Subcommittee on Immigration, Refugees, and Int'l Law (July 30, 1981), quoted in *Plyler v. Doe*, 457 U.S. 202, 218, n. 17 (1982).

172. See, e.g., SCIRP, Final Report, Rec. II.C, p. 72–75; Marshall, "Illegal Immigration," p. 18; Keely, *U.S. Immigration*, p. 60.

The Reagan Administration and a number of other organizations favor a limited amnesty program if it is coupled with a "secure" system to prevent large scale undocumented migration in the future. See Sidney Weintraub and Stanley Ross, *"Temporary Alien Workers in the United States*, p. 88.

173. A key provision of the Immigration Reform and Control Act of 1983, otherwise known as the Simpson-Mazzoli bill, provided for the legalization of undocumented aliens who have resided in the United States for a specific length of time, although the two versions of the bill differed on the length of required residence and the federal benefits to which newly-legalized aliens would be entitled. See Ch. 3, n.31 supra.

174. Aides to David Stockman, Director of the Office of Management and Budget, have estimated the costs of the amnesty bill to be as much as $4.5 to $9.3 billion over four years. See Robert Pear, "Administration Balks at Cost of Amnesty for Illegal Aliens," *The New York Times*, April 30, 1983, p. 8.

175. For discussion of this thesis, see Weintraub and Ross, *"Temporary" Alien Workers in the United States*, p. 88.

Illinois Congressman Henry Hyde conducted a poll of his constituents. When asked "Should illegal aliens presently in the United States be granted amnesty," 84 percent responded in the negative. According to most of these respondents, amnesty was simply a "reward" for unlawful conduct. "Henry J. Hyde Report," May 1981, p. 4.

Another, related argument against amnesty was articulated by a spokesman for the American Legion: "Amnesty for illegals makes no

more sense to us than solving problems of prison overcrowding by re-
leasing all prisoners with a view toward starting with a clean slate."
Paul S. Egan, assistant director of the National Legislative Comm'n of
the American Legion, statement before the Senate Subcommittee on
Immigration and Refugee Policy, Oct. 29, 1981.

176. See Staff Report, pp. 636–642.

177. Robert Pear, "White House Asks a Law to Bar Jobs for Illegal
Aliens," *The New York Times*, July 31, 1981, p. l; Howell Raines, "Rea-
gan Advised to Admit Mexicans as Guest Workers," *The New York Times*,
July 2, 1981, p. D–17.

178. For discussion see Staff Report, pp. 716–17; Marshall, *Illegal
Immigration*, p. 17; Weintraub and Ross, "*Temporary*" *Alien Workers*, pp.
82–98.

179. For discussion see Ch. 4 supra.

180. Statement to Subcommittees on Immigration of the Judiciary
Committees, U.S. Senate and House of Representatives, May 7, 1981,
p. 8. See also Staff Report, pp. 674–681; Vernon Briggs *Foreign Labor
Programs as an Alternative to Illegal Immigration into the United States* p.
4; Weintraub and Ross, "*Temporary*" *Alien Workers*.

181. For discussion see Philip Martin and Mark Miller, "Guestworkers: Lessons from Western Europe," *Industrial and Labor Relations Review*, pp. 315–30.

182. See, e.g., Domestic Council Committee on Illegal Aliens, Pre-
liminary Report (Washington, D.C.: G.P.O., Dec. 1976), p. 42; SCIRP,
Final Report, Rec. II.B.I, pp. 61–69; U.S. Interdepartmental Comm'n
for the Study of Illegal Immigrants from Mexico (Crampton Report);
U.S. Comptroller General, "More Needs to be Done to Reduce the
Number and Adverse Impact of Illegal Aliens in the United States,"
Report to Congress (Washington, D.C.: U.S. General Accounting Of-
fice, July 31, 1973).

183. The employer sanction provisions currently being considered
by Congress apply to all employers, although those with three or fewer
employees are exempt from the record-keeping requirements. Employers are required to examine the identification of every new worker.
For the first three years after the program is instituted, prospective
employees must produce existing forms of identification, such as birth
certificates or social security cards.

Within three years after the implementation of the program, the administration would be required to implement "as necessary" a more
secure method by which to verify employment eligibility. According
to the House version, however, this method cannot utilize a national
identification card. See S. 529, 98th Cong., 1st Sess. § 101 (a)(11), 129

Cong. Rec. S6970, S6973 (daily ed. May 18, 1983); H. R. Rep. No. 115, pt. 4, 98th Cong., 1st Sess. (1983).

184. See Marshall, "Illegal Immigration," pp. 10-ll; Craig Jenkins, "Push/Pull in Recent Mexican Migration to the United States," *International Migration Review* pp. 178–189.

185. For discussion see supra.

186. Testimony before the U.S. Comm'n on Civil Rights, Washington hearing, Civil Rights Comm'n Report, p. 62. See also "Discriminatory Effects of Employer Sanction Programs Under Consideration by the Select Comm'n on Immigration and Refugee Policy," Paper of the Institute for Public Representation, Georgetown University Law Center, in Staff Report, Appendix E, pp. 489–567; MALDEF, "Statement of Position Regarding the Administration's Undocumented Alien Legislative Proposal," 1977.

187. Testimony of John Shattuck, Legislative Director, American Civil Liberties Union, on the Final Report and Recommendations of the SCIRP before the Subcommittees on Immigration of the Senate and House Judiciary Committees, May 6, 1981, pp. 6–7.

188. "Records, Computers, and the Rights of Citizens," Report prepared by the U.S. Dept. of Health, Education, and Welfare (HEW, now Health and Human Services), Secretary's Advisory Committee on an Automated Personal Data System, July 1973, p. 111.

See also "Employer Sanctions, Research Study," Report prepared by the Center for the Study of Human Rights, Notre Dame University Law School, in Staff Report, Appendix E, pp. 57–75.

At its convention in February 1982, the American Bar Association adopted a statement in opposition to employer sanctions, on the ground that "they would be an unworkable, ineffective, expensive and discriminatory procedure for controlling illegal immigration." Robert Pear, "New Drive Under Way in Congress to Revamp U.S. Immigration Laws," *The New York Times*, Feb. 22, 1982, p. 15.

189. See HEW Report, "Records, Computers, and the Rights of Citizens," in Civil Rights Comm'n Report, pp. 66–70.

190. Quoted in FAIR, Immigration Report, vol. 2 (March 1981).

CHAPTER 5

1. Quoted in W. Stanley Mooneyman, *Sea of Heartbreak* (Plainfield, New Jersey: Logos Int'l, 1980), p. 207.

2. Gunther Beyer, "The Political Refugee: 35 Years Later," *International Migration Review* 15 (Spring/Summer 1981), p. 26.

3. William S. Bernard, "The United States and the Migration Pro-

cess," Paper presented at the American Immigration and Citizenship Conference, New York City, 1975, p. 29.

4. Quoted in Aristide R. Zolberg, "International Migration in Political Perspective," in Mary Kritz, Charles Keely, and Silvano Tomasi, *Global Trends in Migration*, p. 9.

5. William Reece Smith, Jr., "The Refugee Crisis: Solving the Problem," *American Bar Association Journal* 67 (November, 1981), p. 1464. For comparable figures see Beyer, "The Political Refugee," p. 26.

6. Staff Report, p. 29.

7. Steven V. Roberts, " 'Feet People' Join Capitol Vocabulary," *The New York Times*, Aug. 15, 1983, p. B–6. The phrase was used in a speech President Reagan delivered in June 1983:

We must not listen to those who would disarm our friends and allow Central America to be turned into a spring of Marxist dictatorships. The result would be a tidal wave of refugees—and this time they'll be "feet people" and not "boat people."

8. As the authors of the Staff Report point out, estimates of refugee numbers are necessarily problematic. The United Nations High Commissioner for Refugees (UNHCR), for instance, calculated that there are currently 16 million refugees in the world; however, this figure includes people who have already been accepted for resettlement, and most likely children of refugees who have been born after their parents migrated. Staff Report, p. 21.

9. See Ch. 5 infra.

10. Quoted in Zolberg, "International Migration in Political Perspective," p. 19.

11. Ibid., p. 20.

12. See Cong'l Research Service, U.S. Immigration Law and Policy 1952–1979 (Wash., D.C.: G.P.O., 1979), pp. 15–25; S. Rep. No. 256, 9th Cong., 1st Sess. 6 (1979); Alex Stepick, "Haitian Refugees in the United States," p. 16.

13. "Text of Reagan's Speech Accepting the Republican's Nomination," *The New York Times*, July 18, 1980, p. 8.

14. For discussion of the United States' refugee policy until 1980, see Staff Report, pp. 201–213; Cong'l Research Service of the Library of Congress, *World Refugee Crisis: The International Community's Response*, by Joyce E. Vialet. Prepared for the U.S. Senate, Committee on the Judiciary, 96th Cong., 1st Sess., Aug. 1979.

15. For discussion see Staff Report, p. 199; The Reverend Theodore M. Hesburgh, Opening Remarks at Wingspread Conference on Immigration and Refugee Policy, The Johnson Foundation, Racine, Wisconsin, March 28–29, 1981.

16. Act of June 25, 1948, ch. 647, 62 Stat. 1009 (1948), as amended by Act of June 16, 1950, ch. 262, 65 Stat. 219 (1950); Act of June 28, 1951, ch. 167, 65 Stat. 96 (1951) (repealed 1957). The act also extended eligibility for refugee status to people uprooted by certain natural calamities proclaimed by the President of the United States.

17. Act of June 27, 1952, ch. 477, 66 Stat. 163.

18. Cong'l Research Service of the Library of Congress, Review of United States Refugee Resettlement Programs and Policies, 96th Cong., 2d Sess. 1 (1980) (hereinafter cited as Library of Congress Report).

19. For discussion see Norman L. Zucker, "The Conundrum of American Immigration and Refugee Policy: The 1980's and Beyond," Paper presented at the National Issues Seminar on "United States Immigration and Refugee Policy for the 1980's," The Brookings Institute, Washington, D.C., Nov. 18, 1981, pp. 2–3.

20. This new policy had been foreshadowed by the President's Escape Program, enacted in 1951 (Act of June 28, 1951, ch. 167, 65 Stat. 96), and its ideological biases were evidenced in subsequent statutes such as the Refugee Relief Act of 1953, and the Refugee Escape Act of 1957, which expedited the admission of those fleeing countries that were either Communist-dominated or located in the general area of the Middle East.

21. President's Commission on Immigration and Naturalization, *Whom We Shall Welcome*, p. 118.

22. I.N.A., § 203, 8 U.S.C. § 1153(a)(7) (1976) (repealed in 1980).

23. Staff Report, p. 214.

24. Library of Congress Report, p. 8.

25. The Refugee Act implemented the United Nations Protocol Relating to the Status of Refugees [*Done* Jan. 21, 1967, 19 U.S.T. 6223, T.I.A.S. No. 6577, 606 U.N.T.S. 267 (*entered into force for U.S.*, Nov. 1, 1968)]. This Protocol, in turn, updates and applies the Convention Relating to the Status of Refugees (*Done* at Geneva, July 28, 1951. 189 U.N.T.S. 150, *reprinted* in 19 U.S.T. at 6529).

26. U.N. Protocol, ibid., art. 1, § 1 (corresponds to Convention, ibid., art. 1, § 2).

27. Library of Congress Report, p. 8.

28. Pub. L. No. 96–212, 94 Stat. 102 (1980).

29. H. Rep. No. 608, 96th Cong., 1st Sess. 6 (1979) (Testimony of Former Secretary of State Cyrus Vance), pp. 1, 9.

30. 94 Stat. § 201; I.N.A. § 101, 8 U.S.C. § 1101(a)(42) (1980). Upon signing the Refugee Act, President Carter emphasized that it provided "a new admissions policy that will permit fair and equitable treatment

of refugees in the United States regardless of their country of origin."
Public Papers: Jimmy Carter 503 (1980–81).

31. 94 Stat. § 201(b) (creating INA, § 207, 8 U.S.C. § 1157(a)(I)(3)
(1980).

32. For discussion see Ch. 5 infra.

33. I.N.A. § 207, 8 U.S.C. § 1157(a)-(e) (1980). [§ 204(b)(2) of the
Refugee Act, however, provided a numerical limitation of 25,000 for
FY 1980.]

34. See "The Refugee Act of 1980: Synopsis," *San Diego Law Review*, pp. 111–13.

35 Staff Report, p. 158. See also Kathleen Teltsch, "Committee
Celebrates 50 Years of Aiding Refugees," *The New York Times*, Nov. 16,
1983, p. B–3.

36. Teltsch, ibid.

37. The act vested the federal government with ongoing responsibility for the resettlement of refugees, and granted up to 100 percent
reimbursement to states for the cash, medical, and other assistance they
provided refugees during their first three years in the country. The act
also allocated grants to voluntary agencies in order to provide them
with at least partial reimbursement for the costs they incurred during
resettlement. 94 Stat. § 311(a)(2), creating I.N.A., § 412, 8 U.S.C. §
1522(b)-(d) (1980).

38. 94 Stat. § 201(b); I.N.A. § 208, 8 U.S.C. § 1158(a) (1980).

39. 94 Stat. § 204(d)(2); I.N.A. § 208, 8 U.S.C. § 1158(a)-(c) (1980).
The Refugee Act also institutionalized a procedure, known as
"withholding," to benefit some aliens ineligible for asylum. This remedy is not available, however, until the government has ordered an
alien's exclusion or deportation. If, at this point, the individual can
demonstrate the likelihood of persecution if returned to his or her
country of nationality, the government is obliged to "withhold" deportation until the threat is eliminated. Withholding thus represents
the "last chance" for an alien, and as a consequence those seeking this
remedy are provided with extensive procedural rights. 94 Stat. §
209(b)(h)(I); I.N.A., § 243, 8 U.S.C. § 1253 (h)(I) (1980).

40. Bernard Gwertzman, "Salvadorans to Gain Refugee Status," *The
New York Times*, Sept. 22, 1983, p. 3.

41. Ibid. See also Table, "Refugee Admissions," prepared for the
author by the Assistant Commissioner, Refugee, Asylum, and Parole,
of the Department of Justice, April 30, 1984.

42. *Kasravi v. I.N.S.*, 400 F. 2d 675 (9th Cir. 1968).

43. Final Report, Recom. V.A.I., p. 161.

44. John Scanlan cites the 800,000 figure, and bases it on the following information: the authorized admission of 234,500 refugees; the

unauthorized entry of—at a minimum—150,000 aliens possibly eligible for statutory asylum; and the admission of roughly 120,000 nonquota relatives of United States citizens under the provision of I.N.A. § 201, 8 U.S.C. § 1151(b). "Regulating Refugee Flow," *Notre Dame Lawyer*, pp. 618, 620 n.26.

45. The Cuban figure includes the weeks extending from April 21-Oct. 31, 1980. The Haitian figure covers the period from April 27-Oct. 31, 1980. See "A Report of the Cuban-Haitian Taskforce," Nov. 1, 1980, pp. 86–92, and 93–98.

46. "Cuban Refugees Get Offer of 'Open Arms' from U.S.," *Facts on File*, 1980, p. 339.

47. Quoted in Robert Wright, "Cuban/Haitian Contracts Granted by HHS," in Lydio Tomasi, ed., *In Defense of the Alien*, p. 112.

48. For discussion see Stepick, "Haitian Refugees in the United States," p. 16.

49. "The Haitian Struggle for Human Rights," *The Christian Century* (Oct. 8, 1980), p. 532.

50. Announcement of Ambassador Victor H. Palmieri, U.S. Coordinator of Refugee Affairs, June 20, 1980, quoted in "A Report of the Cuban-Haitian Taskforce," p. 5.

51. Ibid.

52. Refugee Education Assistance Act of 1980, Pub. L. No. 96–422, 94 Stat. 1799, 1809.

53. For discussion see Zucker, "The Conundrum of American Immigration and Refugee Policy," pp. 4–5.

54. The Florida congressional delegation succeeded in passing the Fascell-Stone Amendment to the Refugee Education Assistance Act. This amendment compelled the federal government to grant the Cuban-Haitian entrants benefits equal to those provided refugees, and to provide states and localities with 100 percent reimbursement for the expenses they incurred assisting the newcomers. Title V of the Refugee Education Assistance Act, 94 Stat. § 1809. See 153 *Cong. Rec.* H10, 122 (daily ed. Sept. 30, 1980) (remarks of Representative Fascell).

55. For discussion see Edward M. Kennedy, "Refugee Act of 1980," *International Migration Review*, p. 141.

56. A. Klement, "Center Helps Law Flunk First Test," *The National Law Journal* (July 7, 1980), p. 1.

57. Interview with an Officer in the Dept. of State, Washington, D.C., conducted by John Scanlon and Gilburt Loescher (May 18, 1980), in Scanlan, "Regulating Refugee Flow," p. 627.

58. "Mass Asylum and American Foreign Policy," (1981) in Scanlan, ibid.

59. 8 C.F.R. § 208–5 (1981). The Guidelines established by the United

Nations for determining the merits of asylum claims stipulate the use of presumptive group determinations. See, Office of the United Nations High Commissioner for Refugees, Handbook on Procedures and Criteria for Determining Refugee Status 13 (1979).

60. Refugee Reports, vol. 2, no. 15.

61. See Kennedy, "Refugee Act of 1980," p. 155.

The Simpson-Mazzoli bill contained a provision to grant permanent residence to those with the status of Cuban/Haitian (status pending). For discussion and citations see Ch. 3 n.31 supra.

Since the Simpson-Mazzoli bill was not passed by Congress, the Reagan Administration may offer legal status and opportunities for citizenship to the Cubans who entered the United States in 1980. According to immigration officials, the Cubans are eligible for legal status under the 1966 Cuban Adjustment Act. This act was passed in order to accommodate Cubans who were either admitted or paroled into the United States since January 1, 1959, and the officials maintained that, as a consequence, its benefits are not available to the Haitians. See Robert Pear, "Cuban Aliens, but not Haitians, Will Be Offered Residency Status," The New York Times, February 12, 1984, p. A1 & A40.

The Administration would certainly encounter serious criticism if it were to adopt a policy that officially disfavored the Haitians, however. Immediately upon hearing that the Administration was considering granting permanent residence status to the Cubans, Congressman Peter Rodino, Chairman of the House Committee on the Judiciary, protested this action in a letter to Attorney General William French Smith. To treat the two groups differently, he stated, would "violate fundamental fairness." Ibid. Congressman Rodino's sentiments were echoed in a New York Times editorial. "The Haitians and the Lucky Law," Feb. 20, 1984, p. A18.

62. Staff Report, p. 214. For discussion of the Cuban settlement, see Fernandez v. Wilkinson, 505 F. Supp. 787, 788 (D. Kan. 1980).

63. From 1970 through 1978 between 5,000 and 10,000 Haitians are estimated to have entered the United States each year. "A Report of the Cuban-Haitian Taskforce," p. 72. Between 1978 and 1980 the number is estimated to have increased to between 15,000 and 20,000 a year. Ibid.

64. See Haitian Refugee Center v. Civiletti, 503 F. Supp. at 510–32.

As the court in Civiletti concluded "[the primary] goal of the [Haitian] Program was to expel Haitian asylum applicants as rapidly as possible," regardless of the validity of the individual claims. Ibid., at 512–513. At the time Civiletti was litigated, not one among the Haitian applications for asylum, cumulatively 4,000 in number, had been granted. Ibid., at 451. This is primarily because the Dept. of State officially labeled all entering Haitians as "economic," rather than "political" refugees. See 126 Cong. Rec. S3961 (daily ed. April 21, 1980) (Report of the United States Coordinator of Refugee Affairs to Congress).

65. I.N.A., § 243, 8 U.S.C. § 1253(b) (1980).

66. For discussion see *Caribbean Refugee Crisis: Cubans and Haitians*, Hearing before the Committee on the Judiciary: U.S. Senate (Washington, D.C.: G.P.O., 1980), pp. 55–65; *Haitian Refugees Need Asylum*, pp. 245–248.

67. *Haitian Refugees Need Asylum*, pp. 245–48.

68. See n. 63 supra.

69. For discussion see 503 F. Supp. at 442–510. During the program the Government processed more than 4,000 applications for asylum submitted by Haitians, although they granted none. Ibid., at 451.

70. For discussion see 503 F. Supp. at 512–513.

71. 503 F. Supp. 442 (S.D. Fla. 1980).

72. 503 F. Supp. at 475, 513–514. As Judge King noted, after reviewing the steps undertaken by the INS during the Haitian Program, "such a policy indicates a predetermination that none of the Haitians could deserve asylum." Ibid., at 514.

73. Ibid., at 513–514. See n. 64 supra.

74. Ibid., at 517.

75. Ibid., at 515.

76. Ibid., at 510.

77. Ibid., at 519.

78. Ibid., at 513.

79. Ibid., at 521–522. See also *Zamora v. I.N.S.*, 532 F. 2d 1055 (2d Cir. 1976). Even without time constraints, most aliens seeking asylum find it extremely difficult to secure the eyewitnesses, documentary evidence, or other data necessary to establish that they are likely to suffer persecution in their native country. For discussion see 503 F. Supp. at 523.

80. *Caribbean Refugee Crisis*, p. 77.

81. 503 F. Supp. at 522–523, 525, 527.

82. Ibid., at 523–524; See Affidavit of Ira Kurzban, "Haitians in Miami: Current Immigration Practices of the United States" (Washington, D.C.: Alien Rights Law Project, 1978), pp. 3–5.

83. 503 F. Supp. at 511.

84. Ibid., at 451.

85. Ibid., at 532.

86. *Louis v. Meissner*, 530 F. Supp. 924 (S.D. Fla. 1981) ("Louis I"); *Louis v. Meissner*, 532 F. Supp. 881 (S.D. Fla. 1982) ("Louis II"); *Louis v. Nelson*, 544 F. Supp. 973 (S.D. Fla. 1982) ("Louis III").

87. 530 F. Supp. 924 (S.D. Fla. 1981).

88. Ibid., at 926.
89. 532 F. Supp. 881 (S.D. Fla. 1982).
90. 544 F. Supp. 973 (S.D. Fla. 1982).
91. For discussion see *Jean v. Nelson*, 711 F. 2d 1455 (11th Cir. 1983), and testimony of William French Smith before the Senate Subcommittee on Immigration and Refugee Policy, and the House Subcommittee on Immigration, Refugees, and International Law, July 31, 1981.
92. 5 U.S.C. §§ 500–706 (1982).
93. 544 F. Supp. at 1004.
94. After the government announced its intention to engage in rule-making, the district court granted a partial stay, which effectively allowed the INS to detain aliens who arrived in the United States between the date the final judgment was entered and the date when the new rules governing detention were promulgated. 711 F. 2d at 1464.
95. 711 F. 2d 1455 (11th Cir. 1983).
96. Ibid., at 1471–75, *citing* 544 F. Supp. at 980–981.
97. Ibid.
98. Ibid., at 1482.
99. Ibid., at 1487.
100. Ibid., at 1488–90, citing findings of Dr. Howard Seth Gitlow in *Bertrand v. Sava*, 684 F. 2d 204 (2d Cir. 1982). 53 tr. 2949.

In the *Louis* cases the Haitian Refugee Center represented all Haitians applying for entry who arrived in the Southern District of Florida on or after May 20, 1981, and who were either then in detention pending their exclusion hearings, or, alternatively, were unrepresented by counsel or represented by the Haitian Refugee Center's Voluntary Lawyer Task Force. Haitians then being detained at the Immigration Service's Processing Center in Brooklyn were not covered by the Center's class action suit because they were represented by independent counsel.

Haitians detained in Brooklyn filed an independent suit challenging the legality of their incarceration. See *Bertrand v. Sava*, 684 F. 2d 204 (2d Cir. 1982). In this instance, however, they received no relief. The Second Circuit found nothing objectionable either in the standards used by the Immigration Service's district director in determining whether or not to parole undocumented aliens, or in the way these standards were applied to the petitioning Haitians.

101. For instance, one attorney, who works closely with Nicaraguans, testified that on many occasions his clients were released on parole while their asylum claims were pending, even when they arrived with fraudulent documents. 711 F. 2d at 1499.
102. 711 F. 2d at 1501. The circuit court addressed claims that the

district court had dismissed, including plaintiffs' contention that the INS is obliged to provide aliens with notice of the right to file for political asylum. Judge Kravitch confirmed that there is "at a minimum, a constitutionally protected right to petition our government for political asylum," ibid. at 1507, and that by failing to inform aliens of this right the government "clos[es] the door entirely on the process." Ibid. This is particularly true when the INS deals with Haitians and other aliens who are typically unschooled in the English language and unfamiliar with American legal processes.

103. New INS regulations, which were finalized on Oct. 19, 1982, provide the following:

An alien who appears to the inspecting officer to be inadmissible, and who arrives without documents . . . or who arrives with documentation which appears on its face to be false, altered, or to relate to another person, or who arrives at a place other than a designated port of entry, *shall be detained.*

47 Fed. Reg. 46,493 (1982); 8 C.F.R. pts. 212, 235 (1982).

104. See Robert Lindsey, "A Flood of Refugees from Salvador Tries to Get Legal Status," *The New York Times,* July 4, 1983, pp. 1, 9. See also pp. 300–302 n.118 infra.

105. "For 1,800 Haitians—Freedom," *Time,* July 26, 1982, p. 14.

106. "Administration Initiates Haitian Interdiction Program," *Immigration Law Bulletin* 3 (Sept.-Dec. 1981), p. 5. On Sept. 24, 1981, President Reagan issued Executive Order #12324 authorizing the interdiction of vessels transporting undocumented Haitians to the United States. According to government officials, authority for this action stemmed from the President's constitutional role in foreign relations, and his statutory authority to prohibit the entrance of people determined to be detrimental to the country's best interests. I.N.A., § 212, 8 U.S.C. § 1182(f) (1980).

107. "Reagan Orders Aliens Stopped on the High Seas," *The New York Times,* Sept. 30, 1981, pp. 1, 28.

108. The United States International Communications Agency announced on October 22, 1981, that in conjunction with the interdiction program it would launch a campaign of its own: It would begin telling Haitians that life in America is intolerable, at least for those whose presence is unauthorized. Bryan O. Walsh, "The Flight from Haiti: An American Response," *America,* Nov. 28, 1981, pp. 336–337.

According to Agency spokesman Joe O'Connell, this campaign of five-minute radio spots represented an "unprecedented attempt to persuade a group of people to stay away from the United States." Ibid., p. 333.

109. For discussion see "Interdiction at Sea Now Operational," *The New American* II, Nov. 1981, p. 1; "Reagan Orders Aliens Stopped on the High Seas," pp. 1, 28; "Haitian Refugees: Detention Policy Defended," *Facts on File*, 1981, p. 981.

110. See Ch. 5 infra. See also Walsh, "The Flight from Haiti," p. 336.

111. Editorial, "Bodies on the Beach," Oct. 28, 1981, p. 26.

112. Art. 33(I) of the Protocol provides:

No contracting state shall expel or return ["refouler"] a refugee in any manner whatsoever to the frontiers of territories where his life or freedom would be threatened on account of race, religion, nationality, membership of a particular social group or political opinion.

Done July 28, 1951, 189 U.N.T.S. 137.

The term is essentially identical to I.N.A., § 243, 8 U.S.C. § 1253(h) (1980), which provides:

The Attorney General shall not deport or return any alien . . . to a country if [he] determines that such alien's life or freedom would be threatened in such country on account of race, religion, nationality, membership in a particular social group, or political opinion.

113. Article 13(a) states that "[e]veryone has the right to leave any country, including his own, and to return to his country" [subject to Art. 29(2) and (3)]. Universal Declaration of Human Rights, G.A. Res. 217 (111), U.N. Doc. A § 810, at 71 (1948).

114. Conference on Security and Cooperation in Europe (CSCE): Final Act, Aug. 1, 1975, reprinted in 73 Dept. State Bull. 322 (1975), 14 Int'l Legal Mat. 1292 (1975).

According to the preamble, signatories are required to

[m]ake it their aim to facilitate freer movement and contacts, individually and collectively, whether privately or officially . . . [and] [d]eclare their readiness to these ends to take measures which they consider appropriate and to conclude agreements or arrangements among themselves, as may be needed.

Ibid., at 1313.

115. See "Administration Initiates Haitian Interdiction Program," p. 5.

116. Gregory Jaynes, "Aides Say That Sea Patrol Has Slowed Haitian Entries," *The New York Times*, cited in *Migration Today*, vol. 9, no. 4–5, 1981, p. 10.

According to Jaynes, since the government announced its interdiction policy in August 1981, the INS has apprehended 1,960 Haitians. During the same four-month period in 1980, by contrast, the service apprehended 6,906. In 1980 a total of 15,093 Haitians were caught by the government, while in 1981, through Dec. 1, 8,023 had been detained.

See also Alan C. Nelson, Commissioner, INS, Letter to the Editor, "A Mandate on Aliens that Immigration Authorities Must Obey," *The New York Times*, May 21, 1982, p 30. Nelson asserts that the administration's efforts have effected a "dramatic decrease" in the number of Haitians apprehended—4,500 fewer in the first quarter of 1982 than in the first quarter of 1981.

117. 503 F. Supp. at 475.

118. Since Civil War erupted in El Salvador in the late 1970s, an estimated 500,000 people—or one-tenth of the country's population—have entered the United States clandestinely. Philip Shenon, "Salvadoran Refugees Striving for Asylum but Being Rejected," *The New York Times*, July 25, 1983, p. 1.

By most accounts, the treatment they have received from government officials has differed only in degree from that traditionally accorded undocumented Haitians. As of May 1982, more than 20,000 Salvadorans have requested political asylum in the United States. As of August 1983, however, no more than 2.5 percent of Salvadoran asylum applications have been approved—primarily because the government insists that, like Haitians, the Salvadorans are economic migrants. Shenon, ibid.

Elliott Abrams, Assistant Secretary of State for Human Rights and Humanitarian Affairs, maintains that

[the Salvadorans'] presence reflects a longstanding pattern of economic migration to the United States stemming from the fact that El Salvador, besides being poor, is the most densely populated country in the Western Hemisphere.

The New York Times, Aug. 5, 1983, p. 23.

In the face of public pressure, however, the Reagan Administration "quietly" informed Congress on September 21, 1983, that the United States would admit up to 200 Salvadorans as political refugees in the fiscal year beginning Oct. 1. Bernard Gwertzman, "Salvadorans to Gain Refugee Status," *The New York Times*, Sept. 22, 1983, p. 3.

The government's alleged mistreatment of the Salvadorans prompted the National Center for Immigration Rights (NCIR) to initiate a lawsuit in 1981 on behalf of an estimated 25,000 Salvadorans who were being detained in the United States. In this case, *Orantes-Hernandez v. Smith*, 541 F. Supp. 351 (C.D. Cal. 1982), Federal District Judge David Kenyon concluded that the Immigration Service had systematically abused Salvadoran aliens in violation of statutory law and administrative regulations. Immigration officials had attempted to coerce them into leaving the country "voluntarily," and frequently succeeded in deporting them within hours after their arrival. Ibid., at 372–373.

INS agents had employed both verbal and physical abuse, Judge Kenyon continued, in an effort to discourage Salvadorans from seeking asylum. Those who nevertheless persisted in this quest were frequently incarcerated for long periods, often at a detention facility in El Centro, California, where conditions were dismal and solitary confinement was integral to "a well-orchestrated national campaign" to effect their mass deportation. Ibid., at 354. The INS was so intent upon ejecting Salvadorans, in fact, that those in detention were denied even the pens and papers necessary to prepare asylum applications.

The judge forbade immigration officials from coercing Salvadorans into leaving the country "voluntarily," or from taking any action without first advising them, in both English and Spanish, of their right to seek asylum. Ibid., at 377. Judge Kenyon concluded with a warning that the INS should "not employ threats, misrepresentation, subterfuge, or other forms of coercion," ibid., at 386, and he instructed the Service to alert the NCIR at least two hours before any Salvadoran is deported.

See also *Nunez v. Boldin.* 537 F. Supp. 578 (S.D. Tex. 1982) (detainable Guatemalans entitled to deportation hearings and to notice of their right to apply for asylum).

119. According to Administration officials, "the vast majority of Salvadorans seeking asylum are not 'political refugees,' who would face persecution if they were returned to their war-torn country, but rather 'economic migrants' fleeing poverty." Robert Lindsey, "A Flood of Refugees from Salvador Tries to Get Legal Status," *The New York Times*, July 4, 1983, p. 1.

120. Quoted in Leslie Maitland Werner, "A Torrent of Requests for Asylum," *The New York Times*, July 7, 1983, p. B–6.

121. Lindsey, "A Flood of Refugees from Salvador," pp. 1, 9.

122. Lawyers Committee Report, "Haitians and Economic Rights in Haiti," *Caribbean Refugee Crisis.* p. 183; "Report on the Status of Haitian Rights in Haiti" (Wash., D.C., Organization of American States, 1980), in *Caribbean Refugee Crisis*, pp. 141–145.

123. "Administration Initiates Haitian Interdiction Program," p. 7; Stepick, "Haitian Refugees in the United States," p. 16.

124. J. Michael Myers, "It's Wrong to Deport Salvadorans Right Now," *The New York Times*, Aug. 19, 1983, p. 20.

Lawrence H. Fuchs, Executive Director of SCIRP, reports that the United States Dept. of State has itself acknowledged the political violence in Salvador. "What Has Gone Wrong with America's Refugee Policy," *Brandeis Review*, pp. 4, 6. According to Fuchs, in its "Country Reports on the World Refugee Situation," which the Department of State gave Congress in September 1981, it stated that between October 1979 and the date of the report more than 15,000 Salvadorans had been killed as a result of political violence, and that refugees were fleeing the country because of death threats issued by forces representing both the left and the right.

125. 503 F. Supp. at 475.

126. For discussion see National Council of Churches, briefing paper, "Human Rights Violations in Haiti," in *Caribbean Refugee Crisis*, p. 243.

127. Ibid.

128. Quoted in "Exiles: Haitians Who Flee a Harsh Regime Need Our Help," *Caribbean Refugee Crisis*, p. 221.

129. "Country Reports on Human Rights Practices for 1979," United States Dept. of State, 1979 Report, p. 344, in Lawyer's Committee Report, *Caribbean Refugee Crisis*, p. 184.

130. Stepick, "Haitian Refugees in the United States," p. 9, quoting Lawyer's Committee Report, *Caribbean Refugee Crisis*, pp. 183–85.

131. 503 F. Supp. at 508.

132. Naomi Flink Zucker, "Some Boat People Are More Equal Than Others," *Progressive* 46 (March 1982), p. 40.

133. Lydio F. Tomasi, *Migration Today* 11 (1983), p. 5.

134. Ibid.

135. Joseph P. Fried, "Afghans Find Asylum Goal Hard to Gain," *The New York Times*, May 5, 1983, p. B-1.

136. Michael H. Posner, "Comments and Recommendations on Proposed Reforms to United States Immigration Policy," *University of Miami Law Review*, p. 885. Posner's figures are based on authorized admissions for FY 1980–1982. See also Presidential Determinations No. 80–28, 45 Fed. Reg. 68, 365 (1980); No. 82–1, 46 Fed. Reg. 55,233 (1981); and No. 83–2, 47 Fed. Reg. 46, 483 (1982).

137. Gwertzman, "Salvadorans to Gain Refugee Status," p. 3. See also Table, "Refugee Admissions," prepared for the author by the Assistant Commissioner, Refugee, Asylum and Parole, of the United States Department of Justice, April 30, 1984.

138. Fuchs, "What Has Gone Wrong with America's Refugee Policy," p. 6; Wade J. Henderson, "Foreign Policy v. Human Policy," *Rights* 28 (June-August 1982), p. 3. See also The Administration's Annual Report to Congress, April 15, 1980, in Lawyer's Committee Report, *Caribbean Refugee Crisis*, p. 194.

139. Stuart Taylor, "China Tennis Player Gets Asylum in U.S.; Peking Aide Protests," *The New York Times*, April 5, 1983, p. 1.

140. "Defecting Russians Tell of Plan That Led to United States," *The New York Times*, July 14, 1983, p. C–15. The article discusses the recent defection from the Soviet Union to the United States of Victoria Mullova, a violinist, and Vato Jordania, a conductor; both fled because "their artistic freedom was being curtailed." Miss Mullova stated that she fled because "I was not given an opportunity to show my art."

141. For discussion see Peter A. Schey, "The Black Boat People Founder on the Shoals of U.S. Policy," *Migration Today* 9 (1981), p. 7.

142. Senator Dennis De Concini, in comments to then Secretary of State Cyrus Vance, emphasized the disparate treatment: "If you are a boat refugee from Cuba, INS automatically considers you a political refugee. If you are a boat person from Baby Doc's Haiti, INS automatically considers you an illegal alien coming to the United States for economic purposes." S. Rep. No. 55, 96th Cong., 2d Sess. 14 (1980). See also Judith Lichtenberg et al., "Persecution v. Poverty: Are the Haitians Refugees?" *Philosophy and Public Policy*, p. 1.

143. Editorial, "Why Poles but Not Salvadorans?" *The New York Times*, May 31, 1983, p. 20. According to administration officials, granting temporary voluntary departure would encourage millions of poor residents from Central America to flee to the United States seeking a better life. Accordingly, on May 31, 1983, the Dept. of State announced that it had reviewed and reaffirmed its policy opposing the granting of such status. Robert Lindsey, "A Flood of Refugees from Salvador Tries to Get Legal Status," *The New York Times*, July 4, 1983, pp. 1, 9.

Senator Edward Kennedy wrote to the Dept. of State in April 1981, requesting that "voluntary departure" be granted undocumented Salvadorans currently residing in the United States. Letter from Senator Edward M. Kennedy, Ranking Minority Member, Senate Judiciary Committee Subcommittee on Immigration and Refugee Policy to Alexander M. Haig, Jr., Secretary of State (April 6, 1981), reprinted in 128 Cong. Rec. S831 (daily ed. Feb. 11, 1982).

The State Dept responded that while violence was widespread in El Salvador, the "widespread fighting, destruction and breakdown of public services" had not reached the level it had in Nicaragua, Lebanon, or Uganda when voluntary departures had been recommended for nationals of these countries. Letter from Alvin Paul Drischler, Acting Assistant Secretary for Congressional Relations, to Senator Edward Kennedy (April 17, 1981), reprinted in 128 Cong. Rec. S831 (daily ed. Feb. 11, 1982).

144. During a House Immigration Subcommittee hearing on Haitian

refugees in 1980, the Department of State's human rights officer on Haiti was asked if he could make any positive comments about the human rights situation in that country. The officer finally responded that Haiti has freedom of religion. Stepick, "Haitian Refugees in the United States," p. 13.

145. For discussion see Lichtenberg et al., "Persecution v. Poverty," p. 2.

146. For discussion see Leo Cherne, "Economic Migrants," *The New York Times*, Oct. 3, 1981, p. 27.

147. *Paul v. I.N.S.*, 521 F. 2d 194, 205 (5th Cir. 1975); See also *Martineau v. I.N.S.*, 556 F. 2d 306 (5th Cir. 1977), and *Zamora v. I.N.S.*, 534 F. 2d 1055 (2d Cir. 1976). For discussion see Note, "Behind the Paper Curtain: Asylum Policy Versus Asylum Practice," *Review of Law and Social Change*, p. 124.

148. Quoted by Gwertzman, "Salvadorans to Gain Refugee Status," p. 3.

149. See n.7 supra.

150. Quoted in Zucker, "Some Boat People Are More Equal Than Others," p. 40.

151. Quoted in Lindsey, "A Flood of Refugees from Salvador Tries to Get Legal Status," pp. 1, 9.

152. See Lichtenberg et al., "Persecution v. Poverty," p. 4. The authors note that because more than 350 million people throughout the world are either unemployed or severely underemployed, "the class of economic migrants is potentially enormous."

153. Countries participating at an international conference in Geneva in 1979 provided another example of successful cooperation. At the conclusion of the conference the parties pressured the Vietnamese government into reducing the number of refugees who were forcibly expelled from the country. They also devised an effective procedure for resettling those who were already in temporary camps in Southeast Asia. For discussion see Whelan, "Principles of United States Immigration Policy," *University of Pittsburgh Law Review*, p. 481 n.72.

154. According to a United Nations report, border patrol officers have a tendency to view with suspicion anyone who requests asylum from countries, such as El Salvador and Haiti, with which the United States has friendly relations. UNHCR, Mission to Monitor I.N.S. Asylum Processing of Salvadoran Illegal Entrants (1981), Reprinted in 128 Cong. Rec. S827, S.820 (daily ed. Feb. 11, 1982).

155. For discussion see Ch. 5 supra. See also Lydio Tomasi, "Editorial," *Migration Today* 11 (1983), p. 5.

156. "Backlog of 200,000 Hope for Asylum in U.S.," *The New York*

Times, February 19, 1984, p. 27. As of February 1983, the INS had almost 170,000 applications for asylum; this means that approximately 200,000 individuals are seeking refuge in the United States, because many applications cover families.

The Simpson-Mazzoli bill contains a provision that would eliminate 140,000 asylum applications by granting resident alien status to those who have lived in the United States for a prescribed number of years. For discussion see Ch. 3 supra.

157. The Senate version of the Simpson-Mazzoli bill, ibid., permits summary exclusion of aliens "still on the threshold," unless they specifically claim asylum. As John Scanlon notes, it thus "permits exclusion without any adjudication and maximizes the possibility that individuals with valid claims will be returned to their country of origin before their claims are raised." "Asylum Adjudication," *University of Pittsburgh Law Review*, p. 264.

The House bill, on the contrary, would permit the Courts of Appeal to review all decisions made by the Immigration Board, including denials of asylum. In common with the Senate version, however, the House bill would not allow collateral review of asylum decisions. See Ch. 3 n.32 supra.

158. See proposed Omnibus Immigration Control Act of 1982 (Reagan Administration bill), S. 1765, 97th Cong. 1st Sess., 127 Cong. Rec. S. 11,993 (daily ed. Oct. 22, 1981). The administration's bill is intended "to permit a swift and firm response" to "future Mariels." Statement of Alan C. Nelson, Commissioner of the INS, before the Senate Subcommittee on Immigration and Refugee Policy 1 (Sept. 30, 1982). The bill has never passed Congress, and has been overshadowed by the Simpson-Mazzoli bill.

The administration's bill consists of ten titles that represent a comprehensive attempt to reduce the influx of undocumented aliens into the United States. According to one provision, once an asylum officer makes a determination, judicial review is no longer available unless the INS commissioner or the Attorney General requests discretionary certification. Administration bill, § 403,127 Cong. Rec. at 511, 966 (daily ed. Oct. 22, 1981).

Another provision radically curtails the availability of judicial review by allowing a federal court to consider an asylum claim only if it is raised during a challenge to an exclusion or deportation order. Even then, the courts may overturn an administration order only if it is found to be arbitrary, capricious, or illegal. Administration bill, § 403(d), 127 Cong. Rec. at 511, 996 (daily ed. Oct. 22, 1981).

159. § 240(B), 127 Cong. Rec. at 511, 996 (daily ed. Oct. 22, 1981).

160. SCIRP recommended that the United States Coordinator for Refugee Affairs, who has access to relevant information (such as State Department reports), be authorized to develop group profiles for use by asylum admissions officers. Final Report, Rec. V.B.3, pp. 172–73.

161. According to one group of researchers, this country's immigration policy could even be regarded as restrictive, considering both its comparatively low population density, and its wealth in proportion to its population (25 percent of the world's total product with only 6 percent of its population). Staff Report, p. 95.

162. For discussion of this proposition, see Lichtenberg et al., "Persecution Versus Poverty," p., 5.

163. "Salvador and Vietnam: Parallels and Differences," *The New York Times*, August 10, 1983, p. 8.

164. Michael Walzer suggests that the United States is also morally obliged to receive other categories of refugees, as well: those whose suffering is a result of United States policy, such as certain of the Indochinese; those whose unsuccessful struggle the United States deliberately promoted, such as the Hungarians after their ill-fated revolution in 1956; and those whose travails are a result of their efforts to champion political principles to which the United States is committed. "The Distribution of Membership," in Brown and Shue, eds., *Boundaries*, pp. 20–21.

CONCLUSION

1. *Nishimura Ekiu v. U.S.*, 142 U.S. 651, 659 (1892).

2. 342 U.S. 580, 587 (1952).

3. Alexander Bickel expanded upon this theme in "The Passive Virtues," when he speculated upon the reasons for the Court's reluctance to challenge federal policy in areas relating to foreign affairs:

[T]he Court's [apprehension arises from its] sense of lack of capacity, compounded in unequal parts of the strangeness of the issue and the suspicion that it will have to yield more often and more substantially to expediency than to principle; the sheer momentousness of it, which unbalances judgment and prevents one from subsuming the normal calculations of probabilities; the anxiety not so much that judicial judgment will be ignored, as that perhaps it should be, but won't.

Harvard Law Review, p. 75.

4. See *Mathews v. Diaz*, 426 U.S. 67 (1976).

5. See, e.g., *Perez v. Brownell*, 356 U.S. 44 (1958). In this case involving a challenge on constitutional grounds to a denaturalization

statute, the government argued that by virtue of its powers over foreign affairs it could deprive aliens of their citizenship when their actions interfered with, or impeded, the conduct of foreign affairs. Although the Supreme Court accepted this argument, it emphasized its duty to examine Congress's action in the area of foreign affairs no less than its action in the domestic sphere because "the restrictions confining Congress in the exercise of any of the powers expressly delegated to it in the Constitution apply with equal vigor when that body seeks to regulate our relations with other nations." Ibid., p. 58.

Again, in *Youngstown Sheet & Tube Co. v. Sawyer*, 343 U.S. 579 (1952) (The Steel Seizure case), the Court held that the President could not seize the nation's steel mills without congressional permission, regardless of their importance in preparing the nation for a wartime emergency.

In another case, *U.S. v. District Court*, 407 U.S. 297 (1972), the Supreme Court denied the President's request to enjoin publication of the Pentagon Papers, notwithstanding their alleged detrimental impact on national security and foreign affairs.

Finally, in *Reid v. Covert*, 354 U.S. 1 (1956), involving the extraterritorial impact of the Constitution when government action affected United States citizens, the Supreme Court held that "The United States [was] entirely a creature of the Constitution. Its powers and authority [had] no other source." Thus, an exercise of power by the United States, even in the area of foreign affairs, is subject to "all the limitations imposed by the Constitution." Ibid., at 5–6.

See also *Delaware Tribal Business Committee v. Weeks*, 430 U.S. 73, 83–84 (1977) ("The plenary power" of Congress in matters of Indian affairs "does not mean that all federal legislation concerning Indians is . . . immune from judicial scrutiny"); *U.S. v. Darby*, 312 U.S. 100, 115 (1941) ("Regulations of commerce which do not infringe some constitutional prohibition are within the plenary power conferred on Congress by the Commerce Clause"); *U.S. v. Curtiss-Wright Co.*, 299 U.S. 304, 320 (1936) (The President's "delicate, plenary and exclusive power . . . as the sole organ of the federal government in the field of international relations" is one that, "like every other governmental power, must be exercised in subordination to the applicable provisions of the Constitution").

6. As far back as 1893, in *Fong Yue Ting v. U.S.*, 149 U.S. 698 (1893), Justice David Brewer expatiated on the evils attending the exercise of unlimited power. In this case the Court majority had upheld the government's right to exclude persons of Chinese ancestry from the country, prompting Justice Brewer to dissent:

It is said that the power here asserted [to exclude the Chinese] is inherent in sovereignty. This doctrine . . . is both indefinite and dangerous. Where are the limits to such power to be found, and by whom are they to be pronounced?

Ibid., at 737–738.

7. *Galvan v. Press*, 347 U.S. 522, 530–532 (1954).

8. "Protection of Aliens from Discriminatory Treatment by the National Government," *Supreme Court Review*, p. 323.

9. 347 U.S. 483 (1954).

10. See, e.g., *Chinese Exclusion Case*, 130 U.S. 581 (1889); *Fong Yue Ting v. U.S.*, 149 U.S. 698 (1893); *Japanese Immigrant Case*, 189 U.S. 86 (1903).

11. See, e.g., *Harisiades v. Shaughnessy*, 342 U.S. 580 (1952).

12. *United States Department of Agriculture v. Moreno*, 413 U.S. 528, 534 (1973).

13. *Perez v. Brownell*, 356 U.S. 44, 64–65 (1957) (dissenting opinion). In a 1922 case Justice Brandeis expressed similar sentiments, noting that the deportation of an individual who claims to be a citizen may deprive him of "all that makes life worth living." *Ng Fung Ho v. White*, 259 U.S. 276, 284 (1922).

14. 403 U.S. 365 (1971).

15. 338 U.S. 537, 542 (1950).

16. This attitude was particularly evident during the civil rights crises in the 1960s, when movements to eliminate racial discrimination through treaties provoked a backlash in Congress that manifested itself in renewed support for the Bricker amendment. According to the principal clause of this amendment, "[a] treaty shall become effective as internal law in the United States only through legislation which would be valid in the absence of a treaty." See S.J. Res. 1, 83d Cong., 1st Sess., 99 Cong. Rec. 6777 (1953).

Former Secretary of State Dean Rusk observed that while the United States has entered into many bilateral treaty agreements that impact upon human rights, major international covenants on human rights are absent from treaties in force. "A Personal Reflection on International Covenants on Human Rights," *Hofstra Law Review*, p. 516.

By not giving internal effect to these treaties, this country contributes to the debilitation of both international law and international institutions. Recently the United States contributed further to this erosion by seeking to deprive the International Court of Justice of jurisdiction over issues relating to its mining of Nicaraguan harbors. Stuart Taylor, Jr., "Nicaragua Takes Case Against United States to World Court," *The New York Times*, April 10, 1984, pp. 1, 8.

17. For discussion see Schechter, "The Views of 'Charterists' and 'Skeptics' on Human Rights," *Hofstra Law Review*, p. 388.

18. See Schechter for a discussion of some of the "revolutionary" results that would obtain if developed countries were to accept at least some degree of responsibility for non-nationals. Ibid., p. 378.

Bibliography

Anand, Ram Prakash. *New States and International Law*. Delhi, India: Vikas Publishing House, 1972.

"Behind the Paper Curtain: Asylum Policy Versus Asylum Practice." *Review of Law and Social Change* 7 (1978): 124.

Bell, Daniel. "The End of American Exceptionalism." *The Public Interest* Fall 1975: 199.

Bernsen, Sam. "Needed Revision of Grounds of Exclusion: Marijuana, Communists, Homosexuals, and Polygamists," in *In Defense of the Alien*. Austin Fragomen, Jr., and Lydio F. Tomasi, eds. Staten Island, New York: Center for Migration Studies, 1980, II.

Bernstein, Tom A. "Political Grounds for Exclusion." *Immigration Law Bulletin* 2 (1981): 11–12.

Beyer, Gunther. "The Political Refugee: 35 Years Later." *International Migration Review* 15 (1981).

Bickel, Alexander. "Citizenship in the American Constitution." *Arizona Law Review* 15 (1973): 369.

———. "The Passive Virtues." *Harvard Law Review* 75 (1961): 40.Boudin, Louis B. "The Settler Within Our Gates [points 1–3]." *New York University Law Review* 26 (1951).

Briggs, Vernon. *Foreign Labor Programs as an Alternative to Illegal Immigration into the United States: A Dissenting View*. Charlottesville, Virginia: Center for Philosophy and Public Policy, 1980.

Brill, Kenneth. "Refugee Law and Policy." *Cleveland State Law Review* 32 (1983–84): 126.

Campbell, Bruce J. *The Golden Door: The Irony of Our Immigration Policy*. New York: Random House, 1954.

Caribbean Refugee Crisis: Cubans and Haitians. Hearing before the Committee on the Judiciary: United States Senate. Washington, D.C.: G.P.O., 1980.

Carliner, David. *The Rights of Aliens*. New York: Avon Books, 1977.

Chapman, Leonard F., Jr. "A Look at Illegal Immigration: Causes and Impact on the United States." *San Diego Law Review* 13 (1975–76).

Commager, Henry Steele. *The Empire of Reason: How Europe Imagined and America Realized the Enlightenment*. New York: Oxford University Press, 1982.

Congressional Research Service. *History of the Immigration and Naturalization Service*. Washington, D.C.: G.P.O., 1980.

Congressional Research Service. *United States Immigration Law and Policy 1952–1979* Washington, D.C.: G.P.O., 1979.

Congressional Research Service. *World Refugee Crisis: The International Community's Response*. Joyce E. Vialet, ed. Washington, D.C.: G.P.O., 1979.

Cornelius, Wayne A. *America in the Era of Limits: Nativist Reactions to the "New Immigration."* Working Paper in United States-Mexican Studies No. 3. San Diego, California: University of California Press, 1982.

Corwin, Arthur F. *Immigrants—and Immigrants: Perspectives on Mexican Labor Migration to the United States*. Westport, Connecticut: Greenwood Press, 1978.

Corwin, Edward S. *The Constitution and What It Means Today*. Harold W. Chase and Craig R. Ducat, eds. Princeton, New Jersey: Princeton University Press, 1973.

"Foreign Direct Investment in United States Real Estate: Xenophobic or Principled Reaction?" *University of Florida Law Review* 28 (1976).

Fuchs, Lawrence H. "What Has Gone Wrong With America's Refugee Policy." *Brandeis Review* 3 (1982): 4–6.

Gordon, Charles. "Right to Counsel in Administrative Proceedings." *Minnesota Law Review* 45 (1961).

Gordon, Milton M. *Assimilation in American Life: The Role of Race, Religion, and National Origin*. New York: Oxford University Press, 1964.

Graham, Otis L., Jr. *Illegal Immigration and the New Reform Movement*. FAIR Immigration Paper II. February 1980.

Greene, Sheldon. "Public Agency Distortion of Congressional Will: Federal Policy Toward Non-Resident Alien Labor." *George Washington Law Review* 40 (1972).

Guha-Roy, N.S. "Is the Law of Responsibility of States for Injuries to

Aliens a Part of Universal Law?" *American Journal of International Law* 55 (1961): 863–891.

Gunther, Gerald. "Forward: In Search of Evolving Doctrine on a Changing Court: A Model for a Newer Equal Protection." *Harvard Law Review* 86 (1972).

Handlin Oscar. *The Uprooted: The Epic Story of the Great Migrations of the American People.* New York: Grosset & Dunlap, 1951.

Hansen, Marcus Lee. *The Immigrant in American History.* New York: Harper & Row, 1940.

Harris, David John. *Cases and Material on International Law.* 2nd ed. London: Sweet & Maxwell, 1979.

Hartz, Louis. *The Liberal Tradition in America: An Interpretation of American Political Thought Since the Revolution.* New York: Harcourt Brace, 1962.

Harwood, Edwin. "Alienation: American Attitudes Toward Alienation." *Public Opinion* June/July 1983.

Hesse, Siegfried. "The Constitutional Status of the Lawfully Admitted Permanent Resident Alien: The Inherent Limits of the Power to Expel." *Yale Law Journal* 69 (1959): 262–297.

Higham, John. *Strangers in the Land: Patterns of American Nativism 1860–1925.* New Brunswick, New Jersey: Rutgers University Press, 1955.

Hull, Elizabeth. "Los Indocumentados: Practices, Recommendations, and Proposals." *Policy Studies Journal* 10 (1982): 638–652.

———. "Resident Aliens and the Equal Protection Clause: The Burger Court's Retreat from *Graham v. Richardson.*" *Brooklyn Law Review* 47 (1980): 1–48.

———. "Resident Aliens, Public Employment, and the Political Community Doctrine." *The Western Political Quarterly* 36 (1983): 221–240.

James, Henry. *The American Scene.* Leon Edel, ed. Bloomington, Indiana: University of Indiana Press, 1968.

Jenkins, Craig. "Push/Pull in Recent Mexican Migration to the United States." *International Migration Review* 2 (1977).

Johnson, Harry. "Some Economic Aspects of the Brain Drain." *Pakistan Development Review* 7 (1967): 379–411.

Kansas, Sidney. *Citizenship of the United States of America.* New York: Washington Publishing Co., 1936.

Keely, Charles B. *The Disposable Worker: Historical and Comparative Perspective on Clandestine Migration.* Staten Island, New York: Center for Migration Studies, 1976.

————. *United States Immigration: A Policy Analysis*. New York: Population Council, 1979.

Kennedy, Edward M. "Refugee Act of 1980." *International Migration Review* 15 (1981).

Konvitz, Milton R. *The Alien and the Asiatic in American Law*. Ithaca, New York: Cornell University Press, 1946.

Kurzban, Ira. *Haitians in Miami: Current Immigration Practices in the United States*. Washington, D.C.: Alien Rights Law Project, 1978.

"The Legal Status of Undocumented Aliens: In Search of a Consistent Theory." *Houston Law Review* 16 (1979).

Lewis, Sasha Gregory. *Slave Trade Today: American Exploitation of Illegal Aliens*. Boston: Beacon Press, 1979.

Lichtenberg, Judith. "Persecution Versus Poverty: Are the Haitians Refugees?" *Philosophy and Public Policy* 2 (1982): 1–5.

Lillich, Richard B. "The Current Status of State Responsibility for Injuries to Aliens." *American Journal of International Law* 73 (1979): 244.

Lipset, Seymour Martin. *The Politics of Unreason: Right Wing Extremism in America*. New York: Harper & Row, 1970.

Lyman, Stanford. *The Chinese Americans*. New York: Random House, 1974.

McCarthy, Kevin. *United States Immigration Policy and Global Interdependence*. Santa Monica, California: Rand Corporation, June 1982.

McDougal, Myres. "The Protection of Aliens from Discrimination and World Public Order: Responsibility of States Conjoined with Human Rights." *American Journal of International Law* 70 (1976): 432–469.

McKenzie, R.D. *Oriental Exclusion: The Effect of American Immigration Laws, Regulations and Judicial Decisions Upon the Chinese and Japanese on the American Pacific Coast*. New York: James S. Ozer, 1971.

Mann, Arthur. *The One and The Many: Reflections on the American Identity*. Chicago: University of Chicago Press, 1979.

Martin, David A. "Due Process and Membership in the National Community: Political Asylum and Beyond." *University of Pittsburgh Law Review* 44 (1983): 165–237.

Martin, Philip L. "Guestworkers: Lessons from Western Europe." *Industrial Labor Relations Review* 33 (1980).

Mooneyman, W. Stanley. *Sea of Heartbreak*. Plainfield, New Jersey: Logos International, 1980.

Nafziger, James A.R. "A Policy Framework for Regulating the Flow of Undocumented Mexican Aliens into the United States." *Oregon Law Review* 56 (1978).

National Commission on Law Observance and Enforcement (Wickersham Commission). *Report on the Enforcement of the Deportation Laws in the United States.* Washington, D.C.: G.P.O., 1931.

National Lawyer's Guild. *Immigration Law and Defense.* Student ed. New York: Clark Boardman Co., 1979.

Posner, Michael H. "Comments and Recommendations on Proposed Reforms to United States Immigration Policy." *University of Miami Law Review* 36 (1982).

President's Commission on Immigration and Naturalization. *Whom We Shall Welcome.* Washington, D.C.: G.P.O., 1953.

Root, Elihu. "The Basis of Protection of Citizens Abroad." *American Journal of International Law* 4 (1910).

Rosales, Simona. "Resident Aliens and the Right to Work: The Quest for Equal Protection." *Hastings Constitutional Law Quarterly* 2 (1977): 1029.

Rosberg, Gerald. "Aliens and Equal Protection: Why Not the Right to Vote?" *Michigan Law Review* 75 (1977): 1092.

———. "Protection of Aliens from Discriminatory Treatment by the National Government." *Supreme Court Review* 1977 (1978): 275.

Rosenfield, Harry N. "Necessary Administrative Reforms in the Immigration and Nationality Act of 1952." *Fordham Law Review* 27 (Summer 1958): 145.

Salem, A. "The United Nations and the International World of Physics." *Bulletin of Atomic Scientists* February 1968: 14–16.

Salinas, Guadalupe. "The Undocumented Mexican Alien: A Legal, Social, and Economic Analysis." *Houston Law Review* 13 (1976).

Scanlon, John. "Asylum Adjudication: Some Due Process Implications of Proposed Immigration Legislation." *University of Pittsburgh Law Review* 44 (Winter 1983): 261–287.

———. "Regulating Refugee Flow: Legal Alternatives and Obligations Under the Refugee Act of 1980." *Notre Dame Lawyer* 56 (1980–81).

Schechter, Lowell F. "The Views of 'Charterists' and 'Skeptics' on Human Rights in the World Legal Order: Two Wrongs Don't Make a Right." *Hofstra Law Review* 9 (1981).

Schey, Peter A. "The Black Boat People Founder on the Shoals of United States Policy." *Migration Today* 9 (1981): 7.

Select Commission on Immigration and Refugee Policy, Final Report. *United States Immigration Policy and the National Interest.* Washington, D.C.: G.P.O., 1981.

Siegel, Jacob S. "Preliminary Review of Existing Studies of the Number of Illegal Residents in the United States." Paper prepared for the Select Commission on Immigration and Refugee Policy, January 1980.

Smith, William Reece, Jr. "The Refugee Crisis: Solving the Problem." *American Bar Association Journal* (November 1981).

Stepick, Alex. *Haitian Refugees in the United States* Report # 52. London: Minority Rights Group, 1982.

Teitelbaum, Michael S. "Right Versus Right: Immigration and Refugee Policy in the United States." *Foreign Affairs* 59 (1980).

United States Bureau of the Census. *Historical Statistics of the United States, Colonial Times to 1970.* 2 vols. Washington, D.C.: G.P.O., 1975.

United States Commission on Civil Rights. *The Tarnished Golden Door: Civil Rights Issues in Immigration.* Washington, D.C.: G.P.O., 1980.

United States Comptroller General. *More Needs to be Done to Reduce the Number and Adverse Impact of Illegal Aliens in the United States.* Washington, D.C.: G.P.O., 1973.

United States Department of Health, Education, and Welfare. *Records, Computers, and the Rights of Citizens.* Washington, D.C.: G.P.O., 1973.

United States Immigration Commission (Dillingham Commission). *United States Immigration Commission, 1907–1910.* Washington, D.C.: G.P.O., 1911.

United States Interdepartmental Commission for the Study of Illegal Immigration from Mexico (Crampton Report). *Final Report: A Program for Effective and Humane Action on Illegal Mexican Immigrants.* Washington, D.C.: G.P.O., 1973.

Walzer, Michael. "The Distribution of Membership." In *Boundaries: National Autonomy and Its Limits.* P. Brown and H. Shue, eds. Totowa, New Jersey: Rowman & Littlefield, Inc., 1981.

Weintraub, Sidney. *"Temporary" Alien Workers in the United States: Designing Policy From Fact and Opinion.* Boulder, Colorado: Westview Press, Inc., 1982.

Weston, Burns H. *International Law and World Order.* St. Paul, Minnesota.: West Publishing Co., 1980.

Whelan, Frederick G. "Principles of United States Immigration Policy." *University of Pittsburgh Law Review* 44 (1983): 447–485.

Wright, Robert. "Cuban/Haitian Contracts Granted by HHS." In *In Defense of the Alien: Refugees and Territorial Asylum.* Lydio F. Tomasi, ed. Staten Island, New York: Center for Migration Studies, 1983, V.

Zolberg, Aristide R. "International Migration in Political Perspective." In *Global Trends in Migration: Theory and Research in International*

Population Movements. Mary M. Kritz, Charles B. Keely, and Silvano M. Tomasi, eds. Staten Island, New York: Center for Migration Studies, 1981.

Zucker, Naomi Flink. "Some Boat People Are More *Equal* than Others." *Progressive* March 1982: 40.

Zucker, Norman L. "The Conundrum of American Immigration and Refugee Policy: The 1980's and Beyond." Paper presented at the National Issues Seminar on "United States Immigration and Refugee Policy for the 1980's." Washington, D.C.: The Brookings Institute, November 18, 1981.

Index

About the Author

ELIZABETH HULL is Assistant Professor of Political Science at Rutgers University, Newark. Her earlier works include articles in *The Unavoidable Question: Immigration Policy in the 1980s,* the *Brooklyn Law Review, Policy Studies Journal,* and *The Western Political Quarterly.*